Not for Glory, Not for Gold

NOT FOR GLORY, NOT FOR GOLD

Keith Miles

C

CENTURY

LONDON MELBOURNE AUCKLAND JOHANNESBURG

Copyright © Williamson Rosen Pty Ltd
Based on a Screenplay by David Williamson

First published in Great Britain in 1986
by Century Hutchinson Ltd,
Brookmount House, 62–65 Chandos Place,
London WC2N 4NW

Century Hutchinson Publishing Group (Australia) Pty Ltd
16–22 Church Street, Hawthorn, Melbourne, Victoria 3122

Century Hutchinson Group (NZ) Ltd
32–34 View Road, PO Box 40–086, Glenfield, Auckland 10

Century Hutchinson Group (SA) Pty Ltd
PO Box 337, Bergvlei 2012, South Africa

British Library Cataloguing in Publication Data

Miles, Keith
Not for glory, not for gold.
1. Running—History
I. Title
796.4'26   EVI069

ISBN 0 7126 1271 8
ISBN 0 7126 1272 6 Pbk

Photoset by Rowland Phototypesetting Ltd,
Bury St Edmunds, Suffolk
Printed in Great Britain by
Richard Clay (The Chaucer Press) Ltd,
Bungay, Suffolk

To athletes everywhere

Prologue

London shivered in the cold and turned its collar up against the relentless surge of a March wind. Dark cloud was low and intimidating and the first stinging hints of rain could be felt in the air. It was not an afternoon for standing about. Wrapped up in long coats and thick scarves, pedestrians hurried along pavements or flagged down taxis or sought refuge in the brightly lit shops and department stores. Cars, buses and the occasional horse and cart jostled for position in the busy streets, anxious to keep on the move and ahead of the storm.

In true British fashion, everyone complained about the weather.

The one exception was the young man who strode down Whitehall with his raincoat flapping around him. Tall, well-built and moving with an athletic fluency, he seemed totally unaware of what was going on around him. His open face was puckered in a frown of concentration. Fear and concern showed in his eyes and his jaw was tight.

He was, quite literally, miles away.

'Can I help you, sir?'

'What?'

The young man came out of his reverie to find himself facing a burly policeman. He was at first jolted by the sight of uniformed authority but he relaxed a little when the policeman gave him a friendly smile and rubbed his gloved hands together.

'You looked a bit lost, sir.'

'Oh. Yes. I think maybe I am.' The young man spoke

I

with a guttural accent but his command of the language was good. 'I want the Home Office. Could you direct me, please?'

'Of course, sir.' The policeman glanced up at the sky. 'With luck, you should just get there before the rain comes.'

Five minutes later the young man was ushered along a corridor at the Home Office and shown into a small room. He was waved to a chair by the official who sat behind the desk but he remained on his feet to make an impassioned plea. The words poured out of him.

'I must not go back to Austria! I have left my country. Please do not send me home again. I cannot go. I wish to stay here!'

'That is for us to decide,' came the crisp retort.

'Do you know what will happen to me if I go back?'

'I know what will happen to you if you don't calm down,' warned the other. 'Let me remind you that you are a guest in this country. And guests are obliged to behave themselves. Is that understood?' He indicated the upright chair and his tone became peremptory. 'Now, please sit down so that I can conduct this interview properly.'

Biting back a reply, the young man took a deep breath and tried to control his feelings of anger and apprehension. After a few moments he sat down and appraised the official more carefully. Slim, poised and greying at the temples, the man wore a smart pin-stripe suit and a smile of cold politeness. He glanced down at a sheet of paper.

'You are Franz Stampfl?'

'That is correct.'

'And you came here from Austria?'

'No – from France. I spent some time there before coming on to England.'

'And you entered this country with a student permit.'

'Yes.'

'That permit has now expired.'

'Can't you renew it?' demanded Stampfl.

'I'm afraid not,' decided the official, staring over at him.

'But you *must*!'

'Don't tell us how to do our job,' cautioned the other. 'We have strict procedures with regard to foreign visitors. I'm

2

sorry, Mr Stampfl, but your visa has expired. You will have to return home.'

'Don't you realize why I *left*!' exclaimed Stampfl.

'That is not my concern.'

'Please, sir. Listen to me.'

'Rules are rules.'

'Just listen!' implored the young man. 'I got out of Austria last year because I hate the fascists. They know that I hate them. The fascists have just taken over my country.'

'I appreciate your position,' said the official with formal sympathy, 'but I have no choice. We go by the book.'

Franz Stampfl leaned forward to whisper. 'If you send me back now, I will be shot.'

The official looked at him steadily then got up to cross to the window. After considering the matter, he turned back into the room.

'Technically, you have no right to be here. Unless . . .'

'Unless?'

'There are only two ways we could allow you to stay in England.'

'Tell me what they are,' urged Stampfl. 'I'll do them both.'

'The first is if you establish an industry here and employ at least twenty Englishmen.'

'A new industry?' Hope gave way to sarcasm. 'Yes, of course. I will go straight out and do it. What sort of industry would you like me to start? I have three pounds in my pocket.' He watched sourly as the official returned to his seat. 'You say that there are two ways. What is the other?'

'You can remain in this country if you can prove to us that you can do work that no Englishman can do.'

'Well, I can certainly do that,' announced Stampfl.

'Can you?'

'Yes, I can throw a javelin ten metres further than any Englishman. I'm a record-holder in the event.'

'But could you be employed in that capacity?'

Sarcasm again intruded. 'Could I be employed to throw the javelin? Your army is very antiquated, sir, but I think that even it has got beyond throwing spears.'

'Then that's it, I'm afraid,' concluded the official, his expression hardening. 'Unless you can fulfil one of the two requirements I have outlined, you must return to Austria.'

The interview was over. Franz Stampfl left the Home Office and took his rage out into the pouring rain. The visit had been a complete waste of time. He should have known better than to expect either mercy or understanding from a British government.

He was now effectively under sentence of death.

There had to be *someone* who would help him.

In the warmth of an Australian autumn a small, wiry man in his late forties cycled along a street in a Melbourne suburb. His tanned skin and general animation gave an impression of health and alertness that was quite false because he was feeling far from well. When he reached the doctor's surgery he got off his bicycle and parked it against a wall before going into the building. A long wait behind a queue of other people did nothing to assuage his natural impatience.

Percy Cerutty was in a mood of profound irritation when he finally got in to see the doctor. He was given an amiable welcome.

'Come in, come in!' said Dr Egan.

'How long does a bloke have to wait around here?' complained the patient with frank bitterness. 'You could be dying before you got any action in this place.'

'Sorry about that, Mr Cerutty. I can't help it if I'm popular.' He appeased the newcomer with a warm smile. 'Take a seat.'

'Right.'

While Cerutty plonked himself down on the bentwood chair, the doctor took a record card from the files and glanced at it. His bushy eyebrows rose in surprise.

'The last time I had you in here was ten years ago.'

'Nearer eleven,' corrected the other.

'What's wrong?'

'If I knew that, I wouldn't be here.'

Over two decades in general practice had taught Dr Egan that a patient's irascibility was often a mask for deep anxiety. Percy Cerutty did not make a habit of coming to the surgery. It must have taken something very serious to get him there.

'What are the symptoms?' asked the doctor solicitously.

'The symptoms are I'm feeling bloody crook.'

4

'Can you be more specific?'

'I've come for some doctoring,' argued Cerutty. 'Get on with it.'

'I will. Open your shirt.'

Cerutty undid the buttons to reveal a thin, bronzed torso with a forest of small white hairs on it. Dr Egan fixed the stethoscope into his ears and applied the business end to the patient's chest. He listened for a long time and his face was clouded. When he had completed his examination he reached for a pad on his desk and began to write something on it.

'Well?' pressed Cerutty. 'What's the problem?'

'Do you get pains in the chest?'

'No.'

'Shortage of breath?'

'Yes. Every time I do anything.'

'We've got a spot of bother, I'm afraid.'

'*We've* got a spot of bother!' yelled the patient. '*I've* got a spot of bother, you mean. What's the bloody trouble?'

Dr Egan looked up from his pad. 'It's your heart.'

As he listened to the diagnosis and to the stern warnings that followed it, Percy Cerutty's anger drained away to be replaced by cold fear. He was subdued and pensive when he left the surgery. Instead of cycling home he pushed his machine slowly through the streets. He had plenty to think about on the long journey back to his little cottage.

His wife greeted him nervously at the front door and took him into the tiny living room with its modest furnishings. While her husband slumped into an armchair Dorothy Cerutty went into the kitchen to make a pot of tea. She knew that he would say nothing about his visit to the doctor until he was ready to do so. It was a question of biding her time.

She served the tea, gave him chance to relax then manufactured conversation. He remained withdrawn and dejected. It was several minutes before he raised his eyes to hers.

'Percy, what exactly did he say?'

'Heart disease.'

'Oh no!'

'That bloody galoot says I've only got two years to live.' He punched the arm of the chair with sudden fury. 'Two bloody years!'

5

'Is there nothing they can do for you?' asked his wife anxiously.

'No. I've got to sit back and let it happen. I've got to take things easy. *Me!* Can you imagine it?'

'You must do as the doctor says, Percy.'

'Why?' he challenged.

'He knows best.'

Her husband gave a snort of disgust and hauled himself out of the armchair. He paced up and down the room and muttered darkly to himself before coming to a halt and swinging around to face her. Pugnacity made him bristle all over.

'Two years!' he shouted. 'I'll outlive that bloody doctor if it kills me.'

Franz Stampfl opened the door and found himself in a rather poky and untidy office. Behind the desk was a big, well-dressed, distinguished-looking man with a bald head and an air of sophisticated determination about him. Stampfl peered at him with respect.

'You are Harold Abrahams?'

'I am.'

'You are *the* Harold Abrahams?'

'Depends what you mean, old chap.'

'Paris Olympic Games, 1924. Gold medal in the 100 metres. Your time was 10.6 seconds.'

'That's me,' conceded Abrahams with a smile. 'And who are you?'

'Franz Stampfl.'

'The javelin thrower?'

'You've heard of me?' said the Austrian with grateful surprise.

'Of course. I keep a close eye on European athletics. You're one of the few javelin throwers in recent years who could give the Scandinavians a run for their money. Pleased to meet you, Franz.'

'Thanks.'

'Now – what can I do for you?'

'Help to prevent me being shot.'

Harold Abrahams had received some strange requests at

the offices of the Amateur Athletic Association but nothing as startling as this. He offered his visitor a chair and gave him his full attention.

'I think you'd better tell me everything,' he suggested.

Franz Stampfl did just that. He spoke movingly about his plight and did not try to hide his emotions. Abrahams, a barrister as well as an athletics administrator, listened with the utmost care and absorbed all the salient details. The Austrian ended his story on an aggrieved note.

'I thought England was supposed to be a free country!'

'Even free countries have laws.'

'But why is your Home Office treating me like an enemy alien? If there is to be a war, I want to fight *against* fascism. That is one of the reasons I came here.'

Abrahams nodded. 'Who put you on to me?'

'Someone told me that you might help.'

'I'll try, certainly.'

'They said that you were a person who got things done.' Stampfl lowered his voice. 'Please, Mr Abrahams. You are my last hope.'

The older man ran a hand across his bald head and pondered. At length he sat up as an idea came to him. He snapped his fingers and pointed across at Stampfl.

'Have you had any experience as a coach?'

'Of course,' replied the other. 'On the continent, I am regarded as one of their very best coaches.'

'Javelin?'

'No, everything. Track and field. I have made it my business to understand the basis of all sports. I have studied hard.'

'The Home Office has to be convinced that you can do something that no Englishman can do.'

'That is true.'

Abrahams heaved a sigh. 'Unfortunately, we already have a lot of coaches of our own.'

'Yes,' rejoined Stampfl, 'and you think they are very good at their job. But they are not.'

'That's a matter of opinion, Franz.'

'Most of your coaches are a disgrace.'

'Those sentiments won't exactly make you popular.'

'I am blunt,' admitted the other, 'and I am always criticized for it. But I tell the truth. Your English coaches are bad.'

'Then you'll have the opportunity to prove how much better you are.' Abrahams flicked through a pile of letters on his desk until he found the one he was after. 'The Metropolitan Police want an athletics coach. How do you fancy trying to lick a bunch of London bobbies into shape?'

'Just tell me where to go.'

'I'll do more than that, Franz. I'll come with you. If you really are such an all-round expert, I'd like to see you in action.'

'You will,' promised Stampfl. 'And thank you.'

They met again next day and made their way to a large sports field in the suburbs. A couple of dozen policemen were going through their training routines. It was a cold afternoon and most of the athletes wore track suits or sweaters.

Stampfl ran his eye over the scene then let his gaze settle on a muscular young man holding a javelin. He drew his companion's attention to the thrower who was so proud of his physique that he was showing it off in white shorts and blue vest. Watched by a few friends, the young man took a short run-up, drew back his arm then hurled the javelin with vicious force. It shot through the air for some fifty yards before burying its nose in the ground. The thrower was delighted with himself and his friends were duly impressed.

Stampfl, however, shook his head and clicked his tongue.

'Do that again!' he called. The thrower looked across at him. 'Please. Throw another one for me.'

Thinking that he had a new admirer, the young man picked up a second javelin and went through the same routine. By putting more effort into it this time, he achieved a few extra yards but his aim had been awry and the second javelin ended up some distance to the right of the first.

'Hopeless!' asserted Stampfl, marching towards him. 'To start with, your run-up is far too short. You must learn to convert speed into power for the throw.'

'What are you on about?' said the policeman defensively.

'Technique, my friend. You have no technique.'

'I'm the best javelin-thrower here!' boasted the other.

'Then you can't have much competition.' Stampfl slipped off his coat and handed it to Abrahams then he selected one

8

of the javelins that lay on the grass and tested its weight. 'Watch this,' he ordered.

Using a much longer and faster approach, he pulled back his arm and released the javelin in an explosion of power. While Stampfl bounced on one foot at the end of his throw, the javelin explored space like a rocket before descending to earth with a thud. It was well over twenty yards beyond the other javelins. The young man gaped in amazement but there was more to come. Choosing another javelin, Stampfl produced an identical throw and chuckled to himself as the steel nose bit into the ground only inches from his first javelin.

'That was terrific!' congratulated the young policeman.

'No, my friend,' said Stampfl. 'It was technique.'

'Could you teach *me* to throw like that?'

'If you're ready to work hard at it.'

'I'd do anything!'

Harold Abrahams smiled as he looked on. He had the satisfying feeling that he had hit on just the right place for Franz Stampfl. Revolted by what was going on in Germany, Abrahams was anxious to do all he could to save Stampfl from being sent home and delivered up to the Nazi regime. In his straightforward way the Austrian was now instructing the young man and his friends in the basics of throwing technique. The new coach of the Metropolitan Police was clearly in his element.

There might be a way to keep him in England, after all.

Wearing nothing but black shorts and running shoes, Percy Cerutty jogged across the green sward in the morning sunshine. The Royal Botanic Gardens were right on his doorstep and he took full advantage of the eighty-eight undulating acres beside the River Yarra. His daily run had made him a familiar sight in the gardens and several people waved to the distinctive figure with his white hair and moustache. Percy ran easily, with a low economical stride, hands held loosely across his chest and pumping gently as he moved along. There was something relaxed and uninhibited about his style and there was a vitality about him that was remarkable in a man approaching fifty.

When he came to the bridge by the corner of Riverside

9

Avenue he swung into Anderson Street. A long, steep incline now faced him and he began to increase the pace steadily until he was almost sprinting flat out. By the time he got back to his cottage in the Domain, he was panting for breath and grinning happily. Percy went into the living room and let out an involuntary whoop of joy that startled his wife so much that she popped her head around the kitchen door in alarm.

'What on earth is wrong?'

'Nothing is wrong, Dorothy. Everything is just perfect. Haven't you seen the morning paper?'

'Of course. The news about the war is dreadful.'

'Forget the war. Look at the date on that paper.'

'Date?'

'Yes. It's my second anniversary. Exactly two years ago I went to see Dr Egan and he told me my heart condition was fatal. According to that idiot I was supposed to've kicked the bloody bucket by now.' He gave a full-throated laugh and slapped his bare chest. 'Yet I'm alive and kicking. Instead of being lifted into my coffin today, I've just got back from a ten-mile run.'

'Dr Egan made a mistake – thank God!'

'He also did me a favour. What he told me made me roll up my sleeves and fight back hard. And you've seen the results, Dorothy. I'm fitter and healthier than I've ever been.'

'Yes, Percy. And noisier.'

'I owe it all to running!' her husband announced with his eyes gleaming. 'I proved that it's possible to get better and better if you really push yourself. And if I can do it for myself, I can do it for other people.' He crossed the room to give her an impulsive hug. 'Dr Egan wrote me off but I came back from the dead. I've not only got a life now – I've got a mission. I'm going to be the best bloody coach that this country or any other, for that matter, has ever seen!'

Chapter One

A thin, lanky, fair-haired boy stood on a deserted beach at an English coastal resort. High above his head white clouds were scudding across an azure sky and gulls cried as they wheeled and dipped and rode on the stiffening breeze. Green waves rolled in with casual power, each one spending itself in a lazy trickle of foam before being drowned by the next. The boy drank in the magic of the whole scene and it filled him with a sudden excitement.

He looked down and marvelled at the intricate patterns of ribbed sand that seemed to reproduce themselves endlessly and faultlessly along the shoreline. The sense of perfection was so overwhelming that it made him take a few steps and leap spontaneously into the air. His shyness made him turn around at once to see if he was being watched but he was quite alone and his solitude heightened his feeling of communion with nature.

As he took a few more steps his excitement began to build and his energy started to flow as never before. He found himself running along the shore with no sense of effort, settling into an easy rhythm and autographing the firm damp sand with his bare feet. It was as if he had found a new source of power and wonder and it gave him an exhilaration that suffused his whole body. He had never known such freedom and such sense of unity with nature.

It was the first of many such moments when Roger Bannister would experience the sheer joy of running.

*

The war blew a gaping hole in British athletics and put an end to the ambitions of countless athletes. Meetings were organized on a limited scale in the services and at club level but there were no major international events to provide greater incentives and tougher challenges. While most of Europe was enmeshed in six long years of ferocious conflict, it was left to neutral Sweden to create many of the sporting headlines. What really captured the attention was the sustained assault being made on the record books by two brilliant middle-distance runners, Gunder Haegg and Arne Andersson – big, powerful men whose intense personal rivalry and extreme fitness drove them on to some phenomenal performances.

In the summer of 1942 Haegg won thirty-two successive races and broke a total of ten world records at a variety of distances. As a result of this astonishing sequence the British press christened him 'Gunder the Wonder'. While Andersson could not match his compatriot's achievement in terms of records, there was very little to choose between them in a mile race, an event that they had revolutionized. Each had set a world's best mark no less than three times. On that sixth occasion, in July 1945, Haegg had clocked 4.01.4 at Malmo. When the barrier of the four-minute mile was smashed, it was generally felt, it would be by one of the two Swedes.

When the war ended the Amateur Athletic Association invited Haegg and Andersson to compete in a match between the AAA, the Army, the RAF and the US Forces. The meeting was to take place at the White City Stadium on August bank holiday and the interest that it generated was quite extraordinary. Starved of top-class athletics and desperate for some excitement to brighten up the war-torn capital, the British public responded in their thousands and not even the threat of a thunderstorm could stop them from converging on the White City.

One particular event dominated the conversation of the hordes as they pressed towards the gates. Patriotism was running high.

'Wooderson is bound to win the mile!'

'They reckon this Andersson bloke is hot stuff.'

'Sydney'll sort him out. He eats Swedes for breakfast.'

'Pity that Haegg is not running the mile.'

'Yes – or Wooderson could take him to the cleaners as well. Old Gunder the Wonder would have some real competition for a change. He's dead scared of Wooderson. That's why he's going in the two miles instead.' The fan gave a confident chuckle. 'Not that he'll be any safer there, mind you. Doug Wilson will beat the pants off him.'

'Do you really think so?' asked his friend.

'Britain is best, mate. If we can win a war against the Germans, we can certainly put a couple of bloody Swedes in their place.'

He had voiced the opinion of many of those around him and there was a chorus of approval. The two men inched forward in the queue and continued a discussion that was taking place everywhere at that moment.

Not far behind them and caught up in the seething crowd were two tall figures with the kind of resemblance that only exists between a father and son. Ralph Bannister was taking the sixteen-year-old Roger to his first big athletics meeting and both had been looking forward to the occasion with anticipatory delight. The family had been evacuated from Harrow to spend most of the war in Bath. To a quiet, withdrawn individual like Roger Bannister who had had some of his most enjoyable outings when he explored the rural charms of Somerset on a bicycle, being part of an exuberant mass of people was a whole new experience. There was an air of collective excitement that he found very infectious.

That excitement was suddenly checked.

'Oh no!' sighed Ralph Bannister.

'What's the matter?' asked his son.

'Look! They're closing the gates.'

'We're not going to be shut out, are we?'

'I hope not.'

But the signs were ominous. Stewards were trying to turn people away from the gates, police were setting up a barrier and some mounted officers were signalling to the crowd that the stadium was full. Over fifty thousand had now passed through the turnstiles and the order for the lock-out had been given.

It was not a popular decision.

13

A great moan of disappointment went up to be followed by a more practical response. Having waited for years for a major athletics meeting, the fans were not going to be denied now. With good-humoured determination they gave a corporate shove and surged forward in such irresistible numbers that the police barrier gave way before them and the gates were forced open. The White City found that it had to accommodate a further seven thousand or more spectators.

Swept along on the human tide, Roger Bannister and his father were carried inside the stadium and elbowed their way to a place on the terraces. It was not the most comfortable position from which to watch the events but that did not matter. They had got in and both were immediately caught up in the atmosphere of a big sporting occasion.

Lifted by the support in the packed stands, the athletes turned on their best performances and kept the crowd thrilled and entertained. Two black athletes caught the eye early on. Aircraftsman Emmanuel McDonald Bailey showed blistering pace in both sprints to finish a close second to the pre-war star, Cyril Holmes, a Company Sergeant Major in the Physical Training Corps. In the 440 yards the towering Jamaican, Flying Officer Arthur Wint, displayed such an elegant and unforced running style that he seemed to amble gracefully to his victory.

But it was the mile that was the blue riband event.

'Do you think Sydney Wooderson can win?' asked the young Bannister.

'Of course,' replied his father.

'But Andersson has held the world record for the mile.'

'So has Wooderson.'

'I know but . . . well, that was a long time ago. Andersson's time is much faster. On paper, he should win.'

'On paper, he might,' agreed Ralph Bannister with a grin. 'But they're not running on paper. They're running on a wet track in front of a partisan British crowd. When this lot get behind Wooderson he'll run with wings on his heels.'

His son still had lingering doubts. 'It would be marvellous if he did win but it won't be easy. They say that he's not been the same since that illness he had last year.'

'Yes. Rheumatic fever is no joke. It really knocked the

stuffing out of him. In fact, the doctors told him to give up running altogether.'

'Then why didn't he?'

'Because he's Sydney Wooderson.'

At that moment there was a rousing cheer of welcome as the British miler came on to the track. When Arne Andersson was introduced to the crowd over the loudspeakers he was given generous applause but it contained none of the affection that Wooderson commanded.

Roger Bannister looked down in surprise at the man who had been the AAA mile champion for five consecutive years before the war. Wooderson was a less than impressive figure. Short, bony and pale, he had close-cropped hair and wore wire-framed spectacles. His long and rather baggy shorts gave him an almost comical appearance. He was thirty-one, his gaunt face making him seem much older, especially when he stood among a group of younger competitors. As he shook Andersson's hand before the start of the race, Wooderson barely came up to the Swede's shoulder.

When the gun sent them away, however, any physical disparity was forgotten. What the British champion lacked in height he more than made up for in courage and stamina. The trim-kitted Andersson soon powered his way to the front to dictate the pace but Wooderson stayed on his heels like a terrier. As the race unfolded the other competitors were forced to play a largely decorative role. It was essentially a contest between two supreme athletes.

National pride was at stake. Showing an indomitable will to win against a bigger and stronger man, Wooderson seemed to symbolize the spirit of wartime Britain itself and the crowd identified totally with him. When he quickened his stride to take the lead just before the bell, everyone urged him on.

'Go on, Sydney!'

'You can do it!'

'Show him who's boss!'

'Run the legs off him!'

But Wooderson could not achieve the impossible. Though he battled valiantly over every inch of the last lap, the superior fitness of the Swede took him back in front and kept him there until the tape. Applause was deafening as the spectators acclaimed a great race and a remarkable performance by a British athlete. Wooderson's grit and sheer zest for running had been astounding.

It certainly fired Roger Bannister's imagination. Wooderson became his hero at that instant and he longed to emulate his example. When his father had taken him to the White City, he had gone with eagerness and high expectation.

When he came away, he had a dream.

Life in the sixth form at University College School, Hampstead, was not an entirely happy experience. After matriculating at the City of Bath Boys' School, Bannister went back to London with his family and found it all rather bewildering. Like a country mouse thrust into a town he was at first quite over-awed by his surroundings. A shy, contemplative youth who tended to live in a world of his own, he became even more isolated at his new day school where his classmates were more boisterous and self-assertive than him. Though he played rugby and did some rowing, he spent most of his time losing himself in his work. At home he was often moody and irritable in a way that went beyond the normal bounds of adolescence.

The headmaster tried to bolster his confidence by appointing him as house captain but the ploy had the reverse effect. Bannister retreated even more into himself and was embarrassed when he had to perform some of his duties. The school had high academic standards and a good reputation but one of its pupils at least could not wait to leave. When he took the scholarship examinations at Oxford and Cambridge he was offered a place at both universities to read Medicine. His main reason for choosing Oxford was that he could take up his place in the coming October instead of having to wait another year, as in the case of Cambridge.

It was to be a fateful decision and one that many members of Cambridge athletics circles came to regret.

Roger Bannister arrived in Oxford on the first day of Michaelmas Term, 1946. He had company on the journey because his sister Joyce was herself a student at the university and she was able to give advice and reassurance. Nevertheless he was lonely and nervous when he first stepped into the lodge at Exeter College to ask where his room was. A couple of other students were chatting to the porter and they seemed so much older and more mature. Like the vast majority of undergraduates they were ex-servicemen whose studies had been rudely interrupted by the war. Still only seventeen, Bannister was a boy among men.

He felt that he was being set apart once more.

'For the second time this century Britain has been through the horrors and devastations of a global war. By the grace of God we have survived that war and you gentlemen will play a crucial part in restoring this shattered homeland of ours to its former greatness . . .'

The Master was addressing the new members of the college on their first evening. Watched by the gilt-framed portraits that lined the walls of the dining room, the freshmen sat on their benches beside the long gleaming tables and listened intently. The Master had great presence and his voice had an authoritative roll to it.

'What you will learn here will not be confined to the knowledge that lies between the covers of books. You will learn, I would hope, that the deepest satisfactions in life come from using whatever talent God has given you, not for your benefit alone, but for the benefit of your family, your friends and your country . . .'

Wearing his full regalia, the Master was standing in front of High Table and letting his words boom around the hall. Scholars and exhibitioners wore long gowns as a mark of distinction and commoners wore short ones. It was their first introduction to college protocol.

'You will learn that on the playing fields the body must be exercised as well as the mind and you will learn that power brings with it responsibility. Above all, I hope that you will leave this college as men of wide interests and vision, men with sound values and a sense of purpose, men for whom the concepts of tolerance, wisdom and justice are sacred.'

He thanked them for their attention, wished them well in their academic careers and then swept out with his gown flowing behind him. A murmur of approval went up and then the undergraduates began to file out.

Bannister was lost in thought as he followed the others into

17

the quadrangle and he did not notice the stocky young man who fell in beside him. His companion had a cheerful manner.

'Enjoy the pep talk?'

'Mm?'

'The Master. Doing his turn.'

'I thought it was quite inspiring,' said Bannister.

'Give or take the odd platitude,' noted the other. 'Are you coming to the JCR?'

'Well . . .'

'I'll buy you a coffee.'

'Oh. Thanks.'

'What are you reading?'

'Medicine.'

'That sounds too much like hard work to me!'

'What's your subject?'

'English. Ostensibly.'

'I'm not with you.'

'I didn't come to Oxford to study, old chap. I came here to enjoy myself for three years. And to row, of course.' They paused at an arched doorway. 'What's your sport? You don't look like an oarsman.'

'I'm not, really.'

'Rugger?'

'Hate it.'

'Well, you must do something,' he insisted. 'A man without a sport is a bit like a ship without a sail.'

'Actually, I was hoping to take up running.'

'Can't you think of anything more *exciting*?' He gave a broad grin. 'Where's the fun in going round and round a track?'

'There'll be cross-country as well, I daresay.'

'That's even worse, old chap!'

'Why?'

They stood aside to let a stream of undergraduates go past on their way to the Junior Common Room then the oarsman leaned in close to give a considered opinion.

'If you want to get the most out of Oxford, take up a *real* sport.'

'Such as?'

'Learn to row or get yourself a hockey stick or join the soccer club. But don't waste your time on athletics.'

'It's not a waste of time.'

'Of course it is!' argued the other, turning away. 'Running will get you absolutely nowhere.'

Bannister shrugged then followed him through the archway.

The next day was a very busy one. There were tutors to see and fellow medics to meet and timetables to work out and thick, expensive textbooks to buy and a dozen other things to do. Occupying such a central position, Exeter College proved to be an ideal base from which to operate. Blackwell's bookshop was right opposite the Broad Street end of the college while the laboratories and science departments were only a short walk away up Parks Road.

Proud to be a member of the most famous university in the world, Bannister was slightly intimidated by it at first and had none of the easy arrogance shown by some of the students from public schools. He felt very much an outsider.

As soon as he was able he went to the place he had resolved to visit at the earliest possible opportunity. Coming out of Turl Street he turned left into the bustling High Street and marvelled at the architectural beauties that were hemmed in familiarly by shops, offices and houses. He strolled past the majestic church of St Mary the Virgin with its soaring spire, past the grandeur of All Souls College with its distinctive golden-yellow stone and past the long, imposing facade of University College on the opposite side of the road.

With a gentle downward gradient, the High curved on past the spectacular domed rotunda of Queen's and the subtler charms of St Edmund Hall before terminating at the splendour of Magdalen with its magnificent tower spearing the sky. Bannister went on over the bridge, took the right fork at the Plain and soon reached his destination.

Iffley Road Running Ground was set back from the main thoroughfare and protected from the noise of its traffic. A row of poplars stood to attention at the far end and beyond them were the damp, luxuriant meadows that fringed the Isis. The cinder track was a third of a mile long and tilted but that did not worry Bannister. What struck him was the combination of peacefulness and defiance. Lying quietly in its own rural glade, the track yet spoke of energy and challenge and athletic achievement.

Bannister knew that many great runners had trained and raced at Iffley Road and some of their names came back to him now. He thought of Arnold Strode-Jackson who won Olympic gold in the 1500 metres at the Stockholm Games of 1912; of the bespectacled Tommy Hampson, who gained his gold medal in the 800 metres at Los Angeles twenty years later; and of the incomparable Jack Lovelock, the fair-haired New Zealander who had once been a medical student at Oxford, and who had dominated middle-distance in his time before capping his career by winning the 1500 metres at the Berlin Olympics of 1936.

So many names, so many memories, so many fine races.

On this humble track in its tranquil setting an important athletic tradition had been forged and Bannister had a sudden impulse to be part of it. He hurried straight back to his college and accosted the first student he saw in the quadrangle.

'Excuse me. I wonder if you could help me?' he asked politely. 'I want to join the Athletic Club.'

'Whatever for!' returned the student with a well-bred sneer.

'Because I . . . like running.'

'Have you seen the doctor about your complaint?'

'No . . .'

'Then you should, my dear fellow. Can't have you indulging in violent exercise. It's demeaning.' His voice became confidential. 'Shall I tell you what *I* do?'

'What?'

'Whenever I have the desire to do anything at all strenuous, I just go and lie down for a while. The urge soon passes off.' He gave a patronizing smile. 'Try it yourself.'

Bannister moved away. His fresh-faced eagerness was a little crumpled now but he did not give up. He went to the Junior Common Room and asked around until he got the information he wanted. It cost a guinea to join the University Athletic Club and the money had to be paid in advance. Rushing to the nearest post office, he bought a postal order for the right amount and sent it off at once.

Over dinner that evening he asked the friendly oarsman to

join him for a run. After many protests the latter succumbed to his persuasion but warned him that he would not make a habit of it. Next day they headed for Iffley Road together. Since he had no track suit, Bannister wore the oil-stained kit he had used for rowing at school. Like his companion, he wore plimsolls on his feet.

They jogged around the track side by side and settled into a comfortable rhythm. With his broad shoulders, heavy chest and bulging thighs, the oarsman presented a sharp contrast to the tall, thin, angular figure beside him. Bannister was thrilled to be running on the celebrated Iffley Road track and there was a real bounce in his stride. His friend, however, did not have the same commitment to athletics and his interest waned after four or five laps.

'Just one more.'

'Okay,' said Bannister. 'Let's stretch it out a bit.'

They increased their pace for the last lap. Though he had a plodding style the oarsman was a powerful runner with plenty of stamina. As they came round the bend into the final straight, he even managed a token burst of speed. Bannister matched it and they passed the finishing line abreast.

They were still trying to get their breath back as one of the groundsmen sauntered over to them. He had been watching them closely and he headed straight for the oarsman.

'Well run! You should stick at it. You've got the power to go a long way in athletics.'

'Thanks – but I prefer rowing.'

'That's a pity,' said the groundsman, then turned to Bannister. 'As for you, son, I'd suggest that you give it up altogether. I hate to say this but you just haven't got the build for running.'

Bannister was jolted. It was hardly the most encouraging start to his athletic career. The blow hurt him very deeply.

Chapter Two

A large field had entered for the race and the runners were moving around nervously before the start. Behind them was the dazzling blue backdrop of the ocean, its surface teased into ripples by the breeze. A few yachts zigzagged their way across Port Phillip Bay. Children played happily on the sandhills. A dog yawned before curling up to sleep in the shade of a cluster of palm trees. Portsea was hot.

Some of the competitors wore peaked caps to shield themselves from the glare and others favoured headbands to absorb the perspiration. All of them looked young, fit, supple and anxious to get under way. Then Percy Cerutty appeared. Naked but for his skimpy black shorts and his running shoes, he caused a lot of comment and amusement. Unperturbed by the fact that he was thirty years older than some of the others, he began to run vigorously on the spot.

Jim Eve, one of the officials, walked over to him.

'Excuse me. Are you an official entrant?'

'Of course I'm an official entrant,' snapped Cerutty, switching to his stretching exercises. 'Do you think I'd be here if I wasn't?'

'What's your name?'

'Ned Kelly.'

Some of the other athletes laughed but Eve was not amused.

'And what's your real name?' he pressed.

'Cerutty. Percy Cerutty.'

'Can't see you here,' said the official, glancing down the list on his clipboard. Then he blinked. 'Wait a minute. Cerutty P.'

'That's me.'

'You do realize that this is a fifty-mile race, don't you?'

'Is it?' joked the athlete. 'I was hoping it was a hundred miles.'

'Aren't you a bit old for this, Mr Cerutty?'

'Look here, young fella,' retorted the other. 'I was running four and a half minutes for the mile when you were still in nappies. And I'm much fitter now than I was then.'

Eve bristled and eyed him coldly. 'If you're going to run you must wear a singlet and it has to have your club colours on it.'

'Who says so?'

'I do. Yes, and your shorts must have a stripe down the sides.'

'What is this – a race or a bloody fashion parade!'

'Those are the regulations.'

'I'll run how I want to run.'

'Not if I disqualify you, Mr Cerutty.'

'You wouldn't dare!'

'There are strict regulations.'

'Then you know what you can do with them!'

The starter was now calling the competitors to the line and Cerutty turned to join them. Eve stood in his way and wagged a finger at him.

'Dress properly or you don't run.'

'Try and stop me.'

Before the official could say another word Cerutty had pushed his way through the ranks of athletes so that he was near the front. They were now under starter's orders. Bunched, tensed and crouching, they were unleashed by the gun and shot forward down the road.

As Jim Eve watched them, another official joined him.

'Was that old fella giving you some lip, Jim?'

'Ah, it doesn't matter! He's never going to finish the race.'

'Are you sure?'

'Positive. I'll give him five miles. Then we'll have to scrape him up off the ground and load him into an ambulance.'

'Poor old bugger!'

'Come on.'

The two men went off to a waiting car so that they could join the convoy that would follow the race all the way to

Melbourne and monitor its progress. They knew that many of those who had set out with such purpose from the starting line would never get within sight of the finish and that each punishing hour would whittle away the numbers more and more.

A small group of runners had opened up an early lead and stayed thirty yards or so in front of a larger group that contained Percy Cerutty, padding along with a frugal stride, his feet hardly leaving the ground and his breathing relaxed. Twenty or more yards behind him was the main pack, a solid mass of athletes who seemed to find safety and comfort by keeping together.

Casualties began before they even reached Sorrento. One athlete tripped, fell and bruised himself so badly he was unable to continue. Another pulled a hamstring and hopped out of the race in agony. A third found a pothole in the road and sprained his ankle. Without even noticing that they had gone, the race continued on its way.

Port Phillip Bay was on their left as they moved slowly up the coast road and there was a cooling breeze coming off the water. Cold drinks were provided for the runners at regular stages and they grabbed paper cups from stewards without checking their stride. Cerutty made sure that he had liquid refreshment at every point so that he could fight off dehydration. He knew only too well the appalling effects it could have on the human body.

As they passed through Rosebud, then through Dromana and on up the peninsula, others came to grief. Inexperienced runners who had gone off too fast too soon now paid the penalty. Cramp started to reduce the field. Heat exhaustion searched for its prey.

Percy Cerutty was running an intelligent race. Maintaining a steady rhythm and conserving his energy with care, he kept in touch with the leading group but made no effort to catch them up. People who lined the route gave him a special cheer when they saw him and he came in for some friendly barracking as well.

'Keep it up, Grandpa!'
'Watch your false teeth don't fall out!'
'Wouldn't it be quicker in a bathchair?'

Jim Eve and his colleague had trailed the runners for well over four hours. Many more competitors had fallen by the wayside now and the survivors were strung out over a distance of two miles. Eve put his foot on the accelerator and took the car all the way to the front-runners. He was astonished to see Cerutty still in contention.

'You gave him five miles, Jim,' reminded his friend.

'It'll kill him if he goes on much longer.'

'He looks to be in better shape than most of them.'

'No. He'll never make it.'

'Care to bet on that?'

But the official did not. Cerutty had just spotted him and given him a brief wave of defiance. The oldest man in the race had no plans to quit just yet.

It was the final stage that was the most cruel. Men who had battled on for forty-five miles and more suddenly found that they had nothing left to give. Their legs turned to rubber or their vision became blurred or their lungs were on fire. One by one they dropped out and had to be given first aid or more serious medical help. They had been robbed of the dignity of completing the course and that was not going to happen to Percy Cerutty. He, too, was in pain but he forced himself to live with it. He had something to prove.

'I don't believe it! He's still there!'

'And in with a chance, Jim.'

'However does the old coot do it?'

'I don't know,' said his colleague, 'but you're damn lucky you didn't put money on him folding up.'

The two officials had driven in ahead to join the large crowd at the finishing line. What they could see a hundred yards away was the bent figure of Percy Cerutty as he closed the gap that separated him from the one runner still ahead of him. The delirious applause was helping to carry the two men home, giving them that vital lift as they fought off exhaustion.

They ran low, legs almost buckling, hardly able to support their body weight. Sweat streamed from every pore of their bodies and their breathing was tormented. But they kept coming and – incredibly – it was Percy Cerutty who was coming more strongly. With a final effort that drained every ounce of energy from him, he managed a small spurt that took him past the leader and through the finishing tape.

'He won!' gasped Eve in utter disbelief.

'Unless you still intend to disqualify him.'

'What?'

'Look at him, Jim. Improper running strip. Disregard for the rules. Verbal abuse of an official.' He grinned at his colleague. 'Fancy going over there and telling him that he's disqualified?'

Jim Eve shook his head. Cerutty was now at the centre of a cheering mob and press photographers were fighting for vantage points.

'The result will stand,' said Eve. 'He deserves it.'

On the verge of collapse, Cerutty nevertheless waved away the hands that reached out to support him. He kept slowly on the move, trying to relax his muscles and to reduce the burning sensation in his chest. The race had turned him into a hero but he was not yet ready for any hero-worship. He needed time to recover and a moment to make a very special telephone call.

An hour later he felt appreciably better. He had rested, taken a shower, changed back into his clothes and drunk some orange juice. As soon as he was strong enough he went off to a public telephone box and dialled a local number. He was put through by the receptionist and heard a familiar voice at the other end of the line.

'Hello . . .'

'Dr Egan?'

'Yes. Who is this, please?'

'Percy Cerutty. Remember me?'

'Indeed I do, Mr Cerutty,' admitted the doctor in surprise.

'You said I'd be in my bloody grave years ago!'

'I'm pleased to hear that you're not.'

'Then here's something else you'll be pleased to hear. For your information, I've just won the Portsea to City marathon. So stick *that* in your breeches and see if it pricks!'

He slammed down the receiver with a grin of triumph.

It had been almost as enjoyable as winning the race.

Wes Santee loped across the fields with the easy stride of a natural athlete. Tall, rangy and with a crew-cut setting off his strong features, he was wearing tee shirt, jeans and a pair of sneakers. Books dangled from a strap in his hand and were swung expertly up when he clambered over a fence. It had been a hot Kansas day and the early evening had not yet taken the full sting out of the sun but Santee did not slacken his pace. Even though he could feel the perspiration trickling down his face, he pushed himself on because he knew that he was late.

He crossed another field, vaulted over the gate and ran on into the dusty yard in front of the ranch house. His father, a big, sinewy man with a weather-beaten exterior, came round the angle of the barn.

'Where you been?' he demanded angrily.

'Sorry, Pa.'

'Shoulda been back an hour ago.'

'Yeah, I know. But —'

'Tell me later,' ordered his father. 'Go do the milking.'

'Sure thing.'

'Then get on with the rest of your chores.'

Wes Santee dropped his books on the wooden verandah and rushed off to a large wooden shed. His shoulder was soon resting in the accommodating flank of a cow as he pulled at her teats and made milk slurp into the pail. While most of his friends had stayed behind at high school to develop their sporting interests or simply to have fun together, he was forced to come home to do his share of work on the ranch. It seemed unfair.

Over two hours later he sat down for the evening meal with his family. His baby sister had already been put to bed and his eight-year-old brother was sent off as soon as the meal was over. Mrs Santee, a bustling, homely woman in a flowered dress, cleared the table and went off to do the washing-up. The teenager knew what was coming.

'Where were you?' grunted his father.

'I . . . had to talk to someone, Pa.'

'Your place was back here.'

'Okay. I know that. But it was kinda special.'

'Nothing is more special than this ranch. Raising cattle means hard work and everyone has to do his share. That includes *you*, Wes.'

'I always do my chores,' reasoned his son. 'Weekends and vacations, you got me here full time.'

'It's not enough.'

'What more can I do?'

'Come home in the afternoons.'

'I can't just walk out of high school!' protested Santee.

'Book-learning ain't everything.'

'Pa – I've got a *right* to an education!'

'I got by without one,' said his father bluntly. 'You start tomorrow. Leave school at noon and get straight back here.'

'No!' argued the other. 'I can't! I won't!'

'You do as you're told, boy.'

'Pa, listen to me. Please. Shall I tell you why I was late back today? Someone wanted to speak to me. My track coach.'

'I told you before. You don't train after school.'

'I wasn't training. Just talking.' He inhaled deeply before he spoke again, knowing that he would meet resistance. 'I *like* running. I'm not just good at it – I'm *real* good. There's not a guy that can stay near me over the mile. The coach says I could be another Glenn Cunningham. Wouldn't *that* be something?'

'You're needed here, son.'

'But I want to take my running further. The coach says I'd be almost certain to win an athletics scholarship. If I got to university and had proper track facilities, I could –'

'That's enough, Wes!' snarled his father. 'We can't meet the payments on this spread with you off at school all day long or dreaming about being Glenn Cunningham. Running races don't pay bills.'

'Pa, you can't hold me back!' argued Santee vehemently. 'It's so unfair!'

'Don't shout like that,' said his mother, coming in from the kitchen. 'You'll wake the baby.'

She calmed them down and then joined the discussion. Her sympathies were divided. Since she had a teaching certificate herself, she knew the value of education and did not want her eldest child to lose out in any way. At the same time, however, she was only too aware of how great a struggle it was to run the ranch. They were in the process of buying the 2000-acre property and it was stretching their resources to the limit.

28

Every hour of help that they could get from their teenage son was invaluable.

It was agreed that Santee might be taken off school on the occasional afternoon but only when it was absolutely necessary. It was not a happy compromise but it did prevent further rancorous argument. Santee accepted his fate with a sigh. Though it was only nine o'clock his parents now went off to bed since they had to be up before dawn. Alone at last he was now able to do his homework.

The ranch house was small, simply furnished and had no electricity. Santee therefore had to work by the light of an oil lamp. He consoled himself with the thought that it was a warm night. During the winter months he had to work while crouched up against the wood stove that was the only source of heat.

It was nearly midnight when he finished his studying but he was not ready for bed just yet. He took out the latest edition of an athletics magazine and gave himself the luxury of flicking through its pages. An article about his hero, Glenn Cunningham, caught his attention and he pored over a photograph that showed the Kansas athlete winning a silver medal in the Berlin Olympics behind Jack Lovelock. Both men had broken the world 1500 metres record that day.

As Santee read the article he was reminded of some of the awesome difficulties that Cunningham had faced early on in life. The rugged athlete whose bold front-running had earned him the nickname of 'The Iron Horse of Kansas' had been badly burned at the age of seven in a school fire that killed his brother. Cunningham's injuries were so serious that the surgeons even considered amputating his legs. After a year of intensive treatment in hospital he was allowed home again. He took up running as a therapeutic exercise and went on to become the fastest miler in the world.

Wes Santee smiled ruefully. It certainly put his own problems into perspective. It also reinforced his ambition to have a successful track career himself and to fight his way to the top no matter what obstacles his father might put in his way.

He slept that night with the magazine under his pillow.

*

Percy Cerutty liked to do things in style. When he held a press conference outside his cottage in Domain Road, he made sure that he stood in the doorway so that any photographs of him would include the sign which he had put up on the adjacent wall. As the sports journalists gathered around him he drew their attention to the sign by tapping on it with his knuckle.

Percy Wells Cerutty
Conditioner of Men, Maker of Champions

'You're not a man for understatement, are you?' asked someone.

'I tell the truth,' asserted Cerutty. 'And I don't believe in hiding my light under a bushel.'

Jill Webster, an attractive young woman in a smart blue dress, asked the next question in her usual direct, no-nonsense manner. She was not deterred by the fact that she was the only female present.

'You made quite a name for yourself as a long-distance runner, Mr Cerutty. What makes you think you'll be any good as a coach?'

'Look here, young lady,' he said testily. 'If you're going to be aggressive from the start, you can just pack your bags and go. What's a young girl like you covering sport for in any case?'

'It's my job.'

'Well, you should be at home looking after your husband.'

'I'm not married.'

'Then you should be. What's wrong with you?'

Jill Webster was unruffled. 'I just want to know what you think you've got to offer.'

'I'll tell you what I think I've got to offer so you put this down in your little pad and just make sure you get it right.' He paused for effect. 'The people who run sport here are mugs, not worth ha'pence. This country is full of fine young men and women who could really put Australia on the map athletic-wise if they weren't told by a lot of drongos that they'll do themselves harm if they train more than twice a week.'

'So your training methods are going to be a lot tougher than the usual ones, are they?' she asked.

'The toughest there have ever been.'

'How do you know they'll work?'

'Because I'm living proof of the fact,' he boasted. 'A fool of a doctor once told me that I'd be dead in two years. Then I took up marathon running. You see the result.' He cackled loudly. 'I'm still above ground while that poor old doctor has rattled the pan.'

One of the male journalists weighed in with a question.

'Do you think that Australia can really make its mark on the world athletic scene?'

'Well, why shouldn't they?' yelled Cerutty, rounding on the man and making him back slightly away. 'Aren't we human beings just like any other human beings?'

Yes, but –'

'Are you saying we're genetically inferior or something?'

'No, of course not. In fact –'

'Europe is tired and worn out,' announced Cerutty. 'They've exhausted themselves with the war and the United States have gone soft. They just sit over there stuffing themselves with doughnuts and watching television.' He extended his arms wide in a dramatic gesture. 'This country has sunshine and fresh air and vigour. Australia is where it's all going to happen. This is the New World and it's high time we started thinking of ourselves that way and turned the corner.'

Jill Webster used her pencil to point to the sign on the wall.

'You claim to be a conditioner of men. What about women?'

'Oh, I've conditioned a few of them in my time, young lady,' he replied with a comical leer. 'But that's another kind of sport.'

'Why are you only interested in male athletes?'

'Because athletics is primarily a test of male strength and endurance. Let's face it, women aren't built the same way.' His lecherous grin drew a chuckle from some of the journalists. 'Not that I'm complaining about the way they're built – far from it! But it's the male runner who will continue to set the fastest times. And thanks to me, many of those runners will be home-grown Australians.'

'Could you give us a couple of names?' pressed Jill.

'I'll do more than that,' said Cerutty obligingly. 'I'll call

31

them over and introduce them.' He turned to a small group of young men who were standing self-consciously in the background. 'Now, this is young Les Perry, the Mighty Atom. Step forward, Les.'

Looking distinctly uncomfortable a short, stocky individual came across and nodded to the journalists. Cerutty increased the athlete's embarrassment by putting an arm around his shoulders.

'Les Perry here ran a three-mile race at St Kilda's Cricket Ground when the temperature was up around a hundred and four degrees. But did he take it easy?' He squeezed Perry's shoulder. 'Did you?'

'No, Perce.'

'No, he didn't! He ran himself into the ground and collapsed on the track. *That's* the sort of man I'm looking for!' emphasized Cerutty with eyes gleaming. 'Someone who's prepared to die!'

'Thanks,' mumbled the athlete and sidled away.

Cerutty turned to a big, muscular young man and beckoned him over. He seemed as uneasy about it all as Perry but he rose to a friendly grin. His coach patted him on the back.

'And this is Don MacMillan. Make a note of that name, all of you. It's one you're going to hear a lot more of in the future.'

'What's your distance, son?' asked one of the journalists.

'He's a miler,' answered Cerutty proudly. 'You people are always drumming up stories in your papers about the four-minute mile. Well, Don MacMillan is the most likely person to beat four minutes.'

This announcement at once startled the athlete himself and caused a buzz of interest. Questions were fired from every angle but it was Jill Webster's voice that cut through the babble.

'Do you really think the four-minute barrier can be broken?'

'Of course it can,' asserted Cerutty with total confidence.

'Athletes have been trying to better four minutes for over half a century,' she argued. 'What makes you so certain that someone can actually do it?'

'Because when mankind sets itself a goal, it always achieves that goal. One day soon Everest will be climbed at last and somebody will run a mile in under four minutes. The human spirit will see to it.'

'And will Don MacMillan be the man to do it?'

'Probably,' replied the coach. 'Who else is there? Gunder Haegg might have done it. He got closest with 4.01.4 seconds. But he and Arne Andersson have been booted out of athletics for infringing the amateur code. So who does that leave?'

'America?' suggested someone.

'They haven't produced a top-class miler since Glenn Cunningham and Bill Bonthron. Forget the Yanks.'

'What about Britain?' asked Jill Webster.

'Sydney Wooderson has shot his bolt. As for the rest of Europe they're still too busy counting their dead to worry too much about athletics. No, *this* is the country where it's going to take place!' he affirmed. 'And I'll tell you this. If Don MacMillan doesn't beat four minutes, then another Australian athlete will. I'll tell you something else as well,' he added with no pretence at modesty. 'When that magic miler does break through the barrier, Percy Cerutty will be the man who trained him.'

And he pointed again to the sign on the wall.

Geelong Grammar School was known for its rigorous academic standards and for its consistently fine sporting records. The emphasis was on hard work coupled with physical exercise in the hope of turning out pupils with a balanced attitude and all-round abilities. While the headmaster kept a close eye on scholastic progress, therefore, he did not neglect the sporting arena in any way. As he was strolling along a corridor one afternoon with his deputy, they reached a window that overlooked the grounds and they paused involuntarily to watch something that was happening down on the running track.

Four senior pupils were engaged in an impromptu race. They were bunched tightly together as they went round the first bend and they seemed well-matched for speed. It was the tallest youth who compelled attention. Slim, elegant and with dark curly hair above a high forehead, he had such an immaculate running style that it made the others look laboured and ungainly.

33

As the four of them went into the back straight he made his move. Finding another gear, he coasted effortlessly away until he had opened up a lead of thirty or forty yards and he was still widening the gap when he reached the finishing line.

The headmaster was delighted with what he had seen.

'That's Landy, isn't it?'

'Yes,' said his colleague. 'John Landy. Rather good, isn't he?'

Chapter Three

A sizeable crowd had braved the bad weather to come to the White City Stadium for the annual meeting between the athletes of Oxford and Cambridge. College scarves of every hue brought some welcome colour to a drab scene and helped to fend off the cold wind. Rain fell steadily and pools of water had built up at several points on the track to rule out any possibility of fast times and tumbling records.

Harold Abrahams looked out from beneath the shelter of the stand and heaved a sigh. Beside him was Sandy Duncan, an affable character in his thirties who was a member of the AAA Coaching Committee and who had been spending a day a week at Iffley Road Running Ground to give advice and encouragement.

'Look at those puddles,' said Abrahams. 'It will be more like cross-country than athletics.'

'Its the jumpers I feel sorry for,' noted Duncan, himself a former champion long-jumper. 'Nothing worse than landing in a sodden pit.'

'Yes, I know all about the hazards of long-jumping,' the older man reminded him. 'My athletics career came to a sudden end in the jumping pit at Stamford Bridge. I went for a big one, lost my footing on take-off and that was it. I heard a noise rather like Smee tearing cloth in *Peter Pan* and my leg was broken.'

'I'm glad you can be so philosophical about it,' said Duncan. 'And there is one consolation. We may have lost a great athlete that day but we gained a brilliant administrator.'

'Thanks, Sandy. Unfortunately, even brilliant adminis-
trators can't make bricks without straw.'

'You can say that again!'

With the Olympic Games scheduled to take place in London
the following year, the problems faced by the AAA had been
highlighted. It was a lean time for British athletics and the
chances of fielding a strong national team seemed rather slim.
Like all the other officials present, Abrahams and Duncan
were hoping that the Varsity meeting would throw up some
new names and kindle some fresh hopes.

'At least we now have a Chief National Coach,' observed
Duncan.

'Yes. And Geoff Dyson is the ideal man for the job.'

'Bit of a parade-ground manner.'

'That'll do no harm. Most athletes need someone to ginger
them up and Geoff will certainly do that.'

The announcer's voice boomed out over the loudspeakers
and a cheer went up as the athletes began to strip off their
track suits for the first event. Sandy Duncan turned to his
companion.

'Who do you think will win?'

'What a question to ask a Cambridge man!'

They exchanged a chuckle and settled down to watch the
100 metres. Notwithstanding the unfriendly conditions, the
athletes ran with flair and commitment, finding that extra
edge that always seems to come when the rival universities
meet. There was continuous excitement on track and field and
the spectators were loud in their appreciation. No outstanding
competitors had emerged but there was a high level of achievement nevertheless.

Six runners now began to get ready for the mile race.

'That tall chap is a bit young, isn't he?' commented Abrahams.

'Yes. That's Roger Bannister. A fresher. Only eighteen.'

'Any good?'

'Too soon to tell. I saw him run in the Freshmen's Sports.
He came second behind Peter Curry.'

'What sort of time?'

'Just under five minutes, I think.'

'Oh dear!' said Abrahams with a grimace.

'It wasn't really that bad. Apparently it was the first time the lad had ever worn spikes and it made him over-stride. He went bounding around the track like a kangaroo. I remember telling him afterwards that he could knock twenty seconds off his time if only he got his stride-pattern right.'

'Let's see if he took your advice, Sandy.'

'Oh, he won't win this,' said Duncan easily. 'Bannister's only the third-string. Lucky to be in the team at all.'

Oblivious to any comments that were being made about him or his chances, Roger Bannister limbered up on the side of the track. He was nervous and diffident and very conscious of the fact that the others were older and more experienced than him. There was a ritual handshake between the six competitors and then they crouched at the line. When the gun set the mile race in motion it was the three Cambridge runners who went into an immediate lead. Bannister stayed well back and was towed around the early laps.

He had never run so fast before and he was aching with tiredness as they approached the bell. Still a respectful distance behind the leaders, he was content to stay there until halfway down the back straight. Then the significance of the occasion seemed to be borne in upon him. After only two terms at Oxford he had won his blue and was representing the university in what was the glamour event of the afternoon. Moreover, he was running on the very track where he had once seen Sydney Wooderson race so courageously in the cause of British athletics.

Bannister felt exhilarated. He had a sudden urge to overtake the others and his body responded at once. Finding a burst of energy that he did not know he possessed, he shrugged off his fatigue and streaked past the figures ahead of him. His long, raking stride took him well clear of all opposition and he was cheered to the echo by the Oxford contingent as he breasted the tape for an emphatic victory.

'Well done, Roger!'

'That was marvellous!'

'You won by twenty yards!'

'Left the Cambridge runners for dead!'

'Fantastic performance!'

He was not able to bask in the adulation because his triumph had brought him near to exhaustion. His chest was a furnace, his limbs had gone slack and the energy that had coursed through him only a short while ago was now completely spent. But as he stood there panting, he was thrilled with what had happened. The race had taught him two important things. He had a will to win. And he was a runner.

When he had recovered enough to shower and dress he was introduced to Harold Abrahams and other top officials. Praise was heaped on him from all sides and he was now taken seriously as an athlete. There was a further treat in store for him.

'Mr Bannister?'

'Yes?'

'I just wanted to congratulate you on your run,' said a big man whose cultured voice still had a New Zealand twang to it. 'I'm Jack Lovelock.'

Bannister did not need to be told that. He had seen the face in dozens of photographs and had recognized instantly that he was in the presence of one of the legendary figures in middle-distance running. He was slightly agog as he shook hands with the great man.

'That was some finishing sprint,' continued Lovelock.

'It wasn't a very fast time, though,' admitted Bannister, hunching his shoulders. 'Over four and a half minutes.'

'Don't worry about that,' counselled the other. 'It was a pretty miserable day for running. Besides, winning is much more important than clocking up a fast time. Do you know what my time was when I took my one and only AAA title back in 1934?'

'What?'

'This will shock you: 4 minutes 26.6 seconds. Me! Jack Lovelock. The world record-holder at the distance.' He laughed at the memory. 'Shall I tell you why it was so slow?'

'Why?'

'Tactics. I was up against two fellas that I was determined to beat. One was a little pipsqueak called Sydney Wooderson who'd had the nerve to beat me at the Southern Championship when he was only nineteen. The other was Jerry Cornes. Remember him?'

'Silver medal in the 1500 metres at the Los Angeles Olympics.'

'That's him. I didn't want to leave anything to chance with those two on my tail. So I slowed the race right down then beat them to the tape in the final dash.' He appraised Bannister through squinting eyes. 'What are you reading?'

'Medicine.'

'Snap! Where?'

'Exeter.'

'My old college as well! I knew you were a man after my own heart. I was a Rhodes Scholar at Exeter and then went on to St Mary's. Medicine and athletics go well together.'

'I haven't found that,' confessed Bannister. 'There's so much studying to do that I have a job to fit my running in.'

'That wasn't what I meant,' explained Lovelock. 'A doctor knows how to listen to his body. How to tune it up and get the best out of it. When you understand the mechanism of human locomotion, it's bound to give you an advantage.'

'I hope so. I could do with it.'

'Well, I must be going.' Lovelock blinked a few times then smiled apologetically. 'Sorry if I keep squinting at you but my eyesight is not what it was. Riding accident. Fell off a horse and banged my head too hard.' He offered his hand again. 'But I can see well enough to be able to watch a fine performance in the mile.'

'Thank you,' said Bannister, giving a farewell handshake.

'Goodbye, then – and good luck!'

'Goodbye.'

Bannister was almost glowing. On the strength of having won a single important race he had met most of the official hierarchy of British athletics and one of the immortals of the track. He had also felt the pulsing excitement of victory in front of a cheering crowd and known the strange joy of pushing himself through the pain barrier.

Medicine would still come first. But he would find more time for his running now. It was a duty.

*

The annual meeting of the Oxford University Athletic Club was conducted with the usual amalgam of boisterousness and seriousness. Though there was a lot of business to get through, the members made sure that it did not dampen their undergraduate high spirits. Their behaviour mirrored the university approach to athletics. Inwardly, they were dedicated to their sport but they were frightened to let that dedication show too much. Nonchalance was the watchword. They hid their true feelings behind a mask of light-hearted indifference.

The chairman's voice rose above the amiable hubbub.

'And now we come to the main item on the agenda . . .'

'What's her name?' yelled one comedian.

'Bring her in!' called a second lewd voice.

He waited until the laughter subsided. 'We come to the election of our new president . . .'

'Hurrah!' shouted a group at the rear end of the packed room.

'There is no need for me to tell you his name . . .'

'Then don't!' suggested someone. 'Give us three guesses.'

'Or to remind you of the great service he has already rendered to this club. Last year he made a name for himself by winning the mile at the White City against three bemused athletes from a university in the Fen Country whose name escapes me at the moment.' He paused to allow room for a few jeers. 'He followed that with a win against the AAA and he has not looked back since.'

'Why?' cried a voice. 'Who's after him?'

'Last term, as secretary of this club, he did an immense amount of work on our behalf and proved what a good organizer he was. All this, I may say, from a young man who, when he first went for a run at Iffley Road, was told by a groundsman that he didn't have the build for athletics!'

The groundsman came in for a barrage of ribald comments and then the chairman waved to the person who was standing nervously on one side in a sports jacket and flannels.

'Gentlemen, I give you – the new President . . .'

'Hurrah!' The cheer was a general one this time.

Roger Bannister cleared his throat and stepped forward to give his speech of acceptance. He looked pale, strained and uneasy. Though he was among friends, his self-confidence

40

seemed to desert him and he was assailed by all his old doubts. He glanced down at the sheet of paper in his hand to remind himself what he was supposed to say. As the noise faded he swallowed hard.

'Gentlemen . . .' he began. 'Let me say how honoured I feel to be the new president of the Oxford University Athletic Club. It is a privilege to be elected and I am very grateful to you all. Oxford has been one of the traditional breeding grounds for British athletics and we must never forget that it was at this university – in 1880 – that the Amateur Athletic Association was founded. Let me take your minds back even further into the realms of athletic history . . .'

He was speaking with a quiet intensity that was totally out of key with the mood of the others. They had come to hear a lively speech and not a lecture. Eyebrows were raised, faces were pulled, murmurs of disapproval began. The longer he went on, the more obvious became the unrest.

'The Greek ideal of sport was that it should be a preparation for life. Indeed, the aim of the Olympics in Ancient Greece was the improvement of the whole man and for a long time specialization in certain events was discouraged . . .'

Aware of the effect that he was having, Bannister became even more nervous in his delivery. Interruptions were starting now and he was finding it difficult to cope. The chairman leaned over to him.

'Relax, Roger,' he whispered. 'Just be yourself, old chap.'

It was sound advice and Bannister took it at once. Abandoning his prepared speech, he cleared his throat once more and spoke in a much less formal and stilted manner.

'Let's forget the past. What you really want to know about is the future. I'd better warn you now that my plans for the club are ambitious. I want to make it bigger and better.' There was a ripple of interest and it encouraged him to go on. 'As I see it, we should have four main targets. One – increase the membership. It's high time we showed the rowing fraternity and the rugger hearties that they're not the only sportsmen at Oxford . . .'

'Hear, hear!' agreed a chorus of voices.

'Two – and I know this is a revolutionary idea – we must try to get professional coaching.' The reaction was immediate

41

and the room was buzzing with protest and agreement. Bannister held up his hands to quell the noise. 'Three – we should revive the Oxford and Cambridge tour of America.'

'Best idea so far!'

'I'll come with you, Roger!'

'Why do we have to take Cambridge?'

The response was warm and positive and it helped to restore Bannister's nerve. This was what the members wanted. Some constructive proposals for the future of the club.

'You said there were four main targets, Roger,' noted someone. 'What's the last one?'

'To improve the track at Iffley Road. Yes, I know it has a wonderful history and we're all very fond of it but it simply doesn't meet international specifications. It's too long. What we need is a 440-yard track with six lanes and it has to be a priority. How would you like to break a world record at Iffley Road only to be told that it can't be ratified because a third of a mile tilted track does not comply with official specifications?'

He had them hanging on his words now and he went on to develop his arguments in a forceful and persuasive way. When he finished his speech he was given rowdy acclaim by a delighted audience. Though his controversial plans would need to be debated more fully, everyone was now convinced that with Roger Bannister as its president, the Oxford University Athletic Club would go from strength to strength.

Improvization was the dominant theme of the London Olympic Games. In a post-war Britain that was beset with shortages and ruled by ration books there was neither time nor money to build special facilities for the XIVth Olympiad. Wembley Stadium, the focal point for the British Empire Exhibition of 1924, became the venue for the athletics and a special cinder track was laid around a circuit that was normally used for greyhound racing. Showjumping was also held at the stadium along with the football and hockey finals.

The nearby Empire Pool accommodated the swimming and the boxing while the basketball was held at Haringey Arena. Cycling events were decided at Herne Hill, wrestling at Earls Court, rowing at Henley and yachting all the way down in

Torquay. Fencing was fitted in at the Palace of Engineering, Wembley.

Fifty-nine countries and almost four and a half thousand athletes were involved, the highest number to date in any Olympic Games. Germany and Japan were notable absentees and Russia was no longer affiliated to the International Olympic Committee. Three more national flags would have fluttered inside Wembley Stadium had not Bulgaria and Palestine withdrawn at the last moment and had Rumania not failed to turn up. The organizers were thrilled with the general response. To have assembled so many competing countries in the wake of a monstrous world war was itself a remarkable achievement.

Athletes had to forego the luxury of an Olympic village and were housed instead at service camps and special centres. They did not pretend to like being billeted at R A F Uxbridge or at colleges in Richmond and Wimbledon but they understood the peculiar circumstances and made allowances for any shortcomings. Discomfort was a small price to pay for the experience of participating in an Olympic Games.

The opening ceremony was held in a heatwave. Summer dresses and shirt sleeves were the order of the day in the giant concrete stands and on the terraces. The stadium was packed to absolute capacity and 6000 athletes from dozens of nations were gathered in the centre of the arena. It was a heartening sight for those who had feared that the Olympic movement might never survive the war.

Lord Burghley, chairman of the organizing committee, invited the King to declare the Games open. Dressed in naval uniform and deeply aware of the international significance of the occasion, George VI spoke words that thundered out over the loudspeakers and that were heard by millions of radio listeners and by the select band who owned television sets.

'I proclaim open the Olympic Games of London, celebrating the XIVth Olympiad of the modern era.'

Tremendous cheers greeted the announcement. As they died away and a hush fell on the huge assembly there was a clanging sound and the massive gates of the stadium were opened to admit the cream of the world's athletes.

In deference to their status as progenitors of the Olympics, the Greeks came first, stepping out proudly in their smart grey suits. The other teams came in alphabetical order, led by the small contingent of Afghans. Argentina came next and provided the first incident of the Games when their flag-bearer forgot to lower his flag in salute when marching past the royal box. A warm welcome was now given to the ordered ranks of the Australian team, the men immaculate in their green jackets and white flannels, the women smart and lithe in their white dresses and straw hats.

And so it went on. Nations who had fought on opposite sides in the war cheered each other with enthusiasm and a great sense of fellowship prevailed. The home crowd reserved its loudest acclaim for the British team as it marched in formation behind the Union Jack.

When the last team had taken its place inside the stadium a trumpet fanfare sounded and 7000 pigeons were released into the clear blue sky. The venerable Dr Garbutt, Archbishop of York, was then called upon to dedicate the Games to the promotion of peace and goodwill among nations.

'No victory in the Games,' he declared, 'can be gained without the moral qualities of self-control and self-discipline. Honour is due not only to the victors but also to the defeated, if in the true spirit of sportsmanship they give at once un-grudging and generous praise to those who have surpassed them in skill and endurance.'

As soon as the dedication was over a tall, blond athlete came on to the track. He wore white shorts and vest and carried the Olympic torch in his hand. Mounting the steps to a specially built podium, he ignited the stadium flame and the voices of a thousand-strong choir soared in perfect unison.

High above the Olympic flame and at the top of the terracing was an enormous board that bore the words of Baron de Courbetin, the founder of the modern Games.

THE IMPORTANT THING IN THE OLYMPIC GAMES IS NOT WINNING BUT TAKING PART. THE ESSENTIAL THING IN LIFE IS NOT CONQUERING BUT FIGHTING WELL

The climax of the ceremony now came when Wing-Commander Donald Finlay, the veteran hurdler who was the captain of the British team, took the Olympic oath.

'In the name of the competitors I promise that we shall take part in these Olympic Games, respecting and abiding by the rules which govern them, in the true spirit of sportsmanship, for the glory of sport and the honour of our teams.'

Roger Bannister was profoundly moved by the whole experience.

He had been invited to become a possible contender for a place in the British team but he had declined on the grounds that he was not yet ready for that level of competition and that he did not want a poor performance in London to jeopardize his chances of going to Helsinki for the next Olympics. Instead of taking part, therefore, he was working as Assistant to Colonel E. A. Hunter OBE, the Commandant of the British Olympic Team. The job involved a variety of duties and, most important of all, it got him into the stadium.

The next fortnight would change his view of athletics completely.

Harold Abrahams moved through the crowd on his way to the stadium. Ten days of competition were now past and public interest had remained high even though there had been very few British successes to celebrate. Abrahams' own zeal was undiminished and he could not wait to get to his seat for another session. As he glanced around the sea of faces he saw one that he recognized.

'Franz!'

'Ah!' shouted Stampfl, spotting the bald head. 'Hello!'

'How are you?' asked Abrahams, shaking his hand then guiding him to a corner where they could talk. 'Are you enjoying the Games?'

'I always enjoy good athletics, my friend.'

'Which country are you supporting?'

'That's the trouble. I have three to choose from.'

'Three?'

'Austria, where I was born. Britain, where I live. And Australia.'

'Of course. I forgot that you spent the war down under.'

'Thanks to your stupid government,' said Stampfl with asperity. 'They shipped me off to an internment camp. Nasty place. In 1942 the Australians gave me a chance to get out if

I joined their army. So I did.' He gave a wry smile. 'It was terrible, Harold. As soon as the war was over, I jumped on the first boat to get back here and take up my coaching again.'

'And you're having a lot of success, I hear.'

'More than your British coaches, anyway.'

'Don't rub it in, Franz.'

'A couple of silver medals and a bronze so far,' chided Stampfl. 'We expect a bit more from the host nation. Your officials haven't been much help, have they?'

'What do you mean?' asked Abrahams warily.

'Jack Crump. Your team manager. Makes a public statement that Fanny Blankers-Koen is too old to make the grade at thirty. What does it make her do? Go out and win four gold medals.'

'She's an amazing athlete.'

'But why did Crump give her that extra incentive? I talked to her husband, Jan, who coaches her. All he had to say before each race was "You're too old, Fanny," and she ran like a gazelle.'

'Maureen Gardner almost pipped her in the 80-metres hurdles, though,' noted Abrahams, recalling one of the few British medallists.

'Yes. And what does Geoff Dyson, your Chief National Coach, do? Runs out and kisses the girl. That's no way to coach!'

'They happen to be engaged, Franz.'

'I know,' said Stampfl with a grin. 'Anyway, Dyson does his best. He just doesn't have enough support.' He warmed to his theme. 'Coaching in this country has never been much good. The approach is too amateur. You need a professional like me in charge.'

'But you're not British,' reminded the other tactfully.

'Neither was Sam Mussabini yet he coached you to a gold medal.'

The bald head nodded. 'Fair point.'

They turned and strolled towards the stadium. Abrahams was glad that he had bumped into his old friend even if the latter's opinions were rather harsh at times. Stampfl loved and understood athletics in a way that set him apart from most coaches.

46

'What's been the highlight of the Games for you, Franz?'

'Oh, that's easy.'

'The Dutch girl winning four gold medals?'

'No.'

'Bob Mathias winning the decathlon for America at seventeen?'

'They were both magnificent competitors but I would pick out someone else. Hermine Bauma.'

Abrahams chuckled. 'Austrian girl. Gold in the javelin.'

'My country. My event.' His eyes twinkled wickedly. 'By the way, how many gold medals did you say that Britain had won?'

The closing ceremony was as emotional in its own way as that which opened the Games. In spite of all the problems and compromises, the XIVth Olympiad had been a resounding success and everyone was sorry to see it end. The joy of celebration was thus mingled with the sadness of farewell as the athletes gathered together for the last time.

As before, every seat was taken and every inch of standing room was occupied. The white Tribune of Honour – a dais fronted by a panel that bore the Olympic logo – was placed on the track in front of the royal box, which was graced on this occasion by the Duke of Edinburgh, the Duchess of Kent, Princess Juliana of the Netherlands and Prince Bernhard. Mr J. Sigfrid Edstrom, President of the International Olympic Committee, spoke from the tribune about the ties of friendship that had been formed between the competing athletes.

After announcing the end of the Games he handed the Olympic flag of embroidered satin to the Lord Mayor of London, Sir Frederick Wells, for safekeeping until the Helsinki Games in four years' time. A fanfare of trumpets sounded, guns sounded a salute and then the mass choir sang the Olympic hymn while the flag in the arena was lowered and the Olympic flame extinguished.

As the final march-out began Roger Bannister watched the athletes with a mixture of pride and nostalgia. He had been in a privileged position to see some extraordinary performances on track and field and he was deeply grateful. Being part of the enterprise – albeit not as a competitor – had

47

made a powerful impression on him. Memories of individual achievements flooded back to inspire him and to strengthen his ambition to take part in the next Olympics, but he took something else away from the stadium that day as well.

Hitherto he had seen athletics as a personal affair that simply involved mastery over himself. The Games had shown him the true importance of sport and its value in international terms. It had broadened his outlook in a way that he had not foreseen.

He had glimpsed a new beauty in the simple act of running.

Chapter Four

A long blast on the whistle brought the game to an end and the players trooped off the pitch and headed for the changing rooms. John Landy had been a key figure in his team's victory yet again. Though he was plastered in mud and had collected more than the usual number of bruises, he was in a happy mood. Australian Rules football was a fast, violent, skilful and demanding sport that seemed uniquely suited to his all-round talents and a game always left him feeling exhilarated. But there was another reason why he loved it. Off the field, Landy tended to be quiet and reserved; on it, he somehow shed all his inhibitions and expressed himself in the most positive and extrovert manner.

'Good game, John!'

'Thanks.'

'We tanned the bloody arses off 'em!'

The banter soon got under way in the showers. The game was discussed in every detail and the players were soon shaking with laughter as they recalled comical incidents or examples of cunning revenges that they had wreaked on members of the opposing team. It was different when they lost. The atmosphere in the showers was more subdued then and the players did not really come alive again until after their first couple of beers.

'Ever thought of taking it up, John?'

'What?'

'Football, of course.'

'No,' said Landy with a self-effacing smile.

'You'd be snapped up by one of the big clubs,' argued his

friend, 'and you'd have a lot more fun than you will with agriculture.'

Landy was sitting in the bar opposite the cheerful face of Len MacRae. The rest of the players were starting to unwind now and raucous jeers went up as someone told a joke. It had been a hard game but the aches and pains were soon anaesthetized by the ever-reliable combination of drink and conviviality. Remorse would not set in until next morning.

'I'm serious, John,' continued MacRae. You could make some money at it. Let's face it, mate. You've won the medal for Best and Fairest in regional football here. That proves you're damn good.'

'I'm not sure that I'd be cut out for league football, Len.'

'How do you know till you've given it a try?'

'No,' decided Landy. 'Too much politics in the professional game. That's not my scene. I just play for the hell of it.'

They were both students of Agricultural Science. After a first year at Melbourne University they had come to Dookie College to do more practical work and had found the place highly congenial. Both of them would be sorry when their second year drew to a close.

'I'll miss this place,' admitted Landy.

'Been bloody great, hasn't it?'

'We've had a ball, Len. Never played so much football and had so many laughs in my life. Even managed to do a spot of work.'

'That's more than I have, mate!'

They laughed and began to trade anecdotes about their time at Dookie. It was Landy's turn to buy the drinks and they adjourned to the bar. Over a second beer they talked about the future.

'Any plans for when we get back to Melbourne, John?'

'I'm thinking of spending more time on my running.'

'And so you should!' encouraged his friend. 'I've always said you could go a long way in athletics.'

'Who knows? If I train properly I might even get to beat you.'

'What do you mean? You're a much better sprinter than me.'

'I was talking about middle-distance, Len. That's what I'm

really interested in and that's where you can lick me.' He sipped his beer and became serious for a moment. 'Football is terrific but it's a team game. When it comes down to it, you always have to depend on the other blokes. If you're a runner, it's different. You're in control, Len. You call the shots.' He shrugged. 'You try, anyway.'

'What about a club?'

'Gordon Hall wants me to rejoin Geelong Guild.'

'Makes sense.'

'Gordon's such an enthusiast. I like that.'

'Nobody's more enthusiastic than John Landy,' noted MacRae. 'Except that you don't let it show so much.'

'Gordon keeps on about this Percy Cerutty.'

'Who doesn't?'

'Sounds like a bit of a bull-shitter to me.'

'He certainly knows how to get publicity for himself. You can't open a paper without finding Cerutty in it somewhere. And he's got a good turn of phrase. You have to hand him that.'

'Yes,' agreed Landy. 'I remember what he said when our Olympic team came back from London. He tore strips off them for not winning more medals. I'm surprised some of the officials didn't sue him for libel.' He grinned. 'Percy Cerutty is a character all right.'

'He's more than that, John. I mean, he must have something if fellas like Don MacMillan and Les Perry believe in him. They reckon he knows everything about athletics. Not just what's going on in this country. He keeps in touch with developments abroad.'

'So Gordon tells me.'

'Apparently he gets all these magazines from Europe and America. Keeps a proper little library at his house.' MacRae took a long drink from his glass. 'To be honest, I've been toying with the idea of going along there myself.'

'Why?'

'I'm curious to meet Cerutty. Maybe he can help me.'

'You don't need any help, Len. You're fast enough as it is.'

'Fast, yes. But I'm such a heavy, clumsy sort of runner. Maybe this bloke can improve me somehow.'

'Well, don't let him improve you too much,' pleaded Landy, 'or I'll never be able to beat you.'

'Why don't you come along as well, John?'

'No thanks.'

'What harm can it do?'

'I just don't think I'd get on well with Cerutty somehow.'

'But all the fellas speak well of him. Tell you what. Why don't we call in at Karang on our way back to Melbourne? We could see Ray Weinberg. He's got some marvellous stories about Percy Cerutty.'

'It'll be nice to see Ray again,' agreed Landy, 'but I'm not going to let the two of you talk me into anything. Cerutty sounds like a bit of a crank to me. And he's always shooting his mouth off. That's just not my style.'

'But supposing he could turn you into a better athlete?'

'He won't get the chance, Len.'

Wes Santee ambled across the campus at the University of Kansas and looked around with satisfaction. He felt at home already. Now that he was about to leave high school, it was time to choose a university and he sensed that he needed to look no further. In his jeans, colourful shirt, cowboy boots and stetson, he was a striking figure and more than one head turned as he moved past. Santee made his way to the college track where a number of athletes were training under the supervision of a short, stout, middle-aged man in spectacles.

The coach called one of the athletes over and discussed his training schedule with him. Santee waited respectfully until the conversation was over then he stepped forward.

'Excuse me, sir.'

'Yes, my boy?'

'I'm looking for Mr Bill Easton.'

'Well, you've found him. Who might you be?'

'Wes Santee, sir.'

'Ah!' Easton's voice took on interest and he appraised the newcomer carefully. 'I've heard a lot about you, Mr Santee. You've run 4.28 for the mile.'

'It was 4.26.4, sir, which is actually a state record. It beat Glenn Cunningham's time that he set in 1930.'

'You don't need to tell me anything about Glenn,' said the

coach with a smile. 'One of the finest athletes this country has produced. You couldn't do better than to follow in his footsteps.'

'That's what I aim to do, sir.'

'Good. Well, if you're as fast as they say you are, Mr Santee, you're going to get a lot of offers from a lot of colleges.'

'I guess so.'

'I'd like you here at the University of Kansas.'

'Thank you, sir. I've heard some very good things about you.'

'I can't work miracles but I can make one promise.'

'What's that, sir?'

'If you've got the talent I can take you to the very top.' He raised a warning eyebrow. 'It won't be no rest cure, mind. I'll be kicking your butt every inch of the way.'

'That don't worry me none, sir.'

Santee liked him immediately. There was an honesty and straightforwardness about Bill Easton that appealed to him a lot. Since he would be going to college on an athletics scholarship it was essential to have a good relationship with the track coach. His instinct told him that he would enjoy working with and for Bill Easton. The coach ran a shrewd eye over him.

'You look strong enough.'

'Hard as nails.'

'Where you from?'

'I live on a farm.'

'That toughens a kid up.'

'Sure does. I know what it is to work hard. I've had to take a lot of time off high school to help out.'

'How come?'

'It's a long story, Mr Easton. My father used to be foreman on the ranch. Four thousand acres. The guy who owned it was sort of family because his wife was my father's cousin. He was great to me. Always giving me ice cream and candy.'

'They're no good to an athlete.'

'Maybe not,' agreed Santee with a grin. 'Anyway, the guy died and somehow his papers weren't in order. So instead of getting the farm, my parents got nothing. It went to someone back in Ohio but they gave us the chance to buy half of it back. That's why it's been such a real struggle these past few years.'

'Did you miss a lot of schooling?' asked the coach.

'A fair bit. I'd go home lots of days at noon.' He brightened. 'But I still got two scholastic letters and four athletic letters. My teachers and my coach were very understanding. If I missed class they let me make it up in my own time.'

'Sounds to me like you're pretty disciplined.'

'I've had to be, sir.'

'Athletics is all about self-discipline. But I guess you've already found that out.' Easton nodded towards a building close to the track. 'Come on up to my office, Mr Santee. When we've had a proper chat I'll show you all our facilities.'

'Thanks.'

'We'll keep you at it if you come here,' added the coach as they walked along side by side. 'We have a weekly schedule with our athletics conference. Then there's the indoor track and field season when we normally just take on one other college. Nebraska or someone. In April we have the relay circuit – the Texas Relays, Kansas Relays, Drake Relays and so on. These meets draw people from all over so the standard is high.'

'I know. But this college always seems to do pretty well.'

'That's because we all work hard together,' explained the coach. 'I'm proud of our athletic achievements but they're all based on the same thing. Team work. Athletes have got to be prepared to sacrifice individual honours for the sake of the team.'

'I'd go along with that.'

'You'd have to, Mr Santee. It doesn't mean that you won't get the chance to make it into the big time. If you're good enough you'll go on to the National Championships. Next thing you know, you might be running on behalf of the United States of America.'

'That's what I plan to do, sir,' said the other seriously.

'That's what you will do, I'm sure,' added the coach with easy confidence. They had reached the building now and he led the way inside. 'There's just one thing.'

'What's that?'

'You wouldn't only be coming here to run.'

54

'I know that, sir.'

'We expect you to study as well so that you leave this college with some qualifications. Athletics is great but it can never be more than just a part of your life. It's important for you to get hold of that right at the start.'

'Yes, sir.'

'Look at Jesse Owens. He won four gold medals in Berlin in 1936. A few years later he was racing horses in a circus sideshow for a couple of lousy bucks.'

'I take the point, Mr Easton.'

'Don't ever let it happen to you.'

'Oh, I won't.'

'This country'll cheer for you and root for you while you're winning them glory but the minute you finish they'll forget you as if you were never there.' They came to the end of a corridor and paused outside a door. 'Athletics in this country is amateur with a capital A so there's not a red cent to be made out of it while you're doing it and even less chance of making some dough after you give it up.'

'The way I see it, Mr Easton, athletics is not an end in itself but it can open doors.'

'I'm glad you appreciate that.' His hard-bitten features split into a warm grin and he offered his hand. 'Welcome to the University of Kansas, Mr Santee.'

'Thank you, sir,' said the other, giving a firm handshake.

'I have the feeling that you and me will get along just fine.'

'So do I.'

Wes Santee followed his new coach into the office.

Les Perry let the iron bar rest across his chest for a few seconds while he adjusted his grip. Legs braced against the strain, he then took a deep breath and used all his strength to lift the weights above his head. His friends clapped and cheered.

'Good on you, Les!'

'Hold it right there while I get a camera, mate.'

'You look like Tarzan!'

'Well, like his chimpanzee, anyway.'

Perry lowered the weights to the floor and shook a fist playfully at the others for trying to make him laugh. They were in an upstairs room at Percy Cerutty's house in Domain

Road. It was John Landy's first visit and there were seven or eight other athletes there as well. Cerutty was keen to impress his new acolyte.

'You've got to be more aggressive in weight-lifting, Les,' he said, moving across to stand behind the bar. 'Work up a bit of venom and then you can lift almost anything.'

By way of demonstration, he inhaled deeply through his nose several times and then looked down at the weights with murder in his eyes. He stooped, took a firm grip and lifted the bar up to his chest. After the briefest pause he gave a fierce grunt and hoisted the weights into the air. They did not stay there for long. Cerutty suddenly left go of the bar completely and jumped back. The weights hit the floor with such an impact that the room shook and there was a yell of protest from down below. The athletes roared with laughter.

'You certainly worked up some aggression there, Perce!'

'Yes, I've never heard your wife sound so aggressive!'

'Show us again!'

'Try it with one hand next time!'

'Instead of no hands at all!'

'Okay, okay,' said their coach, riding over the ridicule. 'I tried to do it too fast, that's all. The point remains that weight-lifting is a valuable exercise. Les has proved that. He's increased his upper body strength by using the weights regularly and his times have started to improve.' He clenched a fist to punch home the message. 'The stronger you are, the better an athlete you become.'

John Landy listened as Cerutty enlarged on this theme. Now that he had been persuaded to come along to one of the coaching sessions, Landy had to admit how enjoyable and instructive it was turning out to be. There was a marvellous feeling of camaraderie among the athletes and Cerutty himself could be quite mesmeric when he really hit his stride. Landy was fascinated.

'Middle-distance running is all about the limits of endurance,' argued Cerutty. 'Look at Emil Zatopek. Gold medal in the 10,000 metres in the last Olympics. Silver in the 5000 metres. Then a gold in both events in the European Championships. And how did he do it?'

'Not by dropping the weights,' suggested Les Perry.

'He did it by total dedication. There's an article about him in one of my magazines. I want you all to read it.' His face was glowing as he recounted the story. 'Zatopek was nothing special five years ago. Then Arne Andersson visited Prague and showed how important all-round physical fitness is to an athlete. Zatopek didn't need telling twice. He trained like a fanatic – even when he was at work.'

'I thought he was in the Czech Army,' noted Gordon Hall.

'He was. And whenever he was on guard duty he used to run on the spot for an hour. Just imagine it. Army uniform, heavy boots, a bloody big rifle over his shoulder – and yet he pumps his knees up and down to develop his stamina.'

'No wonder he runs like he's made of iron,' observed Perry.

'You haven't heard the best bit, Les. In the middle of the Czech winter – when nobody trains outdoors unless they want their balls frozen off – Zatopek goes racing through the snow in a greatcoat and army boots. Relentless self-punishment. Forcing himself to the edge. And if he can do it, then you can.' He clapped his palms together. 'Right. Let's get ready.'

The athletes began to change into their running gear and Cerutty went over to have a private word with Landy. He was well aware of the latter's progress as a runner and had wanted to meet him for some time.

'Glad you could come along, John.'

'Thanks.'

'My spies tell me you're going to be a champion miler.'

'Oh, I don't know about that.'

'Nobody wins the Victorian Schoolboys Mile Title unless they can shift a bit.'

'That was years ago.'

'And you've got steadily better. Gordon says you're one of the stars of the Geelong Guild Club.'

'I enjoy running, that's all,' explained Landy with a shrug.

'You enjoy winning and that's much more important. You're a born competitor, John. All you need to do is to commit yourself whole-heartedly to athletics.'

'Work comes first. I owe it to my parents. They made a lot of sacrifices to put me through Geelong Grammar. I mustn't let them down.'

'What does your father do?'

'He's an accountant.'

'I don't know much about accountants. Since I've always been short of cash, I never had much call for one.' Cerutty's voice took on a conspiratorial tone. 'But I do know about fathers, John. And I bet yours wouldn't feel let down if his son represented his country at the Olympics.'

Landy was taken aback. 'The Olympics!'

'My athletes aim high.'

'But I'm not in that class at all.'

'Not yet, maybe. But given time . . .'

The others were almost ready now and Landy changed quickly to catch up with them. Cerutty then led them down the stairs, flung an apology and a farewell at his wife, and went out into Domain Road. They were soon running at a steady pace around the Botanic Gardens with Cerutty barking at their heels like a sheepdog.

'Keep it up! Stretch those legs! . . . Use those arms, Les! . . . Watch that posture, Don! . . . Put more into it, Gordon.'

Landy soon understood the basis of his coaching technique. He believed in training his athletes to the point of exhaustion, giving them some recovery time and then repeating the process. The accepted view was that hard training either burned people out or made them stale and musclebound. Cerutty was cutting through these beliefs like a knife. He was cracking the whip over his athletes and getting some notable results. He made sure that Landy knew about those results.

'See Don MacMillan up there?' he asked, running alongside his new recruit. 'Came to me as a promising miler and he's Australia's number one at the distance now. In the Centennial Games in New Zealand, Don finished second behind a Pommie runner called Roger Bannister.'

'Yes, I've heard of Bannister.'

'Don Mac will beat him next time.' He waved an arm to include the whole group. 'They're nearly all potential champions here. Les Perry, for instance. Pugnacious little fella just like me. Dead cert for the 5000 metres at Helsinki. Ray Weinberg will be in the Olympic team for the second time as a hurdler. Then there's Neil Robbins, Geoff Warren, Gordon

. . . well, you know them all, John, and I'm sure you realize you're training with the cream of Australia's athletes.'

'Yes, I do.'

'Let's see if you can keep up with them.'

Cerutty moved to the front of the pack and increased the pace substantially, urging them to race him to a clump of trees in the distance. They soon caught him and surged past but he was not too far behind them when they arrived panting at their destination. Landy was astonished that the coach still had enough breath to speak.

'Okay. Two minutes recovery and then the final sprint for home,' he ordered. 'And let's see a bit more attack this time. A bit more aggression. You look at the Aborigines. Great bloody runners. And why? Because they live out in the wilds and they have to chase their food. Quite simple. If they can't run, they don't bloody well eat. Yes, and they know how to work themselves up into a frenzy as well. They sprint after their grub waving their spears and shouting like this.'

He let out a terrifying cry and mimed the throwing of a spear.

'You missed, Perce!' said Les Perry.

'Yes,' added Neil Robbins. 'Your kangaroo just got away.'

'I'm serious about this!' insisted Cerutty. 'We'll all try it. On the last leg, we'll be Abos running down their game.'

'But we've got no spears,' Gordon Hall pointed out.

'We soon will have!' decided Cerutty.

He sprinted off towards a greenhouse that was tucked away behind a high hedge. The athletes relaxed and joked together until something made them gape. Percy Cerutty reappeared with a look of triumph on his face and some long sticks of bamboo in his fist.

'We must strive to make our running more natural,' he declared, giving each person his spear. 'More like the Abos. The comforts of modern civilization have made us softies and cream-puffs.' He held his own stick of bamboo aloft. 'We're going hunting! And we want our prey to know we're after it. So follow me and give it all you've got.'

Brandishing his spear and yelling at the top of his voice, he went racing off. The others looked at each other for a second then followed suit. Landy had never felt so embarrassed in his life but he had to go along with it all.

The Aborigines tore up the hill in pursuit of their next meal, waving their spears and producing some blood-curdling yells. It was all too much for the man who came over the brow of the hill towards them with some books under his arm. He took one look at the wild savages who were approaching him then dropped his books and fled.

Back at the house, Gordon Hall got dressed alongside Landy.

'See, John? I told you that you'd like Percy.'

'Well,' replied the other. 'He's certainly different!'

The euphoria of being selected to represent his country abroad soon began to wear off. Wes Santee had been overjoyed when he was picked to run in an international meeting in Japan while still in his freshman year and he had loved every moment of the flight. To someone who had been raised on a cattle ranch in Kansas, Japan was an exciting novelty and he found something to amaze him wherever he looked. When it came to the actual business of running, however, there were disappointments.

'There's only one coach on the team,' he complained.

'So?'

'What are all those other officials doing on the trip?'

'They just come for the ride, man.'

'But why?'

'Because that's the way it is. The AAU figures that those guys deserve a reward for all the service they've given to athletics and so they get a free holiday to Japan.'

'That's crazy!'

'No, Wes. That's American athletics.'

Santee was standing on the training track with another member of the team, Mal Whitfield. The negro runner was a supreme stylist and he had won the gold medal at the London Olympics in the 800 metres, beating Arthur Wint by three yards. Santee had the utmost admiration for Whitfield who had not lost a single race since his return from Britain.

'I need help, Mal,' he explained. 'Hell, here I am at eighteen making my first appearance at this level and running in a foreign country. I've never even been outside the States before.'

'You'll make out, Wes,' soothed the other.

'Not without some coaching.'

'Then you got it, man.' Whitfield showed perfect teeth in a friendly smile. 'Anything you want to know – just ask.'

Santee was touched. 'Hey, thanks!'

'I know what it's like to be a rookie.'

Mal Whitfield gave him all the guidance that he needed and he did so in a relaxed and easy way. It helped Santee himself to lose some of his tension and he started to enjoy his training. The more they worked together, the more they liked each other and a real bond built up between them. Santee was immensely grateful.

'Could I have a word with you, sir?'

'What's your problem, son?'

'It's about the accommodation.'

Santee had come to see one of the officials, a beefy man with the build of a heavyweight wrestler and a round, flabby face.

'There's someone I want to room with, sir.'

'I guess that can be arranged. Who is it?'

'Mal Whitfield.'

The official stared. 'Is this some kind of joke?'

'No, sir,' said Santee, mystified. 'Mal and I are buddies, that's all.'

'Then be buddies – but don't room with him.'

'Why not?' Realization hit him and made him angry at once. 'Hey! Now, come on!'

'Find someone else,' advised the official.

'Are you saying that we can't share a room because he's black and I'm white? You're actually going to *stop* us?'

'If you'd been more wised up, you'd have stopped yourself.'

'What is all this?' demanded Santee, his rage mounting.

'It's the way we do things.'

'Well, I don't think very much of it! No, sir!'

'We're not interested in your opinions,' snapped the official. 'You're here to run a race and not to tell us how to do our job. The AAU makes all the decisions around here, son, and

61

you got to go along with them for one very good reason.'
Belligerence made his double chin wobble slightly. 'Because
you got no choice! Okay?'

There was a long pause as Santee controlled his temper.
'Okay,' he said quietly. 'But it still stinks.'

Chapter Five

Medicine remained the core of Roger Bannister's life. Even though his reputation as an athlete was growing steadily at home and abroad, his first commitment was always to his work. Having completed his undergraduate studies at Exeter College, he was appointed to a research scholarship at Merton and his work on respiratory physiology enabled him to combine medicine and athletics in a rather unusual way.

'My God! Have I got to run on *that*!'

'It's all in a good cause, Norris.'

'But it looks like some kind of implement of torture.'

'You may not be too far off the mark there,' said Bannister with a smile. 'Come and meet Dr Cunningham.'

Norris McWhirter was a pale, thin, almost ascetic-looking young man with a shock of dark hair above an intelligent face. As well as being a close friend of Bannister's he possessed an encyclopedic knowledge of athletics and was fascinated by every aspect of it. In the role of a guinea pig, he was now being introduced to the one aspect of it that was new to him.

He shook hands with the white-coated Dr Cunningham, who was also involved in the research, then took a second apprehensive look at the treadmill that stood in the laboratory. It seemed to be driven by a motor and was surrounded by all manner of gadgets and tubes. Standing there in shorts and singlet McWhirter was beginning to wish that he had not agreed to participate in the experiment.

'The problem for the middle-distance runner,' explained Bannister smoothly, 'is how to get enough oxygen to the muscles throughout the whole race. We'll start off by examining the factors responsible for the increase of breathing during exercise.'

'What is all this paraphernalia?' asked McWhirter.

'It's quite simple,' said his friend. 'We fit this mask over your mouth so that you can breathe from the gas bags into which we feed different gas mixtures as you go along. When the treadmill starts up, you have to run and we can alter speed and gradient. Your body changes will be monitored at every stage.'

'What's that nasty instrument down there?'

'It's a blood gun which can spring a blade into your finger so that we can measure lactic acid levels.'

'I didn't volunteer to be a blood donor, Roger!'

'You only lose a minimal amount.'

'I suppose this mattress on the floor is for me to collapse on to afterwards?'

'Yes, Norris. I think you'll find it very comfortable.'

The guinea pig tried a last protest. 'Perhaps I'm not the ideal subject for this. I was a sprinter, not a middle-distance runner.'

'You're an athlete. That's what matters.'

McWhirter stepped on to the treadmill with grave misgivings. When he was harnessed up the signal was given and the motor came to life. As the surface beneath his feet moved backwards with a rattling noise he began to run. How long he was kept at it he did not know, but he felt as if he were competing in a marathon during a heatwave. His heart was pounding, his body groaning with pain, his breathing more and more laboured. Sweat poured from him and blood oozed from his finger as a blade was sprung against his skin.

When the speed of the treadmill was increased he had difficulty keeping up with it and when the maximum incline was produced he felt as if he were running up the side of the Tower of Pisa in a pair of hobnail boots. It was agony with a scientific purpose.

When he reached breaking point he fell heavily on to the mattress with every intention of attacking Rip Van Winkle's record. Bannister helped to remove the gas mask from his friend.

'That was marvellous, Norris!'

'Who for?' gurgled the other.

'I can't thank you enough.'

'Tell me something,' croaked McWhirter, each word a separate effort. 'Have you been through this ordeal yourself?'

'Of course. Several times.'

'You must be mad!'

McWhirter closed his eyes again and lay quite still.

Much later, over a cup of coffee in Bannister's rooms, he was restored to his old self. Like everyone else in the world of athletics, he wanted to know how his friend was preparing for the Olympic Games.

'I've stepped up my training and I'm running in as many first-class races as I can. And as you know, I've tried to go abroad whenever possible in order to get used to changes of climate and food.'

'And to feel out some of the competition.'

'Of course. When I've raced against some of my potential rivals, I've been able to weigh up their strengths and weaknesses. Also, I managed to fit in a spot of sightseeing.'

'That never hurts.'

'New Zealand was beautiful. I'd like to have seen much more of it. Funny thing was that I felt homesick when I was there.'

'Dying to get back to that torture chamber you call a lab!'

'Amongst other things.'

'I don't need to tell you the question that everyone is asking about Roger Bannister, do I?' He saw his friend give a resigned sigh. 'What's the answer? Why don't you have a coach?'

'I do, Norris. Myself.'

'So you'll continue to train in splendid isolation?'

'I'll carry on as I am doing.'

'What do you have against coaches, Roger?'

'Nothing. They do an excellent job in most cases. It's just that some athletes need them and some don't.'

'A lot of people are saying that you need one.'

'They're entitled to their opinion,' said Bannister evenly then he gave a quiet smile. 'And so am I.'

Harold Abrahams sat in front of his typewriter and glanced at his notes. As well as being a barrister, an administrator and a broadcaster he was also a prolific journalist who contributed regularly to three newspapers as well as to *Athletic News*. He was writing a piece on Roger Bannister, who had won the Benjamin Franklin Mile in Philadelphia in record time against stern American opposition. The victory had done a lot for British prestige and it gained Bannister enormous publicity. Abrahams had been stirred by the achievement but he did not simply join in the general adulation. As always, he sought to be constructive.

He began to type and the words flowed. When he had finished he read through what he had written and was pleased with his conclusion.

What he needs now is confidence in his own ability. Modesty – a characteristic of Wooderson – in Bannister amounts to an almost complete reluctance to acknowledge his greatness. He has the brains to plan and dominate the Olympic final as Lovelock did in 1936. To beat the world – and I believe he can – he must cultivate a purposeful aggression.

Abrahams folded the article and put it into an envelope.

Percy Cerutty forced his way up the sandhill in the early-morning sunlight with John Landy, Don MacMillan, Les Perry, Geoff Warren and Neil Robbins on his heels. Like their coach, the athletes wore nothing but shorts and their bare feet were sinking deep into the warm sand as they struggled on. When he reached the top of the dune Cerutty let out a banzai cry as he led the charge down the other side. He chose an even bigger challenge this time and headed towards it.

'Exhaustion is pain!' he shouted. 'And pain is all in the mind. If you've got guts and aggression you can run through a brick wall.'

With another ferocious yell he launched himself up the steep incline, his bronzed body glistening with perspiration. The others gritted their teeth and pressed on behind him.

When the athletes got back from their five-mile run they were given a health-food breakfast of oats, nuts, wheatgerm and milk. The indefatigable conditioner of men and maker of champions explained exactly what was in store for them.

'Most people come down here to Portsea for holidays but nobody gets a holiday at my new training camp. You're here to *suffer*. I'm going to teach you fellas what fitness really is.'

'Do we have to eat this kind of stuff all the time?' complained Perry as a nut got stuck between his teeth. 'Don't we get real food?'

'This *is* real food, Les. It's natural, wholesome.'

'And bloody tasteless,' muttered someone.

'It's got goodness in it and that's what counts. Oats, for instance. Give a horse oats and it'll run like the wind.'

'We don't happen to be horses, Perce,' argued Neil Robbins.

Cerutty consulted a sheet of paper. 'This is your programme for the day. One – a run along the beach. We've done that. Two – breakfast. Three –'

'A couple of hours in bed,' suggested Geoff Warren.

'Three!' repeated Cerutty. 'Swimming, surfing and general chores to toughen you up. Chopping wood and so on. Four – training and lectures at the Oval, followed by another swim. Then we have lunch.'

'More nuts!' sighed Les Perry.

'No, it'll be fish and fresh fruit. After lunch – a siesta.'

'Hurrah!' The cheer was general.

'For an hour,' stipulated the coach. 'At four o'clock this afternoon I want you up and ready for an hour of weight-training. Then we have a ten-mile run along dirt roads, ending back at the beach, and we finish with tea at seven and a sort of discussion.'

'Hold on, Perce!' said MacMillan. 'Even Zatopek couldn't stick that pace.'

'Some of you will be running against Zatopek at Helsinki. And when he starts dragging you round for lap after gruelling bloody lap, you'll thank your living stars that I got you fit enough to stand the pace.' He stood up from the table and crossed to a shelf. 'As I've told you before, you blokes are Stotans – that's a cross between Stoics and Spartans. And this is my Stotan philosophy.'

He took some slips of paper from the shelf and handed them around. As Cerutty talked on about his plans and ambitions, Landy studied the Stotal creed as set down by its inventor.

67

1. Realization that, as Wordsworth says, 'Life is real, life is earnest', which denotes that there is no time for wasteful ideas and pursuits.
2. In place of wasteful hobbies there commences a period of supervised and systematic physical training, together with instruction in the art of living fully. This replaces previously undirected life.
3. Swimming will be done all the year round. It is obligatory to swim in the open sea at least once every month. This especially strengthens the will and builds resistance to quitting the task ahead.
4. The programme implies a cessation of late hours. Amusements, both social and entertaining, should be reduced to a minimum and then only in the nature of relaxation from strenuous work.

Landy had many doubts about the philosophic basis of Cerutty's austere creed and he always felt uneasy when the latter began to sound off about Ancient Greece. What he had found valuable was the coach's undoubted skill as a motivator. The sessions at the Botanic Gardens had helped Landy to focus himself on his running and to improve his performances. Cerutty gave him no technical advice about his event and did not dictate his training schedules but he did give the athlete a greater belief in his ability.

It was Landy's first visit to the camp at Portsea and he realized that his week there would be a severe test of his stamina. The main consolation was that he was with a group of very congenial friends.

'Hey, Perce,' called Les Perry. 'Who's this Wordsworth bloke?'

'A Pommie poet.'

'What was his time for the 5000 metres?'

'Wordsworth knew about nature,' insisted Cerutty. 'And he understood about life. It's there to be used to the full. That's always been my belief as well. If anything is going, you've got to throw yourself into it.' He banged the table with his fist. 'The desire for life should show itself in every way – in athletics, in music, in art, in sex, in every bloody thing!'

'What's that about sex?' asked Neil Robbins.

'It's one of the vital functions of life,' announced Cerutty.

'We worked that bit out for ourselves,' said Les Perry.

'Sex is a physical activity,' continued the coach. 'It's another way of expressing yourself. To be sexually outgoing is the same as running a mile in four minutes.'

'But a hell of a lot more fun!' noted Don MacMillan.

Percy Cerutty joined in the laughter then made them clear away the breakfast things. The athletes were staying in a cabin that had been fitted out with tiered bunks. Facilities were very basic and they had to do their own cooking and washing-up. Cerutty himself slept in the house nearby but he kept a close eye on his charges and he was determined that they should prove themselves to be true Stotans in his own mould.

'Tonight we'll find out who the real men are,' he declared.

'How, Perce?' asked Neil Robbins. 'Are you going to get us some real women?'

'I'm going to put you all to the test,' he warned. 'I want you to strip naked, take just one blanket with you and then spend the night out on the beach. Show me you can be Stotans!'

There was a barrage of protest but he overruled it and stuck to his decision. When they had got to the end of a tiring day, therefore, the athletes took a blanket apiece and went out into the darkness. The moon was dancing on the waters of Port Phillip Bay and the waves were making gentle splashing sounds but the friends were impervious to any of the romantic possibilities of the scene.

'It's freezing!' hissed Les Perry.

'These blankets are no damn good,' complained Geoff Warren.

'We'll never last the night out here,' added Les Perry.

The breeze freshened and they started to shiver even more. Some of them tried to shelter in the dunes and burrow into the sand but that did not keep out the cold night air. Neil Robbins decided to run up and down the beach and the others soon joined him. It was Landy who showed the first defiance.

'If this is what he means about being a Stotan, he can bloody well keep it!' he decided as he headed back towards the cabin.

When he reached his bunk he snuggled down under the warm blankets and felt much better. It was now well past midnight and he was soon asleep. Within no time at all, however, his slumbers were disturbed. Percy Cerutty kicked him in the ribs.

'What the hell are you doing in here!' he demanded.

'Trying to sleep.'

'You're supposed to be out there.'

'But it's freezing cold!'

'You young fellas have got no guts,' said Cerutty, shaking his head in disgust. 'Can't you see that I'm doing it for your own good? I'm trying to toughen you up so that you'll make it into the Olympic team.'

'Let's be honest, Perce,' said Landy. 'I haven't really got a hope of getting into the team.'

'That's not the right attitude, John! You can do it if you want to do it. All it needs is enough determination to succeed.' He pulled the blankets off the bed. 'Now get out there again!'

Before Landy could lodge his protest the door opened to admit four shivering athletes. Don MacMillan acted as their spokesman.

'Perce!' be begged. 'Let us in for Christ's sake or we'll all bloody well die of pneumonia.'

After venting his anger on them, Cerutty relented and allowed them to get to bed. Before he left, however, he told them that the next day's programme would be even more punishing. The athletes groaned. Their troubles were still not over. An hour later they were hauled out of their sleep by a tremendous clatter. Someone groped for the light switch and they peered through bleary eyes at the cause of the sudden noise. It was John Landy who had himself been jerked awake as he bumped into a little table.

'Sorry,' he said with an apologetic grin. 'Something I forgot to mention. I'm a sleepwalker.'

They informed him that he was something else as well.

Bill Easton sat behind his desk and read the letter carefully. When he had finished he spoke without looking up.

'You can't go, Wes.'

'That's what I told them last time but they keep inviting me.'

'Then keep turning them down.'

'They'll be flat mad at me, coach.'

'You can live with it. So can I.'

Wes Santee had received an invitation from the Amateur Athletic Union to take part in one of their indoor track and field meetings in New York. He was now a rising star in the athletics world and was much in demand but the University of Kansas had first call on his time and his considerable talent.

'There's too much pomp and ceremony at those meets,' said Bill Easton, handing the letter back to him. 'The officials all wear tux's like they're going to the opera or something. Yeah, and the audience gets all dressed up for it as well.'

Santee waved the letter. 'Says here that the mile is the big feature of the night. That's why they want me.'

'It's always like that, Wes. Regardless of who else might be running in the other events. Remigino or Whitfield – whoever! The mile is king.' The coach removed his glasses and polished them as he talked. 'Last time I was in Madison Square Gardens, they stopped the meet and played the national anthem as they paraded the milers. They got the crowd all whipped up before the race was even started.'

Part of Santee was attracted to the publicity and the razzmatazz but he knew that there was more to it than that. He would act on his coach's advice. Bill Easton had done a tremendous amount for him since he had been at the college and he was the first to acknowledge it. A promising athlete had been transformed into a potential world-beater.

Now in his sophomore year, Santee had acquired a jaunty self-confidence that bordered on arrogance. He tossed the letter on to the desk.

'I don't need to run in these showpiece meets,' he said airily. 'They can't get Wes Santee with a promise of bright lights and the national anthem. They just want to make some dough out of me.'

'That's the name of the game.'

'We fill the seats and they take the profits.'

'I don't like my athletes to be exploited,' affirmed Easton.

'Even if it means upsetting the AAU, I'll protect them all I can.'

'We ain't going to be too popular, coach.'

'That's nothing new. I been punching it out with officialdom for years. Maybe it's something about the Kansas air because Fog Allen, the basketball coach, was the same. Had regular shoot-outs with the AAU. Now they got you and me to get riled at.'

Santee shrugged. 'So? Let them get riled. They always put so much pressure on athletes. Why don't they quit crowding us?'

'Let's forget them for the time being,' said the coach, replacing his glasses. 'Our main job is to get you in shape for the Olympic Trials.'

'I'm ready now!' boasted Santee, slapping his thigh.

'All we got to decide is whether we go for the 1500 metres or the 5000 or both.'

'You know me, coach. I'll take a crack at both.'

'The 1500 is your best event,' reminded Easton, 'and it would give you more chance of a medal at Helsinki. The 5000 is going to have some useful guys in it. Zatopek, for certain. Mimoun of France. Yeah, and there's a British runner called Chris Chataway that they seem to think a lot of over there.'

'I could learn a lot if I got in amongst guys like that.'

'Let's get you qualified first, Wes. For both if possible, but definitely for the 1500. As you know, the Olympic Trials go on results and not times. Doesn't matter if you hold a national record. You have to win on the day to make the team for Helsinki.'

'I don't see a problem there.'

'Neither do I. Bob McMillen will give you a race but you should get through. That brings us to Helsinki. I reckon the man to beat in the 1500 will be Bannister.'

'Yeah,' conceded Santee. 'He sounds real good.'

'There aren't many British athletes who can come over here and win the Benjamin Franklin Mile. No, Bannister is hot.'

'What about this Barthel character?'

'Oh, he'll be a danger man as well. So will Lueg of Germany. So will a couple of others. You won't have it all your own way, Wes.'

'I like competition. Brings out the killer instinct in me.'

'You'll need it,' warned Easton. 'The 1500 metres final looks like being one hell of a race.'

'I know,' said Santee. 'That's why I aim to be in it.'

John Landy knew that something important had happened when he saw his father waving to him. He turned the tractor around and drove it back towards the farmhouse. His mother and his sister, Susan, were there as well and that could mean only one thing. Landy was as surprised as he was delighted. He brought the tractor to a halt and jumped down.

'Congratulations, son!' called Gordon Landy, beaming at him. 'You had a phone call. They've picked you for the Olympic team.'

'Marvellous!'

'We just had to come and tell you ourselves, John,' explained his mother, kissing him on the cheek. 'Oh, we're so proud of you!'

'Thanks, Mum.'

His sister added a kiss of her own. 'I'm going to boast about you to all my friends,' she promised. 'My brother – going to Helsinki!'

'But when did you hear, Dad? What did they say?'

'Simply that you'd been selected, son: 1500 metres.'

'So we'll expect a gold medal,' warned Susan.

'I don't know about that,' said Landy modestly. 'I mean, it's ridiculous, really. I'm not even fit.'

He had been on the farm for some weeks helping his brother with the ploughing and the fencing. His training had suffered badly and he had more or less given up any hope of getting into the Olympic team. Yet he had now been selected. The surge of pleasure that it gave him was incredible. In the middle of his own joy, however, he did not forget his friends.

'What about the others, Dad? Any news?'

'Yes. Percy rang as well.'

'Bet he was amazed to hear about me.'

'No, John. He said you deserved it. He wants to help you all he can. You're to get in touch as soon as possible.'

'I will. What about Les? Don?'

'They're both in,' said his father. 'So is Ray Weinberg.'

'Great! It'll be just like old times.'

'And you'll all be representing your country,' noted his mother. 'I think it's wonderful.'

'There is one small problem, though,' added his father, a shadow falling across his face. 'In fact, it's quite a big problem.'

'What is it?'

'You've got to pay your own way, son.'

Landy was shocked. 'But why?'

'Because the committee reckons they're broke. They can only afford to pay for a few of the athletes. The rest of you have to find your own air fare.'

'How much is it?'

'Seven hundred and fifty pounds.'

Landy recoiled slightly. It sounded like an enormous amount of money to find at such short notice. His excitement at being selected now changed to a fear that he would not be going after all.

His father gave a reassuring smile. 'Don't worry, John. We'll raise the cash for you.'

'But you can't afford all that, Dad.'

'We'll get it somehow,' vowed Gordon Landy.

'Yes, John,' said his mother. 'You did your bit by getting into the Olympic team. We'll do our bit to send you there.'

Chapter Six

Wes Santee completed the first stage of his journey to Helsinki
in fine style. His victory in the A A U championships got him
into the 1500 metres race at the Olympic Trials and his success
in the college championships meant that he would run in the
5000 metres as well. He now had two chances of being
selected for the United States team. His plan was to qualify
for both events and then choose between them, but it was a
plan that foundered on the rocks of officialdom.

Having run brilliantly to take second place in the 5000
metres, he booked himself a ticket to Finland and was quite
elated. When he returned on the next day to race in the 1500
metres at the Olympic Trials he was in a buoyant mood and
convinced that he could win. Bill Easton gave him a few last
words of advice.

'Don't get yourself boxed in on the last lap.'

'I won't.'

'And keep out of trouble. There's been a lot of elbows flying
around in some of the races. Stay well clear.'

'Sure.'

'Okay. Now get out there and show them what Wes Santee
can really do.' He patted the athlete on the back. 'And good
luck!'

'Thanks.'

Santee came out on to the track with the other competitors.
A huge crowd had come to the stadium and he was lifted by
the atmosphere at once. After going through his warm-up
routine he then slipped off his track suit and made his way
to the starting line. Someone moved over to intercept him.

'What's your name, son?'

'Santee, sir. Wesley Santee.'

The official was a short, fussy man with thinning hair. He was smartly dressed in a blazer and flannels and held a clipboard in his hand. After scanning the names on his list, he looked up again.

'Sorry. You're not down here.'

'But I must be.'

'There's no Santee on this list.'

'This is the 1500 metres, isn't it?'

'Yeah.'

'Then I'm in it,' insisted the athlete. 'I qualified in the AAU championships.'

'No, you didn't, son.'

'I did! And I can prove it!'

'You might prove that you won your race but that still doesn't qualify you to run here.'

'Why not?'

'Because the competitors have been picked on their times.'

'Since when?'

'Since we changed the ruling on it,' said the man complacently.

'But you can't do that!' protested Santee.

'We can and we did, son. The AAU runs athletics in this country.'

'Well, it doesn't run it very well!' said the other with sudden vehemence. 'I was told I'd qualified at the championships. Now, you're saying I don't belong in the race.' His anger became a plea. 'Do you know how long I trained to get here, sir? You must let me run.'

'I'd be breaking the rules. Besides, we've got a full line-up.'

Santee exploded. 'Don't you want the best guys representing this country in Helsinki?'

'We'll get them,' replied the official. 'Out of this race.'

'But there's guys here I can beat the socks off!'

'Maybe. They got better times than you, that's all.'

'Let me prove it, sir!' he begged.

'Get off the track, son.'

'Stick me in the line-up! Please!'

'You're holding up the race.'

'Jesus! It's so *unfair!*'

His yell of rage brought another official scuttling over.

'Trouble, Sam?' he asked.

'No, Tom,' replied the first official calmly. 'The kid's going now. Aren't you, son?'

Santee gave up. He was boiling with frustration but helpless to do anything about it. As he strolled back to his track suit he was utterly dejected. Having built himself up for the race he had been kicked out of it by officialdom. It was a devastating blow.

The elation of the previous day had now turned to despair.

They were sending him to Helsinki in the wrong event.

After an enthusiastic send-off at the airport the Australian Olympic team settled down for the long flight and took the chance to get to know each other. There was a mood of joviality and friendliness that betokened an immediate team spirit. The athletics team consisted of thirteen men and four women and they were travelling alongside boxers, wrestlers, weightlifters, swimmers, divers, cyclists, rowers, yachtsmen, fencers, a water-polo team and a lone contender in the modern pentathlon.

John Landy knew many of the athletes already. As they shared some celebratory bottles of champagne together, he sat between Marjorie Jackson, the attractive, dark-haired sprinter from Lithgow, and Les Perry. Don MacMillan was in the aisle, topping up glasses from a bottle.

'Helsinki, here we come!' shouted Marjorie Jackson.

There was a communal cheer and everyone guzzled some more champagne. Whatever problems they might face in Helsinki itself, they were certainly going to enjoy the trip.

'Have you been to Europe before, Marje?' asked Landy.

'No. Have you?'

'Never been out of Australia before, to tell you the truth. I still can't believe I was selected.'

'I can, John. I've seen you run.'

'Thanks.'

'Did they pay your fare?'

'No. We had to find it ourselves.'

'I bet that was difficult.'

'It was. My father contributed a fair bit of the money. But Mervyn Pernell did most of the fund-raising. He's a fantastic character. Mayor of Geelong and friend of just about everybody. Nobody can raise cash like Merv. He and Dad have been marvellous. So have lots of other people. Honestly, I've been so lucky.'

'Sounds like it.' She indicated the pretty, bright-eyed young woman across the aisle. 'Winsome there had to stand on the steps of Melbourne Town Hall and collect her fare in a tin.'

'It's true,' admitted Winsome Cripps.

'That's awful!' said Landy.

'My athletic club went on a rabbit drive,' said Les Perry.

Marjorie Jackson laughed. 'A what?'

'Yeah. Stacks of rabbits around at the moment. You can get two bob a go for their skins.'

'That's a hell of a lot of rabbits to get you to Helsinki.'

'I know, Marje,' agreed Perry ruefully. 'Round about seven and a half thousand.'

Don MacMillan leaned in. 'And Les had to catch most of them.'

They all laughed and the champagne continued to flow.

A few hours later the mood had changed and the general hilarity had given way to a more subdued tone. Some people dozed, others read, others again were feeling the early pangs of homesickness for a country they would not see again for some weeks. Marjorie Jackson grew reflective and turned to her neighbour.

'Does it get to you, John?'

'What?'

'The pressure. Everyone expecting you to do well.'

'It does a bit, I suppose.'

'Australia hasn't won a gold medal on the track for fifty-six years,' she said with a sigh. 'Did you know that?'

'Yes. Last person to do it was Edwin Flack at Athens in 1896. Gold medal in the 1500 metres.' He gave a wry smile. 'My event.'

'According to the press, Australia is not going to wait any longer for another one. *I'm* the bunny who's supposed to break the drought.'

'And you will, Marje!' Landy encouraged.

'I'll do my best, anyway. But it won't be easy. I feel the whole weight of Australia resting on my shoulders somehow.' She shook her head sadly for a moment. 'People up my way have been just great to me. When I broke the world record for the 100 yards, they wanted to show me how proud of me they were. Do you know what they did, John?'

'What?'

'They built me a cinder track in Lithgow so I could train there. Only the poor things didn't have enough money to put lights up so I had to run every night there in the dark.'

'Wasn't that dangerous?'

'Very. All I could go on was the headlights of a car. A friend of mine would park at the end of the straight and I'd run towards the glow.' She shrugged. 'I mean, it's no way to train for an Olympics.'

'Oh, I know,' agreed Landy. 'Our facilities are pathetic, really. There isn't one top-class running track in the whole of the country. No wonder we're so far behind Europe and America. I don't always see eye to eye with Percy but he's right about one thing.'

'What's that?'

'Someone needs to get hold of athletics in Australia by the scruff of the neck and give it one hell of a good shake.'

'Isn't that what Percy Cerutty *has* been doing?'

John laughed. 'It's what he's been trying to do, Marje. Spent his whole life having the gloves on with officials. He's never happy at a meeting unless he's had a blazing row with someone or other.'

'I hear he's coming to Helsinki.'

'Try stopping him. He'll be there as team coach.'

'But we don't have a coach,' she argued. 'They couldn't afford it. All we've got is a team manager and a masseur.'

'Percy will be doing the job unofficially,' he explained. 'He's got this track suit that's identical to ours and he made his wife sew the word "COACH" across the back. He reckons it'll get him in anywhere. And knowing Percy Cerutty, it will.'

'He's an amazing bloke, really. You have to give him that.'

'Yes, Marje. He's unique. A law unto himself.'

*

79

A record attendance of over 46,000 people graced the White City for the AAA Championships. They were seen as a curtain-raiser to the Olympic Games and the British public was anxious to give its athletes a rousing send-off. The meeting was honoured by the presence of Her Majesty the Queen, Patron of the AAA, in the first year of her reign, and she was accompanied by HRH Princess Margaret. Britain's most famous living athletes – Lord Burghley, Tommy Hampson, Sydney Wooderson and Harold Abrahams among them – were mustered in the centre to be presented along with the leading candidates for Helsinki. It was a remarkable sight.

People who had arrived early at the stadium had seen another remarkable sight. As the stands began to fill and officials made their final checks on the arrangements, a small, wiry, white-haired man in his fifties came out on to the empty track. In his usual skimpy black shorts and running shoes he pounded around the inside lane as if he were competing in a race and he had completed a couple of laps before officials realized that he had no right to be there.

They moved towards him in a solid phalanx but he was undismayed. Cheered on by the amused spectators, he eluded his pursuers and kept on running. The officials spent the rest of the meeting trying to get the eccentric old character out of the stadium.

Percy Cerutty had arrived.

Chris Chataway was a sturdy, barrel-chested young man of medium height with the sort of amiable face and wavy red hair that got him noticed at once. He collected many friendly greetings as he walked across the changing room and he acknowledged them with a nod and a grin. Roger Bannister was sitting quietly in a corner as he came up.

'How are you feeling?' asked Chataway.

'The way I always feel before a big race, Chris. Nervous.'

'They can't wait to see you in action out there. They're expecting to watch the Roger Bannister kick that leaves the rest of the field standing.'

'I know. That's the trouble.'

'They have been rather starved of you lately, old boy.'

Bannister's preparations for the Olympics had aroused a lot

of criticism. To avoid the nervous strain of competition he had cut back on the number of races he entered and concentrated more on informal workouts. Time was a problem. Now studying at St Mary's to become a doctor, he was spending long hours attending lectures or working in the hospital wards and it was not always easy to fit in his running around these commitments. He trained alone on the cricket field at Harrow School which was near his home. Inevitably he had been attacked in the press for spurning the help of a top coach.

'Don't pay any attention to them,' advised Chataway. 'Sportswriters usually get it wrong.'

'I know what's best for me,' said Bannister. 'I know the kind of training programme that suits my temperament.'

'Of course.'

'So why can't they just leave me alone?'

'Well, you have rather set the cat among the pigeons this time.'

What had really provoked the sporting press was Bannister's decision to run in the 880 yards at the Championships instead of defending the mile title that he had won the previous year in a championship record time of 4.7.8. Accusations of all kinds had been levelled at him.

He was charged with having made the arrogant assumption that the selectors had already chosen him for the 1500 metres in Helsinki. He was arraigned for trying to avoid his serious rivals like Bill Nankeville, who had achieved a hat-trick of wins in AAA Mile before Bannister relieved him of his title. Most damaging of all, perhaps, was the indictment that his secret training and infrequent appearances in competition were harming the sport because he was putting nothing into it. Athletes were, he was reminded, dependent on the generosity of the public and he was letting them down.

Though Bannister liked to think that he was impervious to press comment, some of it had irritated him but it had not shaken his resolve to plough a lonely furrow. His critics had had their say. That afternoon, in front of a massive crowd, he would have the right of reply.

'I just can't turn it on like a tap, Chris,' he explained.

'Which of us can, old chap?'

'When I commit myself in a mile, I run myself into

81

exhaustion. To the verge of unconsciousness. I can only do that sort of thing a few times a season. That's why I'm saving myself for Helsinki.'

'Makes sense.'

'Not to the press.'

Deafening roars from above signalled the end of another exciting race and the applause sounded like a torrent of hailstones. Chataway looked up and grinned.

'We can't complain about the support.'

'It's marvellous.'

'Gets the old vital juices going.'

'That's adrenalin, Chris.'

'I don't care what it is. All I know is that it makes me want to get out there and do my stuff.'

'Me, too,' said Bannister.

As the applause rang out above them, they headed for the door.

A crowd that had come to see British athletes turning in fine performances were not disappointed. McDonald Bailey won both sprints with electrifying bursts of speed. Bill Nankeville secured the mile title yet again despite an excellent run by John Landy. Chris Chataway got inside fourteen minutes for the 3 miles and thrilled the spectators with the gritty manner of his victory. The long legs of Gordon Pirie took him to a record time in the 6 miles and John Disley achieved a world's best for the 2-mile steeplechase.

Records also fell to British athletes in the 440-yards hurdles, the 2-mile and 7-mile walks, the shot and the javelin. The slight figure of Jim Peters, now well into his thirties, bettered all previous times in the marathon by an astonishing margin.

Roger Bannister was one of the most convincing winners of the afternoon. After unleashing his celebrated finishing burst he sailed away from the rest of the field in majestic style and went through the tape to a hero's acclaim. More than anyone else, he seemed to symbolize British hopes in the Olympics and he was hailed by a patriotic crowd with great pride and affection.

Had he looked at the royal box he would have seen the Queen smiling serenely.

Everyone had been treated to a magnificent day's athletics and the vast majority of them went home in the conviction that Britain would be sending its strongest team ever to an Olympic Games. There were, however, those who dissented from this view.

'What did you think of it, Franz?'

'Interesting.'

'Is that all you can say?' asked Harold Abrahams with a laugh. 'You have a feast like that set before you and your only comment is that it's "interesting". I thought it was inspiring.'

'You would do, Harold. You're British.'

They had met below the stands at the White City as the stadium was clearing and Abrahams was still basking in the glow of it all. Franz Stampfl was amused but not surprised by his friend's reaction.

'As a spectacle it was bloody wonderful,' he agreed.

'That's a real compliment, coming from you.'

'But if you ask my professional opinion as a coach, all I can say is – interesting.'

'There was euphoria in the press box.'

'Journalists always drink too much.'

'They were intoxicated with what they saw, Franz. All those records being knocked over like ninepins. Sportswriters can be pretty cynical – as I well know – but not today. They're talking about seven gold medals.'

'As few as that?' asked Stampfl with irony.

'It does no harm to have confidence in your team.'

'As long as it's not misplaced,' argued the other. 'It's very unfair on an athlete to expect too much of him.'

'We happen to believe our athletes can deliver.'

'Seven times?' asked the Austrian incredulously.

'Well, no. I'm too much of a realist to go along with a figure like that,' said Abrahams. 'And I know how many things can go wrong at an Olympic Games.'

'As in 1948.'

'As – you so rightly remind me – in 1948. We need to wipe away those memories with a really good performance in Helsinki and I feel we've got some people who can do it.' He counted off the names on his fingers. 'McDonald Bailey, Chris

Chataway, John Disley, Jim Peters. Not gold, necessarily, but they could well be among the medals.'

'Don't forget your heel and toe man.'

'Yes. Roland Hardy is a hot tip for the walk. And Gordon Pirie could come good as well. Then, of course, there's Roger Bannister.'

'I was waiting for that name to come up.'

'You must admit that he ran superbly today, Franz.'

'For a man who has no coach he ran magnificently,' conceded Stampfl. 'But I'm not sure that he's got what it takes to win an Olympic final. Not yet, anyway.'

'He has to *believe* in himself,' urged Abrahams.

'No, Harold. That's what you keep saying in your articles but you're wrong. A young man who can hide away and train himself up to that standard must have the most enormous belief in himself. No, I think he has other deficiencies, my friend.'

'What are they, Franz?'

'One – he's not robust enough.'

'That's true, I'm afraid.'

'Takes too long to recover between big races. He needs to build up his strength with weight-training. Two – I'd question his judgement. The mile and the 1500 metres lend themselves to all kinds of tactical exploitation. A positional runner like Bannister has got to know the exact moment when to strike.'

'He usually does know it. As you saw today.'

'I saw him outclass the field in a half-mile, that's all. How will he cope in Helsinki against real competition? Men like Werner Lueg, the world record-holder. And Josef Barthel. They'll try to run the sting out of him so that his kick just doesn't take place. Does he have the tactical skill to avoid that?'

Abrahams smiled. 'What he doesn't have is a coach like you, Franz. Unfortunately. It might make all the difference.'

'A foreigner coaching the pride of the British team?' mocked the Austrian. 'Your people would never stand for it. Bannister would never stand for it either. He doesn't believe in coaches of any nationality. So – he'll have to take his own chance. He might even succeed.'

'You don't sound too convinced about that.'

'I'm not, Harold. And I'm certainly not convinced about the idea of seven gold medals.'

'Britain is sending some fine athletes to the Games.'

'Yes, my friend. But they lack the edge which can only come from regular competition against other countries. The way you do things here – it's hopeless!' He shook his head in disbelief. 'Since 1950 your international programme has consisted of one meeting with France and a tour of the Balkans! Then you expect to go off to an Olympics and pick up seven gold medals.'

'How many *do* you think we'll win?' asked Abrahams quietly.

'None.'

John Landy was finding Ray Weinberg a cheerful companion to have on the top deck of a London bus. They were due to leave for Helsinki that day and were fitting in some last-minute sightseeing before joining the rest of the team to take the coach to the airport.

Weinberg had the well-proportioned build of a champion hurdler and a craggy face that was lit by a ready sense of humour. Having been at the London Olympics he was the ideal guide and kept up an informed commentary. He also took time off to broach a subject that was close to both their hearts.

'Australia is the most amateur country in the world in its attitude towards sport, John,' he complained. 'We're light years behind everyone else.'

'I've found that out since we've been here,' said Landy.

'Perce is mad, we know, but he's been like a breath of fresh air in athletics. It's so hidebound and traditional. Run by officials from pre-war days with pre-war bloody ideas.'

'Yes, Ray. I agree about Perce. It's just that I find him a bit hard to take sometimes.'

'Inevitable.'

'What do you mean?'

'Well, let's face it. You two are not exactly soul-mates, are you? John Landy is a nice, quiet, conventional guy and Percy Cerutty is like the wild man of Borneo. Only wilder.'

'I won't deny he's done a lot for me – I probably wouldn't

be here without him – but I hate it when he shows off in public all the time.'

'That's Perce, I'm afraid. Larger than life.'

'Why does he have to oversell everything, Ray?'

'Because it's the only way he knows.'

'As for all that bullshit about the Stotan philosophy . . .'

Weinberg laughed. 'I'm glad I've never been on one of those weeks down at Portsea. Les reckons it's murder being a Stotan.' He became reflective. 'On the other hand, you have to give the fella his due. He's improved each and every one of us. Take me, for example. Perce never helped me with technique, maybe, but he certainly changed my attitude. For years I just couldn't beat Peter Gardner over the hurdles. Don't know why, John. I tried hard enough. But Peter always had that yard or two over me. Especially when it counted – like at the Empire Games two years ago. Then Perce came along. Told me to work up more anger before a race. Not to shake hands with an opponent until afterwards. I was to be hostile – treat him as an enemy.' He smiled at the memory. 'So I tried it and the stupid thing is that it damn well worked! I finally beat Peter. Thanks to Perce.'

Landy nodded but he remained in two minds about the coach. While he was grateful for the way that Cerutty had encouraged him, he was finding the latter's outrageous behaviour difficult to tolerate. It unsettled him and doubts began to surface.

'I wish I'd had more time to prepare, Ray.'

'You've always kept yourself very fit.'

'Yes, but I only had six weeks to train for the Olympics. It's not enough. I haven't hit my peak form.'

'Well, you haven't done too badly for a bloke who hasn't hit peak form,' observed Weinberg. 'You've not only broken the British 2-miles record since you've been here, you put on a great show at the White City as well.'

'Not as great as you in the hurdles, though.'

'Yes, I've always wanted an AAA title. And it was nice to beat Peter Hildreth on his home patch.' He nudged his companion. 'Don't worry about Helsinki, John. You'll do well, believe me.'

'I hope so.'

'All you have to do is to overcome your little problem.'

'Percy Cerutty?'

'No,' replied Weinberg with a grin. 'That's a side issue.'

'So what's my little problem?'

'You just don't know how damn good you are!'

When Roger Bannister came down to breakfast that morning he had a feeling of quiet satisfaction. His Olympic preparations had been going to plan. The day before, in an informal race designed to tune him up, he had run a three-quarter mile in a time that was four seconds faster than the unofficial world record held by Arne Andersson. It had been an important boost to his morale and had put him in the perfect frame of mind for his trip to Helsinki.

'Good morning, Dad.'

'Good morning, Roger.'

'It won't be a minute, dear!' called his mother from the kitchen.

'No hurry.'

'Take a seat, son,' suggested his father.

'What's wrong?' he asked, alerted by the gentle tone of voice.

Ralph Bannister was holding the morning paper and his son at first thought that it contained yet another attack on his training methods. Even his victory at the White City had not appeased some of his critics.

But it was far worse than that.

'I think you'd better read it for yourself, Roger.'

Bannister took the paper and looked at the item to which his father pointed. The short, formal announcement took his breath away. Owing to the large number of competitors in the 1500 metres at the Olympic Games, it had been decided to break with the tradition of having qualifying heats that were followed by a final two days later. Semi-finals were to be inserted. Athletes would have to run nerve-racking races on three consecutive days.

All of Bannister's preparations had been geared to competing in only two races. Physically and psychologically he was quite unready to run three times. He was mortified. A simple administrative change was threatening to undermine months and months of hard work.

As he put the paper aside he felt that he had just been robbed of his chance to win a gold medal.

Chapter Seven

Politics intruded into the Helsinki Olympic Games of 1952 at the outset. Russia, unexpectedly entering the competition for the first time in forty years, refused to share the Olympic Village with other national teams and was instead housed in a large technical college at Otaniemi, some five miles from the city. Hungary, Poland, Bulgaria, Rumania and Czechoslovakia joined the Russians in the Eastern European camp which was set in a pine forest. A gigantic portrait of Stalin was hung on the front of the building as a mark of Communist occupation.

It was a flagrant breach of the Olympic spirit but it was accepted then forgotten as the Games generated a harmony and sporting atmosphere that were to make it one of the most successful of all Olympiads.

Helsinki did not live up to its nickname of the White Metropolis of the North. Grey skies and heavy rain gave it a dismal aspect on the first day but this in no way inhibited the opening ceremony. Over 70,000 spectators jammed into the stadium to see the flags of sixty-nine nations paraded in front of their respective teams. As each contingent of athletes marched around the track in their smart Olympic uniforms they were drenched by the downpour and had to splash through puddles of water.

But nothing could dampen their ardour or quench their national pride and the opening ceremony remained an extraordinarily moving occasion. The highlight for the spectators and athletes alike was the igniting of the Olympic flame. Into the stadium came a balding legend and the roar was spontaneous when the great Paavo Nurmi was recognized. With his characteristic upright gait, he completed the best part of a lap then reached up to light a flame that burned in its metal bowl just inside the running area.

Nurmi then handed the Olympic torch to an even older reminder of Finland's athletic glories. Hannes Kohlemainen, winner of two gold medals at the Stockholm Games of 1912, went up in the lift to the top of a soaring tower to ignite another flame.

Two of the Flying Finns had set the Games alight.

Silence fell on the excited crowd as the Olympic oath was taken, and then followed an unscheduled part of the proceedings. A young woman, dressed in white, ran gracefully around the track and mounted the rostrum on which the oath had just been taken. Grabbing the microphone, she began to speak in German about the desperate need for peace among nations. Within a few seconds, she was hustled away by stewards in front of the mystified gathering.

Ray Weinberg had watched it all with horrified fascination. He gave a sigh of relief as he turned to John Landy.

'For one horrible bloody moment I thought it was Perce!'

The Australian team soon settled into their accommodation and tried to adapt to the vagaries of a Finnish summer. Bright sunshine had replaced the rain of the first day and it seemed to last interminably. Night was over in a matter of a few hours. It was all very different from the Australian winter that they had left behind them.

The men were staying in the new blocks of flats at Kapyla that constituted the Olympic Village and the women were at a training college close to the stadium itself. Being a relatively small team they blended together easily and the group always gave vociferous support to any of its number who were competing.

'Come on, Marje!'
'Run, you beaut!'
'All the way, girl!'
'Show 'em what you're made of!'
'Keep going! Keep going!'

'You're well ahead!'

'She's done it! She's done it!'

Marjorie Jackson had not only scattered the opposition to win the 100 metres in a time that equalled the world record. She collected Australia's first track gold medal for over fifty years and, by the decisiveness of her victory, put fresh heart into the rest of the team. Shirley Strickland from Perth had taken the bronze medal and Winsome Cripps had finished fourth. It was the first time ever that three Australians had contested an Olympic final.

'That was amazing, Marje!' congratulated John Landy.

'Thanks.'

'No wonder they call you the Lithgow Flash.'

'They'll be celebrating back home when they hear about this,' she said. 'The whole town will go mad.'

'It must be a fantastic feeling.'

'Oh, it is, John. I've actually done it. Suddenly, the pressure's off. I can go out and actually enjoy the 200.' She squeezed his arm. 'I'll be shouting for you when it's your turn.'

'Don't expect that kind of performance,' he warned.

'I won't,' she joked. 'I'll expect a better one.'

She went off to receive more congratulations and Landy watched her go. Her triumph had touched off a tremendous feeling of pride in his country and it made him look forward to his own chance to run in the yellow vest of Australia. Marjorie Jackson had blazed the trail that he was determined to try to follow.

Over 1800 journalists, broadcasters and photographers were covering the Games and there were times when Roger Bannister felt that every one of them was dogging him.

'Could we just take a photo, please?'

'How do you feel about being one of the favourites?'

'Is there any athlete you fear in the final?'

'That's fine – hold it right there!'

'What's your opinion of the track?'

'Why have British athletes done badly so far?'

'Are you happy with your training?'

'Is it true you have a slight cold?'

'Do you feel confident that you could win Britain's first gold medal of the Games?'

It was very tiresome and Bannister learned to dodge it as much as possible. He had still not recovered from the shock of having to run on three consecutive days. Tension and anxiety kept him awake at night and he felt tired during the day. Disappointing performances by the rest of the British team only served to depress him and he became moody and withdrawn. When the heats for the 1500 metres began, he was under considerable nervous strain.

Chris Chataway tried to provide some moral support.

'It's the first four to qualify for the semi-finals, Roger. That makes it a bit easier.'

'Does it?'

'You won't have to kill yourself.'

'Have you seen the times for the first two heats?'

'They had some of the fastest men in them. Your heat should be slower. You may get through just by taking it steady.'

'I hope so.'

Bannister looked around the stadium with weary resignation. Instead of being suffused with confidence, he was wondering how he could qualify in his heat while conserving enough energy for two more races. A supremely analytical runner who knew his own capabilities, he had prepared himself carefully for Olympic competition. His calculations had been dramatically upset and he was now experiencing the quiet panic of a man who has to run into unknown territory.

'Good luck, Roger.'

'Thanks.'

The third heat was over and Bannister would soon be on the track. He prowled around the infield and worked up his concentration for the race. With all his problems he was still representing his country and that fact steeled his resolve to do his utmost.

When the officials called the runners for the fourth heat to the start, he took off his track suit and joined the others. Token handshakes were exchanged. John Landy was among the runners and he gave Bannister a smile. The two men had met briefly in England at a training session in Paddington but they had seen very little of each other at Helsinki. Bannister had kept very much to himself and Landy had been training hard under Cerutty's noisy guidance.

They were called to the line and took up their positions. The gun discharged them and they powered off down the track. Bannister stayed in the pack and was grateful that the pace was not too hard. Landy ran well but his inexperience at this level was very evident and he had none of the tactical skill of some of the others. When the bell sounded it was still very much an open race and nobody seemed willing or able to make a purposeful break.

Bannister was still up with the leaders as they came around the final bend. They were roared down the finishing straight by an enthusiastic crowd and they had to pull out all they could find. The slowest heat of the day produced the tightest finish and split seconds separated the first four. Bannister came third. A crestfallen Landy was in fifth position and out of the event.

Though he had been in no danger of elimination, Bannister had had to drive himself hard and fatigue now hit him. Hands on hips and body sagging, he gulped in lungfuls of air and fought off the pain. He was delighted to have qualified but his elation was tinged with apprehension. Next day he would have to do it once more against sterner opposition and then come back on the following afternoon for the ultimate test.

The British press had talked about seven gold medals but none had materialized. Bannister sensed that he might not be able to rectify that situation.

'You forgot everything I bloody well told you, John,' complained Cerutty bitterly. 'You let me down.'

'I let myself down,' he murmured.

'What happened out there?' demanded the coach.

'They were better than me.'

'That's rubbish and you know it. My athletes are the best in the Olympics and it's high time they started behaving as if they realized it.'

They were back at the Village and a despondent Landy was having to cope with Cerutty's recriminations. He needed sympathy and encouragement at that point and not criticism.

'You blew up, John,' accused the other. 'Why?'

'Because I just wasn't fit enough.'

'My athletes are always fit enough!' asserted Cerutty.

'Six weeks of real training,' said Landy soulfully. 'That's all I had, Perce. It's not the way to go into an Olympics. I'm just not up to it.'

'Of course you are. You broke a British national record, didn't you? Yes, and you all but won that mile at the White City.'

'Those races took it out of me. When I came round that last bend today, I just didn't have anything left to give.' Landy shook his head. 'And it may be the same story in the 5000 metres.'

'Hey, now none of that defeatist bloody talk around here, John Landy!' ordered Cerutty. 'We've still got time to get you honed up for the 5000. I'm banking on you and Les to make the final.' He used a fist to punch the palm of his other hand. 'I want *one* of my boys to win a medal!'

'Don Mac is through in the 1500,' reminded Landy. 'Besides, it's not as if we'll go back empty-handed. Marje got her two golds and she's got a great chance of a third in the relay. Shirl got her gold in the hurdles and a bronze in the 100 metres.'

'But where are the *men's* medals? They're the ones that count.'

'They all count, Perce.'

'Not to me. The Olympic Games is about the highest achievements of man. When they held them in Ancient Greece, they didn't even let the women watch. And do you know what Courbetin said – the fella who actually founded the modern Olympics?'

'Yes. He said that women had no place in them.'

'Only he put it a bit stronger. Courbetin said they'd compete over his dead body.' He gave a hollow laugh. 'Which they have done. No disrespect to Marje Jackson and Shirley Strickland. What they've done is great. But I want an Australian *man* to assert himself. I want you and Don Mac and Les to impose yourself on a race.'

'Will you stop going on at me!' exploded Landy.

Percy Cerutty was taken aback. He had never seen the quiet, self-possessed athlete become so angry before and it made him change his tack at once. He put a consoling hand on the other's shoulder.

'What you need is a fillip, old son.'

'What I need is a rest.'

'But I've got a treat lined up for you,' promised the coach, grinning broadly. 'I'm taking you and a couple of the others to meet the finest athlete in the world.'

Landy was surprised. 'Zatopek?'

'Who else?'

'But he's out at the Russian camp most of the time.'

'So? We drop in and say hello.'

'They'd never let us in, Perce.'

'Ever known me unable to get in somewhere?' asked the other with a chuckle. 'I got in here, didn't I? I get into the stadium every day. Nobody keeps me out, John.'

Landy had to admit it. Percy Cerutty had a remarkable gift for getting into places without any official right to be there. He had demonstrated his gift at the White City, and at St Paul's Cathedral when they had failed to stop him from sprinting up the circular staircase in the tower. Landy's instinct was to keep well clear of this latest escapade but the chance of meeting Zatopek attracted him.

'I'll round up the others,' announced Cerutty.

'Are you *sure* Zatopek will want to see us?'

'Of course. You've seen the interviews he's been giving the press. He's the most friendly guy you could wish for.' He grinned again. 'A bit like me, really.'

Not long afterwards they were both crammed into a car with Les Perry and Don MacMillan as it drove out to Otaniemi. The sun was slanting down through the pine trees to create beautiful prisms of light and there was an occasional glimpse of a furred animal as it flitted through the undergrowth. Landy was absorbed in the natural wonders all around him. Helsinki had proved to be a charming city and the Finns were the most courteous hosts. Landy had felt an instant affinity with the country and was keen to see more of it.

'Zatopek may run in the marathon,' announced Cerutty.

'But he's in the 5000,' said Les Perry, 'and he's already won the 10,000. I know! I chased the back of his vest in that race.'

'He wants a hat trick, Les. I know it's a tall order but I believe the fella can do it.'

'No man can win three gold medals in events as gruelling as those, Perce,' argued Landy. 'Besides, look at the way Jim Peters ran the marathon in Britain. He'll take a hell of a lot of beating.'

'That's where you're wrong. Peters is ill.'

'Since when?'

'Since he arrived. The British camp have been keeping it quiet but they can't hide anything from old Perce. I got talking to one of their athletes and he spilled the beans.'

'What happened?' asked Don MacMillan.

'Seems that Peters got on the plane at London airport and sat there for ages while some senior official was giving a press interview. Peters was in a draught and caught a chill.' His full venom was directed at his favourite target. 'Bloody officials! They ought to be shot.'

'Does that mean Peters won't run?' wondered Perry.

'He'll run. But he won't be one hundred per cent fit. Why in God's name can't they *protect* their athletes? It's criminal.'

They were approaching the Eastern Camp now and the impassive countenance of Joseph Stalin came looming up at them. Landy was diverted by another sight. Because they were enjoying immense success in the Games, the Russians were using it for propaganda purposes. They had set up a huge board to show that their overall medal tally was highest and so the letters CCCP were placed at the top above the USA.

'But the Yanks have picked up golds by the handful in track and field,' said Les Perry. 'The Ruskies haven't done that well at all in the stadium.'

'It's the other things, Les,' explained Cerutty. 'Gymnastics, weight-lifting and so on. The Reds have grabbed everything there.'

The car stopped at the gates as a burly guard held up a hand. Cerutty jumped out and went over to him. They could see him gesticulating wildly and pointing towards the building. At first the guard shook his head but the coach did not give up. When he mimed the act of writing in a notepad, he found the key. The guard nodded and waved the car in. Cerutty rejoined the others.

'See? Told you. Like taking a lollipop off a baby.'

'How did you do it?' said Landy.

'Told him we were journalists who'd come to interview Zatopek. More propaganda for the Soviet bloc, he thought. So we're in.'

When they finally tracked down the Czechoslovak athlete he was in fact in the middle of giving an informal press conference to a small cluster of journalists. Cerutty breezed up to him and blithely introduced himself and his companions. Zatopek greeted them warmly. He was a thin, sinewy man with alert eyes set in a gaunt face and hair that was receding badly. His Slavic heritage showed in his face and his military background in the way that he held himself. Though not big, he conveyed an impression of power and control.

A few officials were standing in the background to keep a watchful eye on the proceedings. One of them brought a tray across and the Australians each took a glass of vodka. When Landy tasted his, he felt as if his throat was on fire. Zatopek was smaller and slighter than he had imagined but he was intrigued by what the Czech was saying. Speaking good if heavily-accented English, Zatopek answered all their questions in a most open and friendly way.

'Twenty miles or so a week is not enough,' he said.

'Not even for a miler?' asked Landy.

'You must do more. Your legs, they are like a bank. You can only take out what you put in.'

'But how do you actually go about it?' asked Perry. 'We read in some article that you do this interval training.'

'That is right, my friend. One fast lap, one slow lap, one fast lap, one slow lap. Again and again.'

'How many times?' said Landy.

'Twenty. Sometimes twenty-five.'

'A day!'

Percy Cerutty watched from the sidelines and began to feel peeved. Though he was thrilled to meet the famous athlete, he was aware that he had been completely upstaged. Moreover, his protégés were now listening intently to Zatopek as if *he* were their coach. Cerutty decided that it was time to intervene.

'Wait a minute, Emil! Those methods may suit you but they're no damn good for my boys.'

'I am only trying to help them,' said Zatopek.

'Yes, well, don't give them all that nonsense about over-training. It's not how far you run – it's the quality of it. Do you run up sandhills? Tell me – do you?'

Zatopek was bewildered. 'Do I run in sandals?'

'Sand–hills. Sand–hills.' Cerutty was losing his temper. 'Don't you understand English?'

'He speaks it very well,' argued Landy. 'How good is your Czechoslovakian, Perce?'

'Keep out of this,' ordered the coach.

'You keep out. What he's saying is interesting so give him a go, will you? We're trying to learn something.'

'You'll learn all you need to learn from me, young Landy.' He pointed at Zatopek. 'What does he know about the way Australians work best? *I'm* your coach, boys. Do what I say or you're out!'

His raised voice brought the officials scurrying over to curtail the interview and shield their star athlete. Landy averted what might have been a nasty incident by raising his glass.

'A toast to international friendship!'

'Friendship!' echoed the others.

They drank their vodkas and left without further disturbance.

America dominated the athletics stadium from the very first day and its achievements in track and field were remarkable. Lindy Remigino won the 100 metres in an eyelash finish from Herb McKenley, leaving McDonald Bailey to salvage British pride with a bronze medal. Andy Stanfield gave the United States victory in the 200 metres and the impeccable running of Mal Whitfield enabled him successfully to defend his 800-metres Olympic title. The same story continued as each day unfolded with world records tumbling freely and the American flag being hoisted aloft during the medal presentation ceremony.

The brilliant successes led to a feeling of invincibility.

'How do you feel about the Games so far, Wes?'

'Terrific. I just love this place.'

'You must be mighty proud of the United States team.'

'Hell – yes! Our guys have so far won over half of the events in the schedule. I feel great just being part of a team like this.'

Wes Santee was enjoying Helsinki and he had certainly cut a dash there in his blue suit, yellow tie, cowboy boots and stetson. He was chatting to a couple of American newsmen at the Olympic Village and he was exuding his usual confidence.

'Wes, are you going to win the 5000 for Uncle Sam?'

'I'm surely going to try,' he drawled.

'Don't you think you're a bit young for this level of competition?'

'I'm nineteen,' he said airily. 'Bob Mathias won the decathlon in London when he was only seventeen. Yeah, and Bob is back on the team this year to win it all over again.' He flashed a smile. 'If I'm old enough to get here, I'm old enough to win.'

'You're not worried by Zatopek's reputation, then?'

'Zatopek's only a human being. Just like me. My times this year are looking good and I'm improving every day.'

'Do you honestly believe you can beat Zatopek?'

'Well, I'll try,' he said good-naturedly. 'And I'll promise you this. If I don't win, I'll give him one hell of a fright.'

Roger Bannister lined up for the final of the 1500 metres and tried to banish his anxieties. He had come through the semi-finals in a punishing race but he knew that this was the one that really mattered. His credibility as Britain's leading miler was now at stake. In defiance of all advice he had trained himself for the supreme test of an Olympic final. Only a medal could justify his solo preparations. A press which had been critical of him before Helsinki would not spare him if he failed. It was a chilling thought.

He summoned up all his concentration as he was called to the starting line. It was a large field and he had already targeted the athletes who would pose the most threat. As current world record-holder at the distance, Werner Lueg, the tall, long-striding West German, began as favourite and he was likely to be the pacemaker. Barthel of Luxembourg, one of the shortest competitors, had shown style in the heats. Don MacMillan had run against Bannister in the Centennial Games so the latter was aware of his potential. And there were a few others.

Bannister had done his homework carefully and planned the race that he would run. Whether his speed and stamina would be equal to it was another matter.

Poised for the release of the starting pistol, he had never felt such tension before. Everything rested on one race. The next Olympic Games would be four years away and that was too far ahead for him. He would be a qualified doctor by then with no chance of finding the time for arduous preparation. This was his one shot at a gold medal. It would be the perfect way to end his running career.

'On your marks – set . . .'

The gun shot them off down the track into a cauldron of noise. There was a lot of jockeying for position at first as athletes sought the comfort of the inside lane. Lueg soon took over as the front-runner and set a pace that was designed to wear down his rivals. Bannister stayed in the pack not far behind him. He still felt strong but there was a long way to go.

Delirium seized the crowd as the bell signalled the last lap and partisan athletes frantically encouraged their colleagues from the infield. As Lueg stormed on down the back straight it seemed as if he might have drawn the sting from the others. Then Bannister moved steadily up until he caught the West German. When he edged up to Lueg's shoulder the British contingent gave a roar of delight as they sensed a triumph at last. Bannister had felt that he lacked self-control during the race but he now had the chance to make up for it with his inimitable kick for home. When he tried to tap that secret source of power which had killed off so many other competitors in so many other races, nothing happened.

Lueg began to draw away and he could not find an answer. More humiliation followed. Barthel overtook him then Bob McMillen, the American, glided past him. Bannister goaded himself on unmercifully and tried to close the gap. After leading for so long, Lueg was passed by Barthel and then the lanky American, a relative outsider, pipped him on the line. Bannister was fourth. A few yards had separated them.

The giant scoreboard high on the banking spelled out the details.

1500 metres Final
1. J. Barthel (Lux)   3.45.2.
2. R. McMillen (USA)   3.45.2.
3. W. Lueg (WG)   3.45.4.
4. R. Bannister (GB)   3.46.0.

What the statistics did not reveal was the fact that a mesmeric race had culminated in a superbly exciting finish. Barthel had won Luxembourg's only medal of the Games. McMillen had swelled the already monstrous tally of the Americans. Lueg had the consolation of bronze for his audacious front-running.

Roger Bannister, however, had nothing. He had run 1500 metres into despair and collapse and was now enveloped by a pain such as he had never experienced before. A pain that was intensified by the knowledge of just how close he had come to glory. A pain that stayed to torment him for a long time.

It was only later that he was able to find some comfort. He had run in a great race in which the Olympic record had been broken and in which he himself had lowered the British record. There was no medal to mark his success but there was still a deep satisfaction to be drawn. He now understood the full meaning of Courbetin's words.

THE IMPORTANT THING IN THE OLYMPIC GAMES IS NOT WINNING BUT TAKING PART.

Bannister had taken part in a memorable Olympic final and it was something of which he could be justly proud.

Chapter Eight

The heats for the 5000 metres gave Wes Santee his opportunity
to thrill the crowd with his positive running and to fulfil some
of the predictions he had been making about himself. Never
slow to blow his own trumpet, he had got himself a fair
amount of attention in the press and he had let the other
athletes know that he was around. It was now time to prove
himself against the best in the world and he was in a confident
mood as he jogged around before the start. While other
competitors were trying to key themselves up and going
through elaborate warm-up routines, he was calm and affable,
itself a form of weapon against the others.

A loud buzz filled the stadium as Zatopek came out on to
the track. Though his thinning hair made him look older than
his thirty years, the Czech runner was still the fittest man at
the Games as well as its most charismatic personality. Santee
waited for him to come over and then offered his hand.

'Mr Zatopek?'

'How do you do?' said the Czech, returning the handshake.

'I'm Wes Santee.'

'I've heard of you.'

'Good. I've tried to make my presence felt.'

'You're going to make it hard for me, eh?'

'Well, I'm going to try,' promised Santee with a smile.

Zatopek nodded. 'Good luck, Mr Santee.'

'Thanks. Good luck to you.'

Emil Zatopek did not need it. Though his heat had been
eagerly awaited by his countless fans, they did not get a

demonstration of the ruthless front-running which had ground his rivals into oblivion in the final of the 10,000 metres. Showing an almost casual indifference, he allowed the Russian, Anufryev, to set the pace in the early stages. Zatopek then speeded and detached four runners from the pack to take with him. Chris Chataway was one of the quartet. As the race neared its end Zatopek waved the Russian through to the front and then made sure that Albertsson of Sweden took second place, contenting himself with having qualified comfortably in third position.

Santee, meanwhile, was still boxed in further back. He had run well but his tactical inexperience had been laid bare and he was never really in contention. Having gone into the race as a potential medallist he had been made to feel like a callow youth.

He took his disappointment well as he congratulated Zatopek.

'I guess I still have a few things to learn.'

'You will learn them, my friend,' said the Czech. 'And I am sure that Wes Santee will be back.'

If Perce Cerutty had been annoyed by John Landy's failure to qualify in the 1500 metres, he was completely enraged by the latter's failure in the tenth heat of the 5000 metres.

'You're a disgrace to your country, John Landy!'

'Don't start again, Perce.'

'You couldn't even make it past the heats,' said the other in disbelief. 'There's guys there you could beat if you ran on one leg and yet they licked you. What happened?'

'I told you before. I just wasn't fit enough.'

'Rubbish! Bloody rubbish! *I* was fit enough to qualify in that heat so you certainly were.'

When Landy had walked off the track he had taken his dejection to the changing rooms beneath the stand but Cerutty had intercepted him for a confrontation. The coach stamped his foot like an Australian version of Rumpelstiltskin.

'Don't you care about your country?' he challenged.

'Of course I do!' retorted Landy.

'Then why didn't you fight a bit bloody harder for it?'

'Perce – clear out, will you?'

'Your father and his friends raised the money to send you here.'

'I know that.'

'And this is how you repay them! You might just as well not have come all this way.'

Landy was struggling to rein in his own temper. He had already put up with a lot from Cerutty and he was near his breaking point. The coach jerked a thumb at his own chest.

'And what about me?' he asked. 'Everyone in Australia knows that I train John Landy. How do you think this makes *me* look?'

'You don't have to train me any more, Perce,' said Landy firmly.

'Eh?'

'From now on I'll be coaching myself – right?'

'Oh, you will, will you?' asked the other derisively.

'Yes. Ten minutes of speaking to Zatopek is worth ten whole years of listening to you.'

Cerutty glowered. 'Well, you get your advice from Mr Zatopek and see how you go.' His finger pointed warningly. 'But don't you come crawling back to me when you find it's getting you nowhere – because I won't have you!'

'That suits me fine, Perce.'

'Running needs guts and you don't have the kind that I expect from my athletes. I only train the best.'

But Landy was not listening. He had turned on his heel and was now striding away down the corridor. The rift between him and Percy Cerutty was long overdue and he had no regrets now that it had taken place. He felt instinctively that it was the right decision. It was also a major turning point in his running career.

John Landy had just taken the essential first step towards becoming the kind of athlete that he was now determined to be.

Drama, excitement and a consistently high level of performance marked the Helsinki Olympics at every stage but it was the final of the 5000 metres which produced the finest spectacle and which seemed to encapsulate the elements of courage, commitment, heartache and luck that are part of the fascination of athletics.

Emil Zatopek could not have been in a better frame of mind for the race. His wife, Dana, had just won a gold medal in the javelin and this gave him an extra spur. He knew that it would be a difficult race. Despite his capacity for successive fast laps he did not have the basic speed to break up a field over 5000 metres. Herbert Schade, the bespectacled German, was capable of leading the field as well as he could. Gaston Reiff, gold medallist in the event at the London Olympics, would watch him like a hawk. Chris Chataway and Gordon Pirie of Britain might have the pace to outsprint him over the last lap.

He therefore played a waiting game. Chataway led for the first lap and the Czech was quite happy to nestle in the pack. Schade took over the lead for the next five laps and then Zatopek decided to inject some speed and dragged the others around in sixty-eight seconds. Schade was then permitted to assume the vanguard again.

The game of cat and mouse continued with clever manoeuvring and subtle changes of pace. Pirie led for a short while but the German soon surged back to take up his preferred position. When the bell rang the pattern of the race changed immediately.

Zatopek kicked, laid back his head and charged off alone. The stadium was in an uproar. This was what everyone had come to see. A lean figure in the red vest of Czechoslovakia. Arms flailing, knees pumping, face contorted, teeth bared, tongue lolling out of the side of his mouth. Emil Zatopek. Running in that unique, hunched style that made him look as if he was in absolute agony.

And then the impossible happened.

At the start of the back straight, three men sped past his right shoulder – Chris Chataway, Herbert Schade and Alain Mimoun, the French Algerian. Zatopek had never suffered an indignity like this in any major race. Certain of victory when he launched himself off at the bell, he was now trailing in fourth position with half a lap to go. He screwed up his features even more and tried to claw back a yard at a time.

Chataway was now in trouble. His bold thrust had tired

him badly and he was hanging on grimly. As they came around the final bend each of the pursuing athletes made his move. For one brief second all four were abreast and then tragedy intervened. Fatigued by his efforts, Chataway tripped on the concrete kerb that lined the infield and he plunged forward to the ground.

A huge communal groan of sympathy went up all round but it changed at once to thunderous applause as Zatopek held off his challengers over the closing yards and flung himself at the tape. He had come back from the dead, routed his rivals and shattered the Olympic record.

Mimoun came second yet again, Schade settled for third, Pirie loped in to take fourth position and a limping Chataway forced himself home after his countryman. Applauding furiously, John Landy and Ray Weinberg gave a special cheer when Les Perry found a last drive for the line to take sixth position.

'What a race!' said Weinberg.

But Landy's eyes were firmly fixed on the winner.

'What an athlete!'

Over breakfast in his hotel, Harold Abrahams read the sports pages of the morning paper. Though he had regularly penned his own reports on events at the stadium, he liked to keep in touch with what other observers were saying. Even if it made him wince.

> The Helsinki Olympic Games have been among the most enjoyable I can remember. The city is beautiful, the hospitality warm and the organization excellent. The one blemish, of course, is the miserable performance by British athletes. Bronze is the best that our men can manage. Among our women, Sheila Lerwill high-jumped her way to our solitary silver.
>
> Why has it all been such a disaster for us?
>
> Countries like Switzerland, Denmark, Belgium, even Turkey stand above us in the overall medal table. A nation as tiny as Luxembourg struck gold on the track. Great Britain, by comparison, has looked anything but great. Our display has been shameful. We have finally run out of excuses.
>
> If over-confidence could win races, then Pirie would have won

the 10,000 metres. If ivory tower arrogance could win races, then Roger Bannister would have won the 1500 metres. If sheer pluck could win races, then Chris Chataway would have won the 5000 metres. Each one of them failed.

In the post mortem that follows this Games, some harsh questions must be asked about our whole attitude to the sport. What is it about our athletes that makes them afraid to win?

Time is running out. With a few days to go, our last hope of gold remains Jim Peters in the marathon. Is he going to redeem our reputation?

Or will he turn out to be yet another Great British Failure?

Abrahams put the article aside and poured himself a black coffee. He felt wounded by the attack but knew there would be far worse to come.

Emil Zatopek did not rest on his laurels. After surviving press conferences and celebrations back at the Eastern Camp he was soon back on the training track to prepare for his assault on the marathon. Like many other athletes, John Landy seized the opportunity to run with the Czech for a few circuits in the hope of learning something from him. Zatopek was always amenable and, since he spoke a number of languages, he was able to give advice to athletes of various nationalities. Landy had cause to be especially grateful to him.

'You run like a comet!' he said at the end of a training session.

'It's not the speed,' explained Zatopek, 'but the consistency.'

'Yes, I've noticed that about European athletes. You don't run as fast as we do in training but you're more consistent.'

'What else have you noticed, John?'

Landy sighed. 'That Australia is a long way behind world standards.'

'You will improve.'

'I have already, simply by watching you.'

'Good.'

'Instead of trying to increase the speed of your laps, you seem to concentrate on shortening the recovery periods between them.'

'It is the only way to build up stamina.'

'And you train every single day?'

'Usually. On a track and elsewhere. I like to run on grass.'

'How many miles altogether in a week?'

'A hundred. At least.'

Landy gave a whistle of surprise. 'A hundred? We do nothing like that. How do you keep it up?'

'I like to win,' said Zatopek simply.

'So do I but I haven't had as much practice at it as you.' They laughed together. 'But my problem is not only stamina. It's technique.'

'Well, don't try to copy me, my friend,' warned the other with a grin. 'I am an effective runner but I am not a pretty sight to see.'

'You have this high arm carriage,' noted Landy. 'So do most European runners. It looks wrong somehow and yet it obviously does the trick. My arm action is very low.'

'Take off a shoe.'

'What?'

'I'll show you how to run better. Take one off.'

'You're not suggesting I run with only one shoe on, are you?' said Landy with a smile, removing one of his track shoes and handing it over. 'Here. Though I don't think it would fit you, I'm afraid.'

'I would not wear it if it did, John. These are sprinter's spikes.'

'All track shoes in Australia are more or less like that. They're made by the same guys who provide the spikes for the Stawell.'

'The what?'

'Stawell. Town in Victoria where they have this famous professional sprint every Easter. The Stawell Gift. One of the richest foot-races in the world. Shirl Strickland's father won it once.'

'Are they comfortable to race in?'

'Fairly. Though they do seem to make me tie up in some races.'

'It's because your legs do all the work. These spikes make you run on your toes. Haven't you noticed the ones we wear?'

'Of course. Shorter spikes and much flatter.'

'They are much easier for a middle-distance runner. If you try a pair, I think you will find that you run with your arms higher. Your legs will not have to do most of the work any more.'

'I'm willing to have a go at anything that will improve me,' said Landy eagerly. 'And if that means a change of track shoe and running style, then that's fine.'

Zatopek handed the shoe back. 'Which event are you going to concentrate on, John?'

'The mile. That's my best distance.'

'Set yourself a target. I always do.'

'Oh, I have. I'm going to bring my time right down. That's why I've been so keen to talk to people like you. I've filled a whole notebook with the things I've picked up here. Everybody has been so friendly and ready to exchange ideas. It's been fantastic!'

'That is what an Olympic Games is all about,' observed Zatopek. 'Sharing. Learning from each other. It makes us better athletes and it makes us better people.'

'It's been a wonderful experience for me – even if I did have problems out on the track.'

The Czech nodded. 'This target you have set yourself for the mile, John. What is it?'

'Oh, it's very ambitious but I'll get there whatever it costs. I'm going to shave a big chunk off my best time until I bring it right down to 4.06.'

'Why not go all the way and break four minutes?'

'I'm not *that* ambitious!' replied Landy with a laugh. 'No, I'll settle for 4.06. Then I'll probably retire from running.'

When the team manager bore down on him Wes Santee braced himself slightly. He had somehow managed to have quite a few brushes with officials in Helsinki and he feared that he might be in for some more hassle now. He was mistaken.

'Wes.'

'Yes, sir?'

'How would you like to run a mile?'

'Why, I'd just love it! Where? When?'

'England. Straight after the Games.'

'You mean, when we take on the team from the British Empire?'

'That's it. At the White City Stadium. We'd like you to run in the 4-mile relay.'

'Terrific! I take the anchor leg in relays all the time back at college. Thanks, sir. This'll give me a chance to prove myself.'

'Yeah,' agreed the manager. 'We did rather throw you in the deep end, kid. Sticking you in an Olympic 5000 metres.'

'Those guys were just too smart for me but they taught me a lot. I wouldn't make the same mistakes again.'

'Good. Well, the coach'll be talking to you about the relay just as soon as we're done here. And remember, Santee. We're not just going to England to put on a show. We're going to beat them and beat them hard.'

'Yes sir!'

'We got a very special reason for wanting to whip the British Empire.'

'Have we?'

'Of course,' replied the manager without a trace of irony. 'We used to belong to it!'

Percy Cerutty sipped at an orange juice and leaned back on his chair in the dining hall at the Olympic Village. Jill Webster was getting an exclusive interview though the volume of the coach's voice meant that it was not too exclusive. Everybody in the hall could hear it.

'So how would you sum up the Australian achievement?'

'What achievement?' he returned.

'If you send only four women and you win three golds and a bronze, that's no mean feat. And there's still the relay to come.'

'If you send thirteen men and you don't win a single medal, that's pathetic. We've come twelve thousand miles or more and we're going home empty-bloody-handed.'

Jill Webster scored her point. 'But some of those athletes were *yours*, Percy. You boasted how well they'd all do. What went wrong?'

'What went wrong is that I didn't have enough time to condition them properly,' he said truculently. 'You can't make an Olympic champion in five minutes. I need more time and

I need more money from the AAU for my training camp at Portsea.' He leaned over to tap the ring-top pad she was holding. 'Make sure you get that last bit.'

'So you don't blame yourself for any failure at Helsinki?'

'Why should I? It's the system that's to blame. It's rotten to the core. And I'm having to fight that system every inch of the way, Jill.' He broke off to finish his orange juice and noticed for the first time how attractive she was in her summer dress. 'Are you married yet?'

'No,' she said easily. 'But I've had plenty of offers. One or two of them were actually for marriage. Coming back to our performance in the Games, what would you single out as the worst faults?'

'Lack of a qualified team coach.'

'Someone like you?'

'I'm the best there is, Jill, and you know it.'

'What other faults?'

'Lack of foresight. Lack of preparation. Lack of money.' He waved a hand towards a group of athletes from the United States team. 'I mean, look at those fellas. Even as college runners they're used to having a manager and a coach and a bloody masseur. The Yanks invest money in the sport. It's bound to pay dividends on the scoreboard. Whereas we invest nothing, so we get nothing!'

Jill Webster scribbled in shorthand then she broke off to finish her coffee and to become aware that a hulking Canadian athlete was giving her a look of polite lechery from a nearby table. She offered him a dismissive smile then turned back to Cerutty.

'Is it true that John Landy has walked out on you?'

'No!'

'According to some of the –'

'Nobody walks out on me, young lady!' he insisted. 'John was not altogether suited to my training methods, that's all. We agreed to part company for a while.'

'That's not the way I heard it.'

'Well, it's the way you're hearing it now!' he yelled.

'Percy,' she said, coming straight back at him. 'Do you mind if I ask you a personal question?'

'Go ahead.'

'How on earth does your poor wife put up with you?'

Instead of being angry or indignant, Cerutty went off into peals of laughter and drew even more attention to himself. He was quite incorrigible. After years of interviewing him, Jill Webster could still not get the upper hand.

She put her pad away in her bag and stood up.

'Thanks, anyway. I've got enough for a story . . .'

'Don't you go printing anything about me and Landy,' he warned.

'People are entitled to know the facts,' she said levelly. 'Besides, it will be interesting to see how John gets on without you.'

'He won't, Jill. He doesn't know it yet but he's just committed suicide as a top athlete. *I* made him and I got him to these Olympics. Without me, he'll go back to being a goodish club runner, that's all.'

'I doubt it, somehow.' She checked her watch. 'Time to go.'

'I'll come with you,' he offered, getting up.

'Promises to be quite a day. Do you think Zatopek has any chance of winning a third gold medal?'

'Of course, Jill.'

'But he's never run a marathon before.'

'That doesn't make any difference,' he assured her. 'Zatopek is a phenomenon. Blokes like him just make it up as they go along.'

Recovered from his chill and delighted with the cool, cloudy weather, Jim Peters, the hot favourite, set a blistering pace in the marathon. He was still leading after ten miles and running with the confidence of a man who holds the world record at the distance. Emil Zatopek suddenly appeared at his shoulder and turned an anguished face to him.

'Do you think we are going fast enough?' asked the Czech.

Peters was too stunned to reply. Zatopek drew away and the British runner, who later dropped out of the race with cramp, never got close to him again. Finland had been the acknowledged home of distance running for some four decades. When Zatopek came into the stadium, therefore, he was given a magnificent ovation by a Finnish audience that could appreciate the true wonder of his achievement.

Three gold medals and three Olympic records.

The Games had begun with the appearance of one legend, Paavo Nurmi, and it had now ended with the creation of another one.

'Did you hear about the Ruskies?' asked Les Perry.

'No,' said Ray Weinberg. 'What have they done now?'

'You know that big scoreboard they had outside their camp?'

'The one that showed them leading on points?' asked MacMillan.

'Yes,' said Perry. 'Trouble is that the Yanks suddenly got those five gold medals in the boxing and overtook them. The Ruskies couldn't bear to advertise that, of course, so they started to take the board down. Only some reporter spotted them and did this story about it. "Russians Caught with their Points Down".'

The others laughed happily. It was one of dozens of Olympic anecdotes that they would be able to tell back home. Helsinki had been fun. They now waited outside the ultra-modern stadium for the signal to march inside in their team uniform for the closing ceremony. Disappointment at their own failure was tempered by the knowledge that they had been involved in a truly great event and that the Australian team had given a better overall performance than many critics had prophesied.

The final medal table made interesting reading.

Country	Gold	Silver	Bronze
USA	40	19	17
USSR	22	30	17
Hungary	16	10	16
Sweden	12	13	10
Italy	8	9	4
Czechoslovakia	7	3	3
France	6	6	6
Australia	6	2	3
Finland	4	6	3
Norway	3	2	0
Switzerland	2	6	6

South Africa	2	4	3
Denmark	2	1	3
Jamaica	2	3	0
Belgium	2	2	0
Turkey	2	0	1
Japan	1	6	2
Britain	1	2	8
Argentina	1	2	2
Poland	1	2	1

Britain's single gold medal had come in the showjumping, where a brilliant clear round by Colonel Harry Llewellyn on Foxhunter had ensured a victory in the team event. The Australians were amused.

'Typical of the Poms!' remarked Ray Weinberg. 'Their best competitor is a bloody horse!'

Marshals now opened the stadium gates and the long procession of national teams began. Sustained and affectionate applause rang out as the Finns saluted athletes who had provided them with an outstanding Olympiad that had been full of spectacle, rich in incident, studded with record-breaking feats and, most important of all, a lasting example of the spirit of international fellowship.

Emotions ran high as the ceremony unfolded and tears were shed in many languages. For some it had been the start of an Olympic career while for others it had been the end. For all of them, however, it had been an uplifting experience that would remain with them for ever.

As the proceedings rolled to their close the band played 'God Save the Queen' and the Australian flag was hoisted up as a sign that the next Olympic Games would be at Melbourne in 1956.

The moment made a profound impression on John Landy. Staring up with pride at his national flag, he vowed that he would bring honour and distinction to his country and to himself. He might have failed on the track in Helsinki but he would now go forward from that disappointment.

His real career in athletics was just beginning.

Chapter Nine

The confrontation at the White City Stadium between a British Empire team and the United States produced a pulsating and entertaining afternoon as athletes strove to reproduce winning Olympic form or to avenge their defeats at Helsinki. To set the seal on a memorable event, a dinner was held that evening at a London hotel and it was attended by all the officials and the majority of the athletes. Rivalries on track and field were soon submerged beneath the goodwill and celebration. The wine flowed freely.

Though there were far too many officials present for his comfort, Wes Santee was nevertheless enjoying the function very much. Seated beside him was Bob McMillen, another lofty runner with a college-boy appearance and the surprise silver medallist in the 1500 metres at the Games. Santee drained his glass.

'What's this stuff we're drinking, Bob?'

'Who cares? It's good.'

'I ran fast out there today. I felt great.'

'That's because you're a miler, Wes. You were more at home with the distance. And you like relays.'

'Yeah. I'm sure glad I got picked for the team. Been a swell day. And I got the chance to meet the British boys properly.'

'What did you make of Bannister?'

'Oh – he's okay,' said Santee without enthusiasm.

'That's what I felt. He's not a guy you could ever get close to, you know what I mean? He's polite and friendly, maybe, but he keeps you at arm's length.'

'All the English seem to be like that, Bob. What the hell's wrong with them? They afraid of us or something?'

'No, it's the way they are, Wes. You take someone like Bannister. When you're with him, he's there and not there. You never get the feeling that you're connecting.'

'Yeah.' He looked up in gratitude as a waiter filled his glass. 'I guess we ought to feel sorry for the guy, really. They threw a lot of shit at him because he didn't come home with a gold medal.'

'Jesus!' exclaimed McMillen. 'I was *in* that race! I know how hard it is to win *any* goddam medal! Bannister ran okay. He just didn't have the breaks.'

'And so they crucify the poor bastard!' Santee clicked his tongue in disgust. 'Some of those sports reporters – they're crazy! They build a guy up so he can't lose and when he does, they knock him down again. That's just about the best way I know to drive him out of athletics altogether.'

'Oh, I don't think Bannister will quit, somehow. That crap about him in the papers will have hurt. He'll want to hit back in the best way possible. Out on a track.'

Santee smiled reflectively. 'I sure would like to find out how good he really is over a mile. I'd like to race him back in the States. And Nankeville. And that Australian, Landy. He looked good.'

'Nice guy, too.'

'I liked him a lot. Landy was kind of easy to have around. You could actually *talk* to him.' He organized the race in his mind. 'Me, Bannister, Nankeville, Landy – and a few of the guys back home. Could be quite a race!' A confident grin spread over his features. 'I'd enjoy beating the pants off them!'

While the dinner was being held upstairs, a much smaller but no less enjoyable celebration was taking place in the dining room. John Landy, Ray Weinberg, Ken Doubleday, also a hurdler, and the four women from the Australian team were having a meal together. They were separate from the main function because they had to slip away early to catch a plane back to Helsinki in order to join their team mates for the flight home. The chance to represent the British Empire at the White City had been a bonus at the end of a long trip and they were in a relaxed and jovial mood. Ray Weinberg poured the last of the Sauternes into Landy's glass.

'It's all gone,' complained Landy, who had done his share of emptying three bottles so far. 'Order another bottle.'

'Waiter!' called Weinberg.

'Don't you think you boys have had enough?' suggested Marjorie Jackson. 'We have to be going soon.'

'There's time for another,' said Weinberg airily. 'That bloke said we could order whatever we liked so let's do it.'

The waiter arrived and a fourth bottle of Sauternes was commissioned. It was soon heightening the party spirit around the table. In the general hilarity, the women were at last managing to forget the incident which had cost the four of them a gold medal in the sprint relay. Shirley Strickland, Verna Johnson and Winsome Cripps had been in devastating form to set up the basis for a victory and it only remained for Marjorie Jackson, double Olympic champion and world record-holder, to run the last leg to certain glory. But there had been a fumble as Winsome Cripps handed over the baton and it had been dropped. Sauternes and good company were an ideal way to blot out the memory of the disaster.

'What time do we have to be at the White City?' asked Weinberg.

'We've already been, Ray,' reminded Winsome Cripps.

He was bewildered. 'Have we? I don't remember a damn thing about it.' He brightened. 'Just as well. The state I'm in, I couldn't jump a hurdle if you gave me a ladder!'

'Do you want a ladder?' asked Landy with an obliging grin. 'I'll order one for you. Waiter!'

'No, John!' hissed Shirley Strickland, laughing.

How they got to the airport Landy and Weinberg never knew because they were both at the blissful stage of inebriation. They kept wandering off down corridors and up staircases and the others had difficulty in keeping track of them. Eventually the whole group drifted into the bar. Landy and Weinberg saw the racks of bottles on the wall.

'How much money you got left, John?'

'Not a lot, Ray.'

'Stick it on the counter, mate.'

They both emptied their pockets of notes and coins before

the gaze of an amused barman. Weinberg leaned over the counter.

'What will that buy?'

'What would you like, sir?'

'Something for a celebration. We're going home.'

The barman collected up the money and disappeared for a minute or so. When he came back he was carrying a magnum of champagne and the sight made the two friends shout with joy. The bottle was opened with an explosive pop and the foaming contents were poured into glasses for the Australian team. Everyone else in the bar showed a kind tolerance as the two men circulated with compulsive bonhomie.

'How do you do, sir?' Weinberg said to an elderly gentleman. 'We're from Australia. Why don't you come and visit us some time?'

'Thank you, young man. But it's rather a long way to go.'

'It'd be worth it,' insisted the athlete. 'My parents are in the hotel trade. You'd have free accommodation and everything.' He moved to the next table to repeat his offer to a middle-aged couple. 'Have you ever been down under? It'd be a marvellous place for a second honeymoon . . .'

John Landy, meanwhile, was demonstrating Australian hospitality at the other end of the bar. Wearing Marje Jackson's hat and carrying the magnum of champagne, he approached two young women.

'Try a drop of this in your cup of tea, girls.'

'No thanks!' said one with a giggle.

'But you've got to help me celebrate. My name is Marje Jackson and I won two medals in the Olympic Games!'

When they eventually boarded the Quantas Constellation that was to take them to Helsinki they were still floating on a magic carpet of pleasant abandon. A shapely air hostess came down the aisle to check that safety belts were all fastened. When she bent over to secure Weinberg's belt for him, he gazed at the vision of loveliness before him and inhaled the subtle aroma of her perfume. The hostess moved on but he continued to stare ahead of him in a state of rapture.

'John?'

'Yes?'

'I'm in love.'

'Thanks,' joked the other. 'I take that as a compliment.'

'Not *you*.' He pointed over the back of the seat. 'Her.'

'Do you want me to tell her about it, Ray?'

'Of course not!'

Later in the flight, he was ready to tell her himself. Every time she flitted up and down the aisle, he gave her an inane grin of admiration. When she served him coffee he put a hand on her arm.

'How would you like to go on holiday?'

'I'd love to, sir,' she admitted.

'Where's your favourite place?'

'Capri.'

'Right,' he decided, trying to get up out of his seat. 'Let's go there straight away. Which way is it?'

She eased him playfully back into his seat and went on serving the other passengers. Weinberg was left to dream about their holiday together on the Isle of Capri and it made him sigh with ecstasy.

Because of heavy fog at Helsinki airport the plane was diverted to Stockholm and the passengers were put on to a coach. Although it was evening there was still good light for a sightseeing tour and the Australians were treated to a captivating experience.

If Helsinki had been beautiful, the Swedish capital was quite stunning. Stockholm's island geography gave it a natural setting that enhanced its wonders. Tall, stately houses vied with dignified civic buildings. Parks, boulevards and tree-lined squares added a rural splendour to the urban magnificence. Water could be seen at almost every turn and the city's reputation as a Venice of the North was amply justified.

Landy and Weinberg competed with superlatives as each new sight came up outside the window of the coach. They saw the cathedral, the Old Houses of Parliament, the Opera House, the Nordic Museum, the City Hall, the Royal Library and dozens of other places that touched off their enthusiasm. Weinberg clicked away eagerly with his camera. He was on his second roll of film when they reached the Royal Palace.

The coach stopped and the passengers all piled out.

Weinberg took several photographs of the palace itself and then stood on the waterfront to focus on Skeppsholmen. He turned back to his colleagues and beckoned them over.

'Line up, everyone. I've got one last shot.'

They allowed themselves to be waved into position and waited for him to immortalize them on Celluloid. When Weinberg raised his camera to peer through his camera, however, his team mates collapsed with laughter.

'Stand still!' he shouted. 'How the hell can I get a picture of you when you're falling around?'

This provoked even greater mirth and he could not understand why. Landy then strolled across to him and tapped the camera.

'Aren't you supposed to take the lens cap *off*, Ray?'

The Sauternes and the warm champagne at the airport had combined to erase most of his memories of the day. A lens cap had now obliterated his careful record of Stockholm. He could see from the glint in Landy's eye that he would never be allowed to forget the incident.

When the town of Lithgow heard that its favourite daughter had won her first gold medal at the Olympic Games it celebrated with a spontaneous symphony of church bells, car horns, fire alarms, factory whistles, ambulance sirens, railway-engine whistles and delirious cheers. By the time that Marjorie Jackson came home with an additional gold medal, Lithgow was a sea of welcoming banners and shining faces.

Her car was given a police motorcycle escort on the 150-mile journey from Sydney and she was cheered all the way along the route. Outside her home town she switched to an open car that was filled with flowers and she made her triumphal progress through the streets. All 14,000 inhabitants seemed to have turned out to greet her along with many others from neighbouring areas.

There would be civic receptions for her in Adelaide and in Melbourne but it was her welcome in that small town in the Blue Mountains that meant most. In routing the best sprinters in the world, Marjorie Jackson had put Lithgow on the map. Its people let her know what they thought of her.

John Landy got no ovation. He returned to a warm welcome from his family who waved away his apologies for not having done better and who remained proud that their son had represented his country. He had brought presents back for all of them but the most important items in his suitcase were for himself. When he unpacked in his bedroom he took them out to examine them once again.

His new pair of track shoes would alter his whole running style and his notebook that was bulging with new ideas would change his attitude to his sport. Helsinki had been worth it.

Roger Bannister stood with a group of other medical students around a bed in a hospital ward as the consultant made a thorough examination of the patient. The pressure of his studies had given him little time to continue his running and he could find no immediate incentive to amend the situation. His Olympic defeat had left him with a sense of anti-climax as well as with a natural resentment at being told that his preparations had been at fault. The next major international events in the athletics calendar would be the Empire Games in Vancouver and the European Games in Berne. Both would take place in 1954, the year of Bannister's final medical examinations.

'If you could step in a little closer, gentlemen . . .'

The consultant brought them into a semi-circle around the patient so that he could explain the nature of the case and the course of treatment that he had prescribed. There was a brief discussion and then it was time to move off to another ward. The patient, an old man in striped pyjamas, gave a resigned smile. In a teaching hospital like St Mary's he was having to get used to the idea of an audience.

'You won't need to train if this keeps up, Roger.'

'What's that?'

'All this trailing around the wards we seem to do,' said the colleague who walked beside him down a long corridor. 'We must have clocked up at least a mile already this morning. It's a training session in itself for you.'

'And much more tiring than my usual one,' admitted Bannister.

'How is the running going at the moment?'

'It's not, really.'

'Oh?'

'I've been cutting back on it lately.'

'Well, of course, the season is more or less over now and you have earned a rest.'

'That isn't the reason, actually.'

'What is?' He turned a cynical grin on his colleague. 'Don't tell me that you want to devote more time to medicine.'

'All right, I won't. But that happens to be the truth.'

The other laughed. 'Then you must be the only medical student I've ever met who feels like that. All the others go out of their way to do anything rather than buckle down to their studies. I do.' He probed a little. 'There's more to it than that, isn't there?'

'Perhaps.'

'You're not thinking of giving it up altogether, are you?' asked the student in surprise. 'Is that what you plan to do?'

'I haven't decided.'

'Not that I'd blame you, mind.'

'What do you mean?'

'Well, let's be frank, old chap. Some of the papers did rather give you a bollocking after Helsinki. If that had happened to me, I'd have raised two fingers to the lot of them.'

Bannister smiled. 'It *is* a big temptation, I must confess.'

'So what *are* you going to do?'

'I don't know.'

'Oh, come on . . .'

'I don't, honestly.'

'That doesn't sound like you, Roger. You're always so single-minded about everything.'

'Not this time.'

'Supposing – just supposing now – that you had won the 1500 metres at the Olympics. What would you have done then?'

'Retired, probably.'

'Finished at the top.'

'Yes.'

'Now that *does* sound like you. And that's why I bet you'll go on. So that Roger Bannister can finish on a high. Not a low.'

The white coats swept into another ward and converged upon the next patient. It was turning out to be a long morning.

Since Franz Stampfl had established his own coaching scheme, he had been getting a steady stream of athletes keen to profit from his expertise. His pre-eminence as a coach was being recognized more and more and the fact that his ideas often ran counter to the accepted theology of athletics made him a controversial figure. It was a role that Stampfl enjoyed.

Training sessions were held at the Duke of Yorks Barracks in Kings Road, Chelsea. As well as a running track, he had the use of a drill hall and of the rifle range up on top of it. It was in the latter that he coached hammer throwers and shot putters so he had rigged up huge safety nets to forestall any accidents.

'Good evening, Franz.'

'Hello, Harold. Come to watch the fun?'

'You seem to have far more athletes around than when I last dropped in. How many are there altogether?'

'Hundreds. I've lost count.'

Stampfl had been talking to a hammer thrower about his point of release but he broke off when he saw Harold Abrahams approaching. The hammer thrower mimed his action in the background as the two men chatted. In another corner a group of shot putters grunted and groaned as they heaved the solid metal through the air.

'You've been coaching up at Oxford again, I'm told.'

'If you can call it that,' said Stampfl. 'When I was starting my scheme here, two of the first people to roll up were Chris Chataway and Chris Brasher. They asked me to go up to Oxford. On a contract.'

'I seem to remember doing the same thing way back in 1938,' recalled Abrahams. 'Except that I had the sense to send you to Cambridge as well. I wasn't having my old university disadvantaged.' He paused to watch a shot land with a muffled thud on a rubber mat. 'How is it going up at Oxford?'

Stampfl shrugged. 'I haven't done anything yet.'

'I heard that you were going every day.'

'Oh, I am. They wanted me to stay there but I did not wish

to do that. So I travel up by train.' He spread his hands in a gesture of helplessness. 'But I do nothing, Harold. They get me to Oxford then they don't use me.'

'They ask advice, surely?'

'Yes, they chat to me all the time – but we could do that on the telephone. I am never allowed to *coach* them. It is ridiculous. Those students still like to think they are continuing the tradition of the gentleman athlete.' He gave a scornful laugh. 'They should look at Roger Bannister and see where that tradition got him.'

'I'm glad you mentioned Bannister,' said Abrahams. 'It's about him that I wanted a word.'

'Why?'

'Because he and I had a heart to heart the other day.'

'That is an achievement, Harold. He's been hiding himself away for months. Is he still sulking about Helsinki?'

'Bannister doesn't sulk,' replied Abrahams. 'He's far too self-critical to do that. No, he simply wanted to keep his own counsel for a while. And take a hard look at his future.'

'It is a sensible thing for any athlete to do.'

'He has a problem. Motivation. The Empire Games is two years away. He needs something to aim at in the short term. Something that will revive his interest and provide that motivation.'

Stampfl saw what was coming. 'And you want to ask me if I think it is possible. Is that it?'

'Do you, Franz? Can the four-minute mile be broken?'

'Of course. All records can be broken in the end.'

'But is Bannister the man to do it in this case?'

'I would doubt it.'

'Why?'

'Because of what I was just saying.'

'The gentleman athlete syndrome?'

'Yes,' replied Stampfl. 'Bannister has immense talent but he also happens to be a romantic. Running is like a crusade to him.'

'Is that such a bad thing?'

'Romantics do not win Olympic finals, Harold. Nor do they break through impossible barriers like the four-minute mile. It's the realists who always come out on top.'

'I'm not sure that I altogether agree there.'

'Look at the Americans. Not an ounce of romance in their souls and they end up as Olympic champions.'

'Heaven forbid that British athletics should go the way of America!' protested Abrahams with passion. 'What with scholarships and sponsors and all the rest of the commercial claptrap, they've all but killed off the amateur code.'

'I'm not suggesting you have to go in for all that nonsense. What I am saying is that America takes athletics seriously enough to put some money into it so that standards can be raised.'

'They put money in so that more money can be made,' argued Abrahams. 'But we're wandering away from the point. You say that Bannister will not make it.'

'Not unless he has a realist to help him to do it. Someone who can plan the whole thing from start to finish. Someone who is cool and objective and quietly ruthless.' He flashed a disarming grin. 'Don't worry. I am not applying for the job. I have enough on my plate as it is.' There was a pause. 'How committed is Bannister?'

'He's started training again in earnest.'

'On his own?'

'Yes.'

'Then he's wasting his time.'

'But he's increased the severity of his work markedly,' argued Abrahams. 'He's concentrating on interval running.'

'It makes no difference,' returned Stampfl. 'Breaking the four-minute barrier is like climbing Mount Everest. The only way that either peak will ever be reached is by a team effort. Bannister needs help. Athletes prepared to run with him and for him.'

Abrahams sighed. 'Not much hope of that, I'm afraid. He's still very much the lone wolf.'

'Then someone else will get there first, Harold. There are lots of good milers about. In Europe. In America. In Australia, even.'

'We've got to beat them to it!' urged Abrahams with burning conviction. 'For heaven's sake – the mile race *belongs* to Britain. It all began here. The first great miler was Walter George who set a world record all the way back in 1884. It's in our blood, Franz. The four-minute mile is part of our birthright.'

'Your birthright, Harold,' said Stampfl. 'Not mine. I am an Austrian so you must forgive me if I see it another way. The four-minute mile is up for grabs, my friend. It will go to the man who wants it the most – whatever his nationality.'

'I'd like him to be British.'

'Of course. It would bring tremendous prestige to you and that is something British athletics could do with at the moment. But you will not see that barrier smashed by a medical student who trains on his own between lectures.' He signalled to the hammer thrower that he would be joining him soon. 'One other thing.'

'What's that, Franz?'

'You mentioned Walter George.'

'The Wiltshire Wonder.'

'He set that world record when he was an amateur.'

'So?'

'Two years later – if I remember rightly – he knocked almost six seconds off that time.' A smirk appeared. 'As a professional.'

Abrahams grinned. 'Sorry, Franz. I'm not rising to the bait this time. Besides, I've held you up long enough. Our friend here is dying to throw his hammer and he's been very patient.'

'Stay and watch,' invited Stampfl. 'Terry is my best thrower. When he came to me he was sending the hammer everywhere but in the right direction. He has much more control now.'

He nodded to the young men then took Abrahams behind the cover of a thick net. Other athletes took cover as well. Terry wrapped his fingers around the handle then started to breathe in deeply through his nose. When he felt he was ready, he suddenly jerked on the handle and sent the chain and ball into a horizontal plane as he rotated at speed. Leaning backwards as he swung, he came round for the third time and released the hammer with maximum force.

Whatever he had been taught about control had somehow been forgotten this time. Instead of landing in the net at the far end of the range, the hammer climbed upwards with accelerating power and went straight through the roof.

The hammer-thrower groaned, the other athletes laughed

wildly, and Franz Stampfl stared up at the gaping hole above him.

'Look at it!' he shouted. 'It's Friday evening. They won't be able to mend the roof until Monday!'

'Sorry,' muttered Terry.

'You'll get us thrown out by the Army, you bloody fool!' yelled the coach. He turned to his friend. 'What's the weather forecast for the weekend?'

'Rain,' said Abrahams with amused sympathy. 'Heavy showers.'

It was shortly after midnight when John Landy finished his studying for the night and put away his books. Because his involvement with the Olympics had interfered with his academic work he was having to repeat his final year at Melbourne University and he was making certain that he would be ready for his examinations this time.

Changing into his running gear, he slipped quietly out into the darkness and made his way to Central Park, Malvern, which was nearby. When he got to the oval he put on the track shoes that he had brought back from Europe and began his training routine.

After jogging for the first lap he pushed himself hard for the second then recovered by jogging again for the third. Fast and slow laps were alternated for an hour and a half. Landy's running style was at once more comfortable and effective now. His flatter foot action was complemented by a higher arm carriage that gave him more balance and thrust. There was now more relaxation in his stride and none of the tension that he had felt before in his thigh and calf muscles. Again, his new style was more economical, preserving strength and distributing energy much better.

He had not wavered from the target he had set himself of 4.06 for the mile. What had given him extra impetus on his return was the hostility with which his failure at Helsinki had been treated in the press. It had wounded him deeply and sent him out to train on his very first night home.

Landy had stuck at it seven days a week ever since.

The Olympic Games had exposed his inexperience and shattered his self-confidence. He had promised himself that he would never again be so ill-prepared. In the future he would always be the fittest man in the race. As well as the fastest.

As he made his way back home in the stillness of the night he had the satisfaction of knowing that he had undergone a complete metamorphosis as an athlete. A good runner had become a dedicated one. A hobby had become a mission. A sport had become an extension of his personality.

John Landy had gone to Helsinki as a raw recruit.

He had returned as a fanatic.

Chapter Ten

With a cigar in his mouth and a glass tankard in each hand, Chris Chataway threaded his way through a busy lounge bar to where Roger Bannister was standing. He handed one of the drinks to his friend then removed his cigar.

'Thanks, Chris. Cheers!'

'Cheers, old boy!' They sipped their beers. 'Lovely!'

'Why do you keep smoking those foul things?' asked Bannister good-humouredly. 'They can't be doing you any good.'

'Are you speaking as a doctor or as an athlete?'

'Both.'

'I happen to like cigars,' said Chataway breezily. 'One of the pleasures of life and I've never been one to deny myself pleasure. I'm not like you, Roger – I don't go into monastic seclusion when I train. I give myself rewards.' He held up the cigar. 'Like this.'

'Doesn't it affect your respiration, Chris?'

'Only when I smoke during a race!' They traded a laugh. 'Besides, lots of good athletes like a whiff. I saw plenty of ciggies about at Helsinki. Look at Denis Johansson, for instance. He smokes like a chimney and yet he's Finland's best miler.' He inhaled again then expelled the smoke into the air. 'How are things, anyway?'

'Fine.'

'Still working night and day?'

'I have to, Chris.'

'Your own fault for choosing medicine, old boy. You should have read PPE like me. Three years of fun and then a crash programme of work just before your Finals.'

Bannister smiled. 'I know you too well to believe that.'

'What?'

'You're the sort of chap who likes to give the impression that he does no work but who beavers away like mad in secret. It's the same with your running, Chris. You pretend that you don't really train then you put in the slog when nobody is looking.'

'Someone *is* looking now, Roger. I've got a proper coach.'

'Franz Stampfl?'

'Yes. He helped me before Helsinki, as you know. And he's been coming up to Oxford to give general advice. I finally decided to take the plunge and put myself in his hands.'

'Good. He may stop you smoking.'

'Franz has made an amazing difference. He lives and breathes athletics. Terrifying enthusiasm.' He paused to take another drink. 'I must confess that there are times when I've thought about giving it all up. As you must have.'

'Oh, yes,' said Bannister with feeling.

'That kind of attitude doesn't last two minutes with Franz. He makes you *want* to run. And he's got me doing things I'd never have thought possible. Weight-training, calisthenics and so on.'

Bannister was delighted to be able to fit in time for a drink with his friend. Chataway was always lively company and his cheerful ebullience was always a tonic. But they were very different runners. As he listened to his friend praising Franz Stampfl's methods, Bannister was not shifted from his belief that he himself did not need a coach. When Chataway challenged him on the subject he had his answer ready.

'Why don't you let me introduce you to Stampfl?'

'No thanks.'

'He might be able to help you, Roger.'

'I'm doing fine as it is.'

'Still determined to go it alone, eh?'

'I'm temperamentally unsuited to being coached.'

'Don't give me that!' said Chataway jocularly. 'What you mean is that you want to keep all the glory to yourself.'

'That's one way of looking at it,' admitted Bannister. 'But the way I see it is this. If I come to grief – as I did in Helsinki – then I only have myself to blame.'

'That's true.' He took one last puff at the cigar and stubbed it out in a nearby ashtray. 'So how is the training?'

'It's going very well, Chris.'

'Still doing intervals?'

'Yes, I run about ten fast quarters every day.'

'How fast?'

'Around 63 seconds.' Chataway was impressed. 'Physiologically, it makes great sense to stress the body by speed and partial recovery. If anything is going to improve your chance of out-sprinting the others at the end of a fast race, then that will.'

'No supplementary training of any kind?'

'I've never bothered with weights or exercises, Chris. I've always remembered what Sydney Wooderson once said in an article. That the best preparation for any runner is simply to run, run, run.'

'That approach didn't do him any harm,' conceded Chataway.

'I'm getting stronger and faster all the time.'

'But with no chance of proving it in a race. If only we had proper indoor facilities like the Yanks. Those chaps can run on quality tracks all the year round. And it shows.'

'They may have better facilities,' argued Bannister, 'but they don't have a better attitude than we do.'

'Yes they do. They're only interested in winning.'

'I didn't mean that. You can't fault them on competitiveness. I noticed it the first time I went to America. Princeton in 1949. It was an eye-opener. They all had this total commitment to the idea of winning. It was very refreshing in its own way. I found American athletes so alert, so interested in life.'

'So why is our attitude better, Roger?'

'Because we're still, at heart, amateurs,' explained Bannister. 'When I went over to Philadelphia to run in the Benjamin Franklin Mile, they were staggered that I didn't have an entourage with me. My manager, coach and so on. That's the kind of world they live in. Where athletics is a kind of business that's geared to turning out a superior product. I just couldn't stand the college atmosphere over there so I asked to be moved out to a hotel.'

'I bet that made you popular,' noted Chataway.

'I still won the race,' recalled his friend. 'But do you take my point? The American system is effective, I grant you, but is it beneficial to the athletes themselves? I mean, whatever happened to the love of running?'

Chataway grinned. 'It's been patented by a chap called Roger Bannister. The last of the idealists.'

'I take that as a compliment.'

'You're the only person I know who would.'

They laughed and continued to compare notes about their respective training schedules. Bannister then checked his watch and saw that he had to get back to the hospital.

'My trouble is that I have to squeeze my idealism in between ward rounds and lectures. Medicine is a taxing discipline. Still, at least I know what I'll come out as at the end of it all.'

'Dr Bannister, I presume?' joked Chataway.

'What about you, Chris? What will you do with your degree in PPE? Politics, philosophy or economics?'

'Politics might be fun,' remarked the other. 'But that can wait for a bit, I feel. No, my thoughts have been turning towards a career elsewhere. I might try to make a living out of the elixir of life.'

'Athletics?'

'No, Roger.' He held up his tankard and swished its contents around. 'Brewing!'

Len MacRae waited for his friend to complete his training and then strolled across to him. They were in Central Park on a warm afternoon.

'Now that's what I call precision running, John!'

'Thanks.'

'You've always had a good running style but it looks bloody beautiful now.'

'It works, Len. That's the main thing. I don't get the same sort of fatigue in my legs any more.'

'I wish I could move like that. Perce keeps working on me but I still lumber along like a carthorse.' They strolled across to where Landy had left his track suit. 'Er, he was asking after you, by the way.'

'Perce?'

'Yes. Said you'd be welcome to drop in any time.'

'No thanks, Len.'

'Oh, come on. Why don't you two bury the hatchet?'

'I've got nothing against Percy Cerutty,' said Landy. 'He's a great coach. In his own way, he's a great man. But he's just not the person to get the best out of me.'

'He got the best out of Don Mac,' noted MacRae.

'I know.'

'A new Australian mile record of 4.09. The press gave Don some marvellous write-ups. And Perce, of course – he made sure of that!'

'I'm pleased for both of them,' observed Landy. 'But I prefer to go my own way. Besides, 4.09 is good but it's nothing special in world terms.' He rattled through a list of names and times as if they were kept at the forefront of his mind. 'Slykhuis ran 4.2.2 three years ago. Gaston Rieff has done 4.2.8. Olle Aberg has run 4.4.2. You've got Neilson, Lamers and Roger Bannister on 4.4.8. And then there's guys like Barthel, Lueg and Bob McMillen who've turned in some pretty fantastic times for the 1500.' He began to pull on his track suit. 'And then you've got me.'

'Think you can beat Don's record?'

'I have to, Len. As an act of faith. My target is 4.06.'

'That'll take some running on our rotten bloody tracks.'

'I'll do it somehow.'

'You deserve to, John. Never known a fella train so damn hard as you. Especially when he's studying for his exams at the same time.'

'I've got to pass those, Len,' said Landy seriously. 'I mean, athletics is important to me – bloody important – but I've only got a few more years in it at most. Whereas I'll be involved with agriculture for the rest of my life.'

They walked side by side towards the gate in the distance, chatting easily about old times at Dookie. Landy suddenly stopped in his tracks and then shot off towards a clump of bushes nearby. He vanished behind them for a couple of minutes and MacRae was mystified. When he came back, Landy's hands were cupped together and he had a smile of triumph on his face.

'What the hell did you do that for, John?' wondered MacRae.

'My collection.'

'Of what?'

'These little beauts.' He parted his hands a fraction to give MacRae a glimpse of a butterfly that was fluttering about in its prison. 'It's a great hobby.'

'I know. Interested in them myself.'

'Butterflies?' said Landy in surprise.

'Yes. I have this huge collection of them.'

'Where?'

'In my stomach. Just before a bloody race!'

The aircraft looped around to give the passengers a glimpse of Lake Erie before heading for the runway at Cleveland Airport. Wes Santee and Art Dalzell felt the bump as the wheels made their first jarring contact with the tarmac. Dalzell was a close friend from the University of Kansas as well as being a first-rate miler. The two athletes were gaining quite a reputation on the athletics circuit.

'How many miles do you figure we've flown this year?'

'Too many, Wes.'

'Yeah. I hate it. Flying always tires me.'

'Me, too. Then they expect us to come up with record-breaking performances. Man, I haven't enough strength to run to the john!'

He yawned as the aircraft taxied to a standstill.

Santee and Dalzell had been invited to compete in an indoor mile at a track in Cleveland, Ohio. The organizer, who had spoken to Santee over the telephone, had made it quite clear that he wanted something very special for his patrons. Santee, in his exuberant fashion, had promised him that he would not be disappointed.

'What do you reckon we're aiming at, Wes?' asked Dalzell, as they waited for their things in the baggage hall. 'About 4.10?'

'I think the guy said the Cleveland record was about 4.08.'

'Shit, man! That's fast!'

'You're my rabbit, Art. My star pacemaker. You have to get me there somehow.'

'Any ideas how?'

'Sure,' said Santee, leaning forward to grab a travel bag as it came past him on a conveyor belt. 'Let's run the first quarter in 62, the second quarter in 62, and the third quarter in 62.'

'That gives us 3.06. You'll have to shift, Wes.'

'I figure I can run the last quarter in about 58 so we'd end up well under the record with 4.04.'

Dalzell grinned. 'We'd also end up with one of the fastest indoor miles ever run. You really think you can do it, Wes?'

'I'll let you know when I wake up properly,' said the other, stifling a yawn. 'Hey, here comes your bag right now . . .'

They were met by one of the officials and driven to the track. The organizer was there to greet them. A big, bluff man with dark, greasy hair that was slicked back over his head, he pumped their hands and guided them in to have their first view of the running circuit. The athletes assessed the length of the track at a glance.

'Twelve laps to a mile,' noted Santee.

'That's it, son,' agreed the organizer. 'It's a great running surface. We get a lot of good things said about it.'

'I'd hate to run anything longer than a mile on it,' drawled Dalzell. 'A guy could get dizzy going round in circles that many times.'

'You just concentrate on serving up that record,' suggested the organizer. 'I got every seat sold on account of you two.'

'Hey, now hold on, sir,' said Santee politely. 'We'll do our best but we can't give you a guarantee.'

The man was blunt. 'I don't want a guarantee. I want a record.'

'An *attempt* at a record,' added Dalzell.

'Say, what is this! Your coach told me you guys were the hottest milers around. I mean, I've got a deal here. I paid for results.'

'You might have a better chance of getting those results if our coach was with us,' explained Santee politely. 'Art and me run that little bit faster when Bill Easton is there to kick our ass.'

'Come on, guys,' argued the organizer. 'This is amateur athletics we're talking about. We can't afford to fly your goddam coach up here as well. You want that kind of treatment, take up pro football.'

The athletes gave up. They had been invited there as the

main attraction of the meeting and they were expected to break the Cleveland record for the indoor mile. No excuses would be accepted.

Long before the meeting was due to begin the stadium was filled and the organizer was wandering about oozing a kind of bullying charm and promising everyone that they were in for a magnificent evening of athletics. The two friends from Kansas sat in the changing room and made their final plans. They had practised on the track and liked it. The record might be in danger after all.

Eventually they were called out for the mile race.

'Know something?' said Santee.

'What?'

'I started to run better since Eisenhower got elected.'

'Is that good or bad?'

'Wish I knew.'

The other athletes knew that they were just also-rans in the race and one or two of them resented the fact and resolved to try to cause an upset by beating the two star milers. Their resolutions foundered as soon as the gun fired. Art Dalzell streaked into an immediate lead and Santee sat in behind him.

After only three laps they had opened up an appreciable lead. Santee looked up at the clock as they pounded past the line and he gave a shout of joy. They were bang on schedule.

'Hey, we're doing good!' he called.

'Thanks.'

'Keep it up, Art. Keep pushing.'

'Yeah,' gulped the other.

They forged on around the track with the crowd howling them on. Three laps later they were still hitting the time that they had planned. The two athletes were delighted with themselves but the organizer was now puce with rage. A half-mile in 2.04 did not seem to him to be a realistic basis for a record run. Each time the Kansas duo hared past him he yelled abuse at them.

'Go faster! You promised you'd go fast, you bastards!'

They completed another lap and saw his wild eyes blazing with vengeance. He raised a fist as they got close.

'Give me my goddam record, you schmucks!'

After nine laps the time stood at 3.06. Wes Santee then

took over. Shedding Dalzell like a booster rocket, he shot away with gathering speed and opened up a gap at once. The crowd were now whipped up into a frenzy as they saw his long, smooth stride eating up the yards at a furious pace. Dalzell was still running, as were the other athletes, but all eyes were on Santee.

When the organizer saw the time after two more laps his anger turned to uncontrolled joy and he jumped up and down excitedly.

'That's my boy! Just look at that kid go!'

Santee found a last burst of energy to increase his speed and he positively screamed around the last lap before diving at the tape. His time had been 4.03.6.

Lungs bursting and body shuddering after the effort it had just been forced to make, Santee bent over and tried to ignore the figure who was dancing around him with glee.

'We did it, son! We gave them a promise and we delivered!'

A weary Art Dalzell now crossed the line and the organizer was on him in a flash, squeezing him hard and kissing both his cheeks.

'Oh, you beautiful rabbit! You're the greatest person in the world! *Both* of you are! You guys have made me so happy!'

Like Santee, Dalzell could force no words out of a dry mouth that felt as if it were smouldering. When they had recovered enough to be able to acknowledge the pandemonium of the applause, the athletes saw that the organizer was still celebrating.

Later, in the showers, Santee was peeved.

'It makes you sick, Art.'

'Why, man? You just run one of the fastest indoor miles ever.'

'Yeah, and what happens?'

'I get kissed by that crazy guy in a tuxedo.'

'And why? Because we gave them what they paid to see.' Santee turned off the shower and reached for a towel. 'Sometimes I just hate the way they run athletics in the States.'

'Only sometimes?'

'It's a racket!'

'I know. They press buttons and we're supposed to get records.'

137

'Look what happened in there tonight, Art. I had a pace-maker and it made all the difference. My rabbit pulled me around and I get close to a world record.'

'Sounds to me like you got one hell of a good rabbit!'

'I have. And we came through for them. But where does it get us?'

'We'll grab us a few headlines, maybe.' He laughed. 'They might even invite us back to Cleveland to please the crowd once again.'

Santee was bitter. 'If I'd run that time in England, they'd probably have given me a knighthood. Over here, they just slap me on the back then go off and count all the dough I just made for them.'

He was glad when they flew out of Cleveland, Ohio.

Though he would be the last person ever to admit it, Percy Cerutty had not had the happiest of Olympics. Apart from having to watch his athletes fail in succession, he had quarrelled with Landy and had the occasional row with a few of the others. In watching American and European coaching methods he had realized that some of his own techniques were rather outmoded and he had suffered the humiliation of not being taken so seriously by the world's media as his rivals from other countries.

A worse blow came when he finally returned home to the little house in Domain Road. His wife had left him. After years of putting up with his temper, tantrums, love affair with athletics and habit of dropping heavy weights on the floor above her head, the long-suffering Dorothy Cerutty had moved out for good. Percy immediately went around to see her and tried to woo her back with a ferocious argument. But his wife had finally had enough.

'John has finished his exams now, Perce.'

'Good. How did they go?'

'Very well from what I hear. He can let his hair down a bit now. Start to run a few races.'

Les Perry was down at Portsea with a bunch of other athletes. He and his guru were having a quiet moment together beside the sea. In his own mind Cerutty had not yet accepted that Landy had left him.

'We ought to get him down here again, Les.'

'He won't come. That one week at Portsea was enough for John.'

'Couldn't he stand the pace?'

'I think it was the Stotan philosophy that got up his nose.'

'A man has got to have a set of values!' argued Cerutty with finger-pointing vehemence. 'My Stotan creed is not just designed to make you run faster. It should mould your entire life. I hold that suffering and dedication are the only ways to understanding, compassion and courage.'

'Yes, Perce,' said Les rather wearily.

'And those three things add up to a lovable personality.'

'Is that what *you've* got, Perce?'

'Of course!' barked the coach. 'And I've got the most priceless quality of all out of the Stotan creed – character!' He gazed out across the bay and pondered. 'Landy will never make it on his own.'

'Don't bank on it. He's been training like a maniac. Says he's never felt so fit in all his life.'

'You're a much better athlete than him, Les. Always will be.'

'I'm not sure about that,' admitted the other.

'Look at Helsinki. Landy got eliminated in the heats whereas Les Perry ran in two Olympic finals.'

'I know but I didn't even manage to finish the 10,000 metres.'

'You're a natural runner, Les. You throw yourself into a race body and soul. Not Landy. His approach is too intellectualized. He's a bit like that English miler, Bannister. Too analytical. Too obsessed with the *theory* of his event.' He gave a snort of contempt. 'It's practice that counts, not bloody theory! That's why Landy will never really get there. You're a much better bet.'

'We'll soon find out, anyway.'

'How?'

'At Olympic Park next week. I'm running against John in the A Grade mile. We'll be able to see what all his interval training has done for him.'

'No top athlete can survive without a coach,' insisted Cerutty.

'He won't come back, Perce. You'll have to accept that.'

'Why should I be bothered!' stormed the other. 'I've got enough people to train as it is. Besides, I can tell you this, old son. John Landy needs me one hell of a lot more than I need him!'

They began to stroll along the shoreline together. Cerutty's outburst had concealed his disappointment and feeling of rejection. He hated the idea that someone should walk out on him. There was another very important consideration. The trip to Helsinki had depleted his already limited financial resources. He needed to make the Portsea Training Camp into a going concern and the most effective way to do that was for his athletes to bring it kudos.

His judgement was shrewd. He knew that John Landy had the makings of a champion. It would be very galling to him if he drew no benefit out of the latter's success.

He looked up at something in the water. Two shapely young women had come romping out of the surf and ran up on to the beach. His eyes glistened with frank appreciation.

'Les.'

'Yes, Perce?'

'I think I may have to get married again.'

Harold Abrahams had finally found a moment to have a brief chat with Roger Bannister. They were looking at the heavy coating of frost that covered the running track in Paddington where Bannister usually trained.

'The British winter strikes again!' groaned Abrahams. 'You'd need ice skates to get round that.'

'When is the A A A going to build us a decent indoor track?'

'Just as soon as we receive your cheque for a quarter of a million pounds, Roger. At the moment, I'm afraid, we couldn't afford to build an indoor dog kennel.'

They swung round and headed back towards St Mary's Hospital. The two men liked and respected each other very much and always enjoyed their time together. Since Abrahams had become aware that Bannister was hoping to break the four-minute barrier for the mile, he had shown a particular interest.

'How is it going?'

'Until the bad weather came – very well.'

'Time is against us, I'm afraid. It would be deeply annoying if you were to miss the boat.'

'Yes,' agreed Bannister. 'I've been reading about some of those times that Santee has returned.'

'Denis Johansson is over there at some college as well. He's run 4.04, remember. And like Santee, he's ready to blow his own trumpet a bit. He's on record as saying that he'll get there first.' Abrahams screwed up his face with well-bred contempt. 'We can't have the four-minute barrier being broken in *America*!"

'It would be intolerable,' agreed Bannister with a smile.

'They'd ram it down our throats at every opportunity.'

'I know, don't worry.'

'Not America, *please*. I think I'd prefer it to happen down in Australia before that.'

'I don't think there's much chance of that.'

'You never know. It's their summer right now. Their athletics season is well under way.'

'That makes no difference. Don MacMillan is their top miler and his best time is only 4.09. Their national record.'

'Who else have they got?'

'Nobody of any real class. There's John Landy but he's still very green. It would be a miracle if he were to break four minutes.'

'So we can rule out the Aussies?'

'Definitely,' said Bannister with assurance. 'The danger lies in America and Europe. We can forget about Australia.'

Chapter Eleven

John Landy lay sound asleep as a ray of bright sunshine sliced through the crack in his bedroom curtains and bisected the carpet. There was a gentle knock on the door but he was much too far away to hear it. A louder knock still failed to elicit a response. The door opened slowly and then his mother stepped in. Concern puckered her features.

'John,' she called. 'John!'

'Mm?' He began to stir.

'John, wake up!'

'What is it?' he burbled, surfacing for a brief moment.

'I thought you were running today.'

'I am, Mum.'

'Do you know what time it is, dear?'

Landy moaned as his head throbbed with pain. 'We had a few drinks at Bob Prentice's last night.' The pain intensified. 'A few too many, obviously.'

'It's eleven-thirty, John.'

'Never!'

'You overslept.'

The information cut through his hangover and brought him fully awake. His alarm clock provided corroboration. He got out of bed at once then put his hands to his head as a steel ball seemed to roll around inside his skull.

'I'll make you some breakfast,' said his mother.

'No time, Mum. I'll have to grab something on the way.'

'But you can't go out like that, dear.'

He managed a weak smile. 'I'll be all right.'

'Let me get you some aspirins . . .'

Mustering all his strength he went to the bathroom, dressed, packed his running kit into a bag, trotted downstairs, waved away the bottle of aspirins that his mother offered him and went out into a December morning. The sun had now retreated behind some clouds and there was a light breeze.

Landy's headache was forgotten as he hurried along the street until he came to a milk bar. He dived in through the door.

'Got anything to eat?'

'Hot or cold, mate?'

'Hot.'

'We've got pies.'

'Two, please.'

'They mightn't be all that hot yet.' The proprietor fingerprinted one of the pies in the small oven to test its temperature and gave a reassuring grin. 'They'll do.'

'Thanks.'

'Sauce?'

'Just a little.'

The man poured a generous dollop of brown sauce on to the pies and then set the impromptu meal on a paper bag. Landy paid him and raced out. He was just in time to jump on a train as it headed towards the city. The pies were bolted down on the way.

'Come on, John!'

'Where've you been, mate?'

'Don't miss your race!'

'We need the bloody points.'

His clubmates from Geelong Guild were relieved to see him and chided him affectionately for being late. He changed quickly into his gear then went out on to the track at Olympic Park. Friends hailed him from every side and he waved back. Though not large, the crowd was vocal as it watched a high-jumper clear the bar at the first attempt. Les Perry, wearing the running vest of Williamstown Club, was standing in the infield as Landy approached.

'I was hoping you'd cry off, John,' he joked.

'I was hoping you would.'

'Keep out of the inside lane,' warned his friend.

'Why?'

He looked down and got his answer. It was a cinder track made of crushed red scoria stone. Wet and soggy, the inside lane had been churned up by the passage of many feet.

'Let's give those bastards something to write about,' suggested Perry, nodding towards the press box. 'They had a good go at us after Helsinki. Our chance to get back at them now.'

'I know,' said Landy.

As he began his warm-up he realized how much better he felt. His headache had vanished and the pies were no longer sitting so heavily inside him. Notwithstanding his rush to get to the stadium, he sensed that he was going to run well.

'Competitors for the mile . . .'

The announcement took a cluster of athletes to the starting line. Rivalry at inter-club meetings was intense and the crowd was composed of partisan sections. Individual runners collected loud exhortations from their supporters as they lined up. Percy Cerutty's voice was as prominent as ever.

There was the usual bumping and elbowing as they tensed themselves for the gun. When it came, they went off in a sudden plunge of speed. The mile was the premier event and it had an element of real excitement from the outset.

Les Perry had gone off at a pace that would not have disgraced a half-mile. Showing that reckless commitment that had first aroused Cerutty's interest in him, he powered his way around the track with his spikes stabbing hard into the cinders. Landy soon tucked in behind him, both men running wide, almost a yard out. The rest of the field started to string out in their wake.

Landy's elegant, flowing, upright style was in complete contrast to the bustling thrust of the short figure ahead of him. He felt comfortable as he dogged Perry's footsteps and he was running well within himself. When the lap time was announced over the loudspeaker, therefore, he was rather surprised at the speed they had maintained: 59.02!

Encouraged by a fresh roar from the crowd, Perry surged on but Landy stayed with him all the way. An inter-club race between many competitors had now changed into a fascinating duel between two Olympic athletes. The loudspeaker was waiting for them again.

'Two minutes one second!'

Marginally slower but still a remarkable lap in the conditions. Perry was now feeling the effects of his bold pacemaking and he began to weaken slightly. Landy trailed him until the right moment came and then he accelerated into the lead with majestic stride and pulled away with ease.

There were now only two competitors left in the race: John Landy and the Australian National record.

'Three minutes three seconds!'

Caught up in the noise and the excitement, Landy did not hear the time and did not therefore realize just how close he was to a world-record schedule. What he did know was that he was running as never before. Olympic Park was now galvanized into frenzied cheering and club loyalties were discarded by Australian spectators who sensed that they were witnessing the most astonishing mile run in their history.

All those long and unremitting hours of training now started to yield their reward. Power and aggression coursed through Landy as he launched his attack. After coasting around the last lap he produced a searing burst down the finishing straight that turned the applause into hysteria and enabled him to breast the tape seventy yards ahead of Les Perry.

The effort had drained him but the sheer exhilaration of what he knew he had done buoyed him up. Friends and officials were rushing to congratulate him. Spectators were standing to acclaim him. There was a huddle around the timekeepers and an agonizing wait until they were ready. Len MacRae was the first to bring the news to Landy.

'Did I break the record, Len?'

'You smashed it to pieces, John. You ran 4.2.1!'

Landy went into a euphoric daze. On a slow track and with no assistance in the closing stages he had run the fastest time in the world that year and come within a whisker of Gunder Haegg's world record. To a man whose previous best mile time was 4.11.0, it was all rather overwhelming.

Faces surrounded him, hands patted him, voices cheered. Within minutes he was signing a form applying for recognition of his record then he posed for a photograph with Hugh Weir, the bespectacled and trilby-wearing President of the Amateur Athletic Union of Australia. Four laps of the Olympic Park track had turned an inter-club race into an event of international significance and Landy had his first taste of the overpowering nature of fame.

He found it difficult to concentrate and had not yet fully comprehended the importance of what he had done. Len MacRae put an arm around his shoulder and told him.

'That was amazing, John!' he shouted. 'On a better track you'd have run the first four-minute mile.'

Landy grinned happily. He had a new target now.

News of the achievement flashed around the sporting world to cause a mixture of surprise, disbelief and fear. Athletes in many countries had set their sights on being the first to break the four-minute barrier and they were not pleased at the thought that the feat might now be accomplished by an unknown runner from the southern hemisphere.

'Have you *seen* that time!' demanded Wes Santee.

'Calm down,' advised his coach.

'It was 4.2.1!'

'Maybe their stopwatches don't work too well down there.'

'It's been ratified.'

'Yeah, I know,' said Bill Easton with a puzzled frown. 'It don't make sense, though. I mean, Landy was nothing in Helsinki.'

'Well, he sure is something now.'

'Could be just a freak run.'

'I can't take that chance.'

'What do you mean?'

'That I'm getting the other side of four minutes for the mile and I'm getting there first!' He sat down in front of Easton's desk. 'You've got to let me work on it, coach.'

'Sorry, Wes.'

'But I'm so close. It only needs a final push.'

'You know the score. You're part of a team here.'

Santee's urgency increased. 'We're talking about a world record! About smashing through a psychological barrier that's held guys back for years. I've run 4.02.4. I *know* I can get there.'

'So do I, Wes. And you will.'

'Then I need to concentrate on the mile.'

'You can't just drop out of everything else.'

'Why not?'

'Because the college needs you for the relays. We've got to get those points on the board.'

'Coach,' Santee reminded him. 'We win the relays, the University of Kansas comes out on top. I break the four-minute mile, and all America comes out on top.'

'Sure. But you're forgetting something.'

'What's that?'

'You're here on a scholarship to run for this college.'

'It's holding me back!'

'I don't see it that way,' returned Easton firmly. 'You're a great athlete, Wes, we all know that. But you wouldn't have got where you are without this college. We expect you to remember that.'

'I do.'

'Then stop trying to make our whole athletics schedule revolve around one man. It's not as if you don't get the chance to run the occasional mile race.'

'That's not enough, coach.'

'It'll have to be.' Easton leaned forward in his chair and adopted a more sympathetic tone. 'Relax, Wes. You'll still make it somehow. The four-minute mile will keep a little longer.'

'Not a hope in hell!' said the athlete with a rueful smile.

'Why?'

'Because John Landy has given every miler in the world an extra incentive. Those guys will all be trying that little bit harder from now on. Pretty soon, one of them is bound to beat four minutes.' He gave a resigned sigh. 'And while he's doing it, Wes Santee will be running in a goddam relay somewhere!'

Norris McWhirter slowed the car to turn the corner and then moved up through the gears again. He was giving Roger Bannister a lift home to Harrow and, like the excellent journalist he was, he made sure that he was getting an interview on the way.

'How surprised were you, Roger?'

'I was astounded. No disrespect to Landy, but I thought he

was a very ordinary athlete when I saw him run over here.'

'He gave Bill Nankeville a good race at the White City.'

'Yes, but what was Landy's time? It was 4.12 or something. He didn't seem to have the makings of a world-class miler.'

'Then how do you explain it?'

'I don't,' admitted Bannister. 'I'm still trying to come to terms with it. Under the circumstances it was a quite phenomenal run.'

'How has it affected your own plans?'

'It's put a bomb under them, Norris. If Landy can slice nearly nine seconds off his best time, there's no knowing what he can do.'

McWhirter smiled. 'Bit like the prospect of execution, eh?'

'Yes. Concentrates the mind wonderfully.'

'So what's the drill?'

'Step up my training even more and hope for the best.'

'If there's ever anywhere you want to go – to a meeting or a cross-country race or anything – Ross or I will be glad to give you a lift. Don't be afraid to ask.'

'Thanks. It's very kind of you both.'

'Not at all. It's an investment.'

'In what?'

'A vital piece of athletics history. We'd like a small stake in the first mile to be run in under four minutes.'

'Then perhaps you ought to offer Landy a lift as well!'

Bannister was very fond of Ross and Norris McWhirter. Since the time that he had first learned to tell the identical twins apart, he had found them warm, friendly and very supportive to him. No journalists were as well informed about the athletics scene as the McWhirters and their passion for the statistical aspect of the sport was legendary. The offer of help was no idle one. Bannister knew that Ross and Norris McWhirter would be tireless in their efforts to do what they could for him. It was a comfort.

'If only we could get you away for a few months,' opined McWhirter, beeping his horn as a cyclist pulled out in front of him. 'Somewhere warm and sunny where you could train properly.'

'Not a chance, I'm afraid.'

148

'Don't tell me,' mocked the other gently. 'Medicine comes first.'

'It does. In the final analysis, athletics is not the be-all and end-all.'

'I agree, Roger. It's far more important than that.'

Bannister laughed. 'Fair comment.'

'The ideal place for you at this time of year would be down under. But I suppose Australia wouldn't appeal to you one bit.'

'That's where you're wrong. I like the Aussies. I remember the first time I really came across them. It was at the Centennial Games in New Zealand. The Aussies seemed to have so much fun together. That sort of camaraderie never happens in a British team.'

'Does that mean we can get you on the next flight to Sydney?'

'No, it doesn't. If I get below four minutes – and I know that it looks doubtful at the moment – I'd want it to be in this country.'

'Any particular track?'

'Need you ask, Norris?'

'Oxford.'

'Yes.'

'Of course. You helped to rebuild that track at Iffley Road. And that's where your athletic career really began. Oh yes, it would be the perfect place.' A professional consideration nudged him. 'And it would make a marvellous story.'

'You're unlikely to be able to write it, though.'

'Why?'

'Because the chances of it happening at Iffley Road are very slim. The most probable place would be at the White City during a big race.'

'That's trusting to luck, isn't it, Roger?'

'In what way?'

'Supposing you never get the standard of competition you need to give you that added stimulus?' He glanced across at his passenger. 'Do you really think you're going to break four minutes under normal race conditions?'

'What's the alternative?'

'Make it into a team effort.'

'You know my views on that, Norris.'

'I was hoping that John Landy might have altered them.'

'I'd just like to do it on my own.'

'Pacemakers could help. So could a coach.' He slowed the car to a halt at some traffic lights. 'Why be so independent about it?'

'Force of habit.'

'Gunder Haegg was not too proud to use pacemakers.'

'Landy is. So am I.'

'Oh well,' said McWhirter, easing the car forward as the green light beckoned. 'Since you're determined to do it the hard way . . .'

'It isn't that, Norris.'

'Then what is it?'

Bannister shrugged. 'I suppose I'm a perfectionist. And that makes me very intense about everything I do. Intense and possessive. I want to get it absolutely right and that means doing it all by myself. Can you understand that?'

'Very easily.'

'I need to be in complete control. It's my one big weakness.'

'No, Roger,' corrected his friend. 'I think that it's your main source of strength.'

It was extraordinary. One race had transformed John Landy's running career. A failed Olympic competitor was now being hailed as the top miler in the world. Starved of heroes among its male athletes, the Australian press fell on him voraciously and made a meal of his triumph.

On Saturday afternoon at Olympic Park, Melbourne University student, John Landy, made world news running a mile in the staggering time of 4.02.1. Next morning he went out into the country to collect butterflies.

Landy is an agricultural science student who, by reason of unstinted application and personal sacrifice, has managed to run faster and faster despite the increasing mental strain of university examinations.

It takes moral and physical fibre of a high order to do this.

Look back through your record books and you will find that

men who have really 'scaled the heights', who went through life on an even keel, were those who combined sport and study.

There were C. B. Fry, the late Jack Lovelock, Rev. Bob Richards, Lord Burghley, 'flying parson' Gil Dodds and a host of others.

Landy is cast in the same mould. He plans ahead and he knows where he is going.

John Landy sat in his bedroom and read through the cuttings. The adulation was at once gratifying and unnerving. Praise was welcome after so much criticism but he had suddenly become public property and that alarmed a private person like himself. He simply could not recognize the real John Landy in some of the florid descriptions that were given and he was not at all sure that he could live up to some of the fulsome predictions that were being made about Australia's new superstar. It was all rather bewildering.

He gave a wry smile as he glanced at another cutting. Percy Cerutty had not missed the chance for self-publicity. The conditioner of men and maker of champions gave the impression that he was masterminding Landy's training programme.

Trainer Cerutty is confident that Landy will do the trick. Cerutty said that training methods were improving all the time. He said that he had built up Landy by making him run up and down sandhills and by using heavy iron dumb-bells.

'As training methods improve, we are gradually reaching the super performances of tomorrow,' said Cerutty.

'Professor Cotton and Forbes Carlile are doing a lot of worth-while work at Sydney University,' he added.

However, Cerutty said that it was useless to expect Australians to compete successfully in world athletics unless they had all the incentives and opportunities accorded to athletes in Europe and the USA.

Landy put the cutting aside. In running the third-fastest mile of all time he had not only proved that he was a supreme athlete. He had shown himself that he could do it without the benefit of Percy Cerutty at his side. The way forward was to continue with his strict regime of daily interval training. He would not be running up any more sandhills in Portsea.

Like Roger Bannister he derived great satisfaction from the idea of being his own man and choosing his own options. He would not easily surrender his independence again.

It was the essence of his running.

A blustery wind and an overcast sky could not deter spectators from turning up in such large numbers at Olympic Park on that first Saturday in the New Year that they caused a traffic jam. Tempers became frayed, horns sounded, arguments started. The commotion was still going on when two of the athletes approached the stadium carrying their running gear in their bags. One of them was frankly alarmed.

'Look at the size of the crowd!'

'Marvellous!'

'They must think that Zatopek is running.'

'He is – but we call him John Landy.'

'All I did was to win a few races,' argued the other modestly.

'Yes, but you won them in record times,' replied Les Perry. 'That's why you've got such a big fan club.' A thought struck him. 'Unless they're all coming to watch *me*!'

Landy hoped that he would not be recognized as he made his way towards the entrance but his hope was soon dashed. Men, women and children called and waved and tried to get to him. With a polite grin to hide behind, he burrowed his way to the gates with Les Perry and the two of them were admitted. Even now he was not safe. As they walked down the corridor towards the changing room a bevy of sportswriters ambushed them.

'How do you feel, John?'

'Any chance of beating four minutes tonight?'

'Did you have a couple of pies to eat this time?'

'What are your tactics for the race?'

Landy shrugged. 'My tactics are to win. And I feel fine.'

'You don't sound it,' noted Jill Webster. 'Have you got a cold?'

'A bit of one,' he confessed.

'Will that affect your performance?' she wondered.

'I hope not.'

'There are thousands of people out there today, John. They're counting on you for something special.'

'I'll do my best,' he promised.

Before they could fire any more questions at him, he and Les Perry had squeezed themselves through the door of the changing room. Landy was grateful to escape.

'That's *all* I need before a big race!' he complained.

'I've got no time for those people,' said Perry in an aggrieved tone. 'When you broke that record last month, I came in second with a personal best of 4.13. Just think of it, John. Five years ago, 4.13 would have got me the star treatment from that lot and now they just ignore me.'

'Time moves on, Les.'

They laughed at his unintentional pun.

As soon as he stepped out on to the track Landy could see how difficult it would be to run a fast time. The wind was gusting down the back straight and would be in the faces of the athletes as they went down it. The track was hard, unwatered and looked as if it had not been tended for some time.

Landy had other problems. Suffering from a heavy cold, he had had a bad night with very little sleep. To turn on a world-class performance this time would be a small miracle. And yet that was what the crowd had come to see. It depressed him slightly.

When the starting pistol fired it detonated an explosion of noise in the stands that carried the athletes along with it. Les Perry again shot into the lead to run an even faster lap than during the first race. Landy was towed around behind him at a punitive pace while the rest of the field were involved in a different race altogether.

At the halfway mark the time was an incredible 1.59.04 and the announcement seemed to instil fresh determination into Landy. To the delight of the crowd he suddenly cut loose on his own and began the long race home towards immortality. The wind buffeted him down the back straight but his stride pattern did not falter. As he glided around the bend the wind was behind him to help him sail past the main stand with graceful power.

His time at the bell was 3.01.0 and it sent the spectators

into ecstasy. They were now certain that four minutes would at last be beaten and they acclaimed the young Australian who was about to do it. But Landy was starting to struggle. The wind was more troublesome down the back straight this time and he slowed noticeably, only to pick up his rhythm again as Les Perry, having burned himself out and retired from the race, urged him on from the infield.

Landy was now a hundred yards clear of the others, running on courage and fending off pain and fatigue. He went through the tape to a hero's welcome then slowed to a trot as he waited for his time.

Unknown to him, he had already achieved one notable mark. His time at the 1500 metres had been almost a second faster than Barthel's in the Olympic final. His time for the mile was now arousing disbelief among the officials. They checked and double checked their stop watches in sheer astonishment.

'First – John Landy . . .'

A hush fell on the stadium as the loudspeaker reverberated.

'In a time of 4.02.8!'

Disappointment all round was hidden beneath a torrent of applause and the athlete gave a tired smile of gratitude. Up in the press box sportswriters were already mentally composing their stories about a gallant loser who made a valiant attempt that failed. Running in adverse conditions, with a heavy cold and without serious opposition, Landy had clocked a time that was almost superhuman. But it was not enough for many of the journalists.

Fame had delivered him into their hands and he learned a salutary lesson that day. A hero must earn his hero-worship afresh each time.

Whenever he ran, he was expected to go faster.

Chapter Twelve

Bill Easton poured himself another beer and absent-mindedly watched a television commercial for a new washing powder. Seated beside him was Wes Santee, leaning forward so that his elbows could rest on his knees. They were in the living room at the coach's house and they were waiting for a sports programme. Santee was edgy.

'Maybe he won't even be in the show.'

'He'll be in it.'

'But why should we bother to watch the little creep?'

'Because I say so, Wes.'

'We know what he's like.'

'Shut up – it's starting.'

The commercial had been replaced by a familiar credit sequence that was backed by theme music which had been scored for brass. A well-groomed presenter appeared on the screen and detailed the sports coverage that was to come.

'Our first item, however, concerns that perennial question in the world of athletics. Is the four-minute mile possible?' He swivelled in his chair to face his studio guests and another camera gave a wide-angle shot of the interview. 'With me in the studio is a young man who believes he may have the answer to that question. His name is Denis Johansson. He hails from Finland but he's studying here in the States at Purdue University.' He flashed an unctuous smile. 'Welcome to the programme, Denis.'

'Thank you.'

Johansson was a lean, dark-haired athlete of medium height with ruddy cheeks and an almost debonair quality. When he spoke his accent was pronounced but his English was quite good. Beside him was a vivacious, blonde American girl who had evidently graduated at the Academy of the Dumb. She was gazing at the Finn with undiluted lust.

'Jesus!' Santee slapped his leg in irritation.

'What are you studying over here, Denis?' asked the presenter.

'Physical education.' He smirked at his companion to show that she was involved in the practical aspects of his work. 'But I am also in this country to show some of your athletes how to run.'

'That sounds like fighting talk.'

'I am confident, that's all. What is wrong with confidence?'

'Come here and I'll show you!' snarled Santee, glaring at the set.

'Smart-looking broad,' conceded Easton.

The presenter continued. 'If we can just turn to the four-minute mile, Denis . . .'

'It will be broken very soon, sir,' said Johansson smoothly. 'And you are looking at the man who will break it.'

'That's a bold prediction.'

'I do not believe in false modesty. It is dishonest.'

'Just listen to him!' complained Santee.

Johansson smirked again. 'I just know I will do it.'

'And what makes you so sure?'

'My country is Finland. We produced the great Paavo Nurmi, who was a member of my own club in Turku. We produced many other brilliant middle-distance runners. There is a tradition. I am part of it.'

'Carrying on from where Nurmi left off.'

'And doing the one thing he failed to do. Breaking through the four-minute barrier for the mile.'

'He's got something,' admitted Easton. 'You have to give him that.'

'I will!' promised Santee.

'Denis,' said the presenter. 'If you're as good as you say you are, how is it that the American public hasn't heard more about you?'

'Because your sports reporters do not know their job.'

Easton laughed. 'He certainly knows how to win friends!'

'Your press here pays a lot of attention to runners like John Landy and Roger Bannister and your own Wes Santee. There is no doubt in my mind that I can beat all of them.'

'You'll be racing against Wes Santee in two days' time.'

'*He* will be racing against me.' The smirk. 'Trying to, anyway.'

'Are you telling us that you are going to win?'

'I don't think there's any question about that.'

'Who *is* this guy!' exclaimed Santee.

'Hear him out,' suggested the coach.

'I expect win comfortably.'

'But Wes Santee has been running some very fast times for the mile recently, Denis.'

'No faster than mine.'

'If your times are so similar, what makes you so convinced that you can beat him?'

'Well, times are one thing,' replied Johansson airily, 'but races are quite another. A man-to-man contest calls for strength and maturity. I'm a few years older than Santee so I have both. In my opinion he is too immature, both physically and psychologically, to be a top-rank miler.'

Bill Easton had to protect his television from attack.

'Do you think it's possible that the four-minute mile could be broken when you and Wes Santee meet?'

'Something will be broken!' vowed Santee.

'It's more than possible,' Johansson announced. 'And if it is broken, then I will do it. Santee would have no chance.'

'Why is it that you have so little respect for him?'

Easton switched off the programme before his living room was demolished. Santee was now on his feet, circling vengefully and punching items of furniture to release his anger. When he had calmed down enough to stand still he pointed a long finger at the coach.

'I'm going to beat that sonofabitch!'

'Sure.'

'I'll burn him right off at the finish.'

'You got the fastest finish in the world, Wes,' agreed Easton, 'but your first two laps sometimes let you down. When you race against Johansson, I want you to go off fast – real fast. Okay?'

'Okay, coach.'

'Get your breathing going early. Make sure you're in a position on the last lap to use your finish.'

'I'm going to tan his Scandinavian hide!' announced Santee.

'Still feeling riled up?'

'You bet!'

'Now you see why I wanted you to watch that smart-ass on TV,' explained the coach with a grin. 'I think it worked.'

Santee nodded grimly. 'It worked.'

Two days later Wes Santee streaked away from a fading Johansson to record a season's best for the mile of 4.02.4. The Kansan was delighted. The Finn somehow remained affable. And the coach was disappointed that there was no sign of the dumb blonde.

Chris Chataway nibbled at his food and then pushed the plate away.

'Do you eat this kind of thing every day, Roger?'

'Yes.'

'No wonder you're so emaciated!'

'I don't have time for a three-course lunch at the Savoy, I'm afraid,' said Bannister. 'My lecture finishes at twelve-thirty and I usually have to be back at two. So I dash to the track to fit my training in and then pop in here for a quick bite.'

'A quick bite is all that this grub merits.'

'I told you to have the salad.'

They were sitting in a small restaurant in Paddington near the track where Bannister had just completed his daily training stint. His mind, as ever, was on the four-minute barrier.

'I'm convinced that I know the best way to do it, Chris.'

'So do I, old boy. Ride a bicycle.'

'I'm serious. The key to it lies in running four quarters at roughly the same speed.'

'That will take a bit of doing!'

'I know but I'm sure it's the answer. An athlete's oxygen consumption rises steeply as speed increases. To keep his oxygen requirement down to a minimum, he must run the slowest average speed he can to achieve his target.'

'Four quarters at one minute each.'

'That would be impossible,' said Bannister, 'but I do think we could get close to it.'

'We?'

'Sorry, I'm just hypothesizing. If I could hit the three-quarter mark round about three minutes, I'd be in with a definite chance.'

'Then why don't you try it, Roger?'

'Because I can't expect the other competitors to oblige me by running three laps at roughly the same speed.'

'I'd do it for you,' volunteered Chataway.

'Would you?' His friend was touched.

'Well, I'll try, anyway. I certainly won't get to the bell in three minutes but it will be as close to that as I can manage.' He could see that Bannister was tempted. 'Unless you still have those absurd scruples about using a pacemaker.'

'No . . . I've accepted that I may need help.'

'Could I have that in writing?' asked Chataway. 'I could sell it to Harold Abrahams for a small fortune!'

'How soon would you be ready, Chris?'

'You tell me. It's your show.'

'In a fortnight?'

'A fortnight! That's asking a lot. I'm not exactly used to sprinting for three-quarters of a mile.' He looked across at the other and smiled. 'However, since it is in a good cause . . .'

'Oxford versus the AAA.'

'I can't think of a more appropriate meeting.'

'We'll need to plan it very carefully.'

'But *not* in this place, Roger,' insisted Chataway. 'If I'm to be your pacemaker, I need to build myself up with proper food.' He became serious. 'Do you really think it's on, old boy?'

'I've been training for it long enough.'

'I know. And you've been living with the fear that you may open the paper one morning and discover that someone's beaten you to the draw.' He pulled a face. 'Someone like our Mr Santee, for instance.'

'Yes,' sighed Bannister. 'He's really on form at the moment. I suppose I should just be grateful that it's winter now in Australia so Landy is quiescent. But Santee is a big worry. They say that he can run the last lap like a quarter-miler.'

'But you've got something he'll never have, Roger.'

'What's that?'

'Me, of course!'

'Thanks, Chris. I can't say how grateful I am.'

'Then don't,' advised the other. 'What you don't realize is that I have an ulterior motive.'

'Oh?'

'Yes, I'm not just doing this in the spirit of self-sacrifice, you know. My fantasy is this. I lead for three laps to reach the bell in just over three minutes.'

'And then?'

'You try to overtake me but find my kick is even better than yours. While you're wondering how I did it, I'm through the tape in under four minutes to claim myself a nice little niche in the record books. Good?'

Bannister was amused. 'I'll believe it when I see it.'

'Yes,' said Chataway as fantasy gave way to realism. 'So will I.'

During the mile race in the annual meeting between Oxford and the AAA, Chris Chataway went flat out for three laps in a total time of 3.05.2. Roger Bannister brought his kick into play and blazed around the track in 58.04 seconds to finish with a mile time of 4.03.6. It was a significant improvement on his best time and he was thrilled.

Over a drink together afterwards, Chataway was in jovial mood and treated himself to a cigar by way of celebration.

'Just as well you're not a qualified doctor yet, Roger.'

'Why?'

'That time of yours. It's in direct contravention of the Hippocratic oath.'

'In what way?'

'Well, you're supposed to *save* lives. When the news gets out that you've just run 4.03.6, there'll be heart attacks all over the world.' He puffed on his cigar. 'Changed your mind about the idea of a pacemaker?'

'Oh, yes,' admitted Bannister. 'You were an enormous help.'

'Can't promise to do that again in a hurry, though,' warned the other. 'I have my own running career to think about.'

'I appreciate that.'

'But if you do decide to have another crack at it, try Chris Brasher. I daresay he'd be willing to pace you.'

'I'll bear it in mind.'

Chataway raised his glass. 'To the best mile of your career!'

'Cheers!' Bannister sipped his beer then became thoughtful. Today was very important to him. One more step towards the top of Everest.

He sensed that he could get there now.

Two days later Edmund Hillary and Sherpa Tensing reached the summit of Everest. They were part of the expedition led by Colonel John Hunt and the feat was portrayed as a magnificent team effort.

Harold Abrahams stood beside Franz Stampfl as they watched a couple of sprinters completing a 100 yards. The former was impressed.

'Not bad! Not bad!'

'I won't say that either of them will be the next McDonald Bailey but they're coming along. There's so much technique involved in sprinting.' He turned to his companion. 'As you well know.'

'Yes, I spent months honing my technique, Franz.'

'You still have an Olympic gold medal to remind you that it was all worth it,' noted Stampfl.

'And to remind me how much I owed to Sam Mussabini.'

'I'm glad that somebody remembers his coach!'

'Sam used to make me *want* to run, somehow.'

'A coach's job is largely inspirational, Harold. The technical side of it is only about twenty per cent of the work.' He glanced around at the dozens of young men who were going through their training routines. 'The vital thing – as I don't need to tell you – is to win the confidence of the athlete. Everything flows from that.'

'Sam was everything to me, Franz. Guide, philosopher, adviser, friend, father confessor.' Abrahams smiled at the memory. 'He was practically a saint.'

'No. He was just a good coach.' Stampfl grinned. 'And I'm

sure that he could be as ruthless and black-hearted as the rest of us have to be.'

'Oh, he could!'

Harold Abrahams had called in once again at the coaching clinic for a chat with Stampfl. He always found the Austrian's views very refreshing and liked to hear progress reports about certain athletes.

'How is Chataway coming along?'

'You've seen for yourself. He gets better all the time.'

'Is it too soon to be making predictions for Vancouver?'

'Far too soon – and that is why I will make one. Barring injury, Chris Chataway will win the 3 miles at the Empire Games.'

'Any other predictions?'

'I think that British athletes could do very well.' He lifted a warning eyebrow. 'Provided that they are properly coached.'

'That brings us back to a certain young medical student.'

'I was waiting for you to mention Bannister.'

'This could be the season that he does it, Franz.'

'Yes,' said the other, unpersuaded. 'It could be.'

'He's already run that splendid 4.03.6.'

'Only because he was paced by Chataway. Three weeks later at the White City, all that Bannister could manage was 4.09.4. And now, I hear, he's pulled a muscle.'

'Yes, he's out of action for a while.'

'Santee isn't. Johansson isn't. Neither are all the other mad milers who are chasing the dream of a four-minute mile.'

'Bannister is well aware of that, I can promise you. That's why he feels that it's now or never. From the middle of July onwards, he's going to have to concentrate even more on his medical studies.'

'What are you saying to me, Harold?'

Abrahams pondered. 'I think he could profit from your help.'

'Any athlete could.'

'Well?'

'Let him ask for it.'

'Unfortunately, he'd never bring himself to do that.'

'Well, I am certainly not going to approach *him*,' insisted Stampfl with a measure of indignation. 'I have never asked anybody for a coaching job – except that time I came to you before the war. I have my pride, Harold. People approach me.' He indicated the athletes all around. 'As you see, I do not turn them away. I can't afford to.'

'Fair enough,' concluded Abrahams.

'Besides, maybe you are looking at the wrong person.'

'I'm not with you, Franz.'

'Roger Bannister. The way you go on about him, anybody would think that the whole of British athletics revolves around him.'

'Of course it doesn't. But the four-minute mile is something unique. A Holy Grail, if you like.'

'You don't have to sell it to me.'

'But you must appreciate what it would mean if Bannister could bring it off. It would give the whole sport a shot in the arm.'

'You're doing it all over again,' warned Stampfl.

'Doing what?'

'Putting too much on the poor man's shoulders. It was the same at Helsinki. Because this country was desperate for some kind of success, you all looked to Bannister to provide. You saddled him with the burden of winning and it was a terrible pressure to bear. Don't make the same mistake again.'

'It was his decision to go for four minutes.'

'Then let him get on with it.'

Abrahams nodded. 'There may be something in what you say, Franz.' He watched the other shrewdly. 'Will he do it?'

'Not this season, perhaps.'

'Everest has finally been conquered. That has to be seen as a good omen. Hillary got to the summit.'

'Only with the help of Tensing,' reminded Stampfl. 'That's what Bannister will need. A Sherpa. Maybe two.'

'I think he realizes that now.' They exchanged a handshake. 'Well, thanks for your time. I'll let you get on with your gainful employ.' Something jogged his memory. 'Oh, you said just now that I might be looking at the wrong man.'

'That's right. Take your eyes off Bannister for a moment.'

'We've got nobody else who can run a four-minute mile.'

'No, but you do have another highly talented athlete.'

'Chataway?'

'Him, too, of course. But I was thinking about Gordon Pirie.'

'Yes. Gordon is a superb runner, I grant you.'

'He's already started to make headlines this season.'

'Unfortunately they're not always the right kind of headlines,' complained Abrahams. 'I do wish he wouldn't keep making intemperate remarks to the press.'

'He's a Yorkshireman. Speaks his mind.'

'You know what journalists are, Franz. Every time Gordon makes a new boast or has a go at officialdom, they blow it up ridiculously into a major story.'

'I can see that you're talking as an administrator now, Harold, and not as a gentleman of the press yourself.' The other conceded a smile. 'You have it your way. Keep watching Roger Bannister in the hope that he's the one who'll find the Holy Grail, as you call it.'

'And what about you?'

'I'll stick with Pirie. I believe that *he* could be the man who takes athletics by storm this year.'

The ample frame of Don MacMillan was lounging in an armchair behind a newspaper when the landlady knocked on the door and came in.

'Phone call for you, Mr MacMillan.'

'Oh. Thanks.'

'Will you please tell your friends not to call so often?' she asked wearily. 'It's a long walk up those steps.'

'Try shouting.'

She took offence. 'I do have other guests as well, you know!'

MacMillan smiled and followed her downstairs. He was staying at a small boarding house in Bloomsbury and its telephone was in the hall. He picked it up and spoke into the receiver.

'Hello.'

'Don?'

'Yes.'

'Roger Bannister here.'

'Hello, Roger!' greeted MacMillan with mingled pleasure and surprise. 'Good to hear from you.'

'How are you enjoying life in England?'

164

'It's great. If I was back in Melbourne right now, I'd be shivering in my shoes.'

'What did you think of the Coronation?'

'Fantastic! I'm so glad I was here for that. We don't have anything quite like it down in Australia.'

'I can imagine.' The voice at the other end of the line became more tentative. 'Er, how is your training coming on?'

'Oh, I potter along.'

'Pretty fit as usual?'

'Fairly. Why?'

'I just wondered if you'd be at all interested in helping me out?' There was a slight pause then Bannister came out with it. 'I'm planning another attempt at four minutes.'

'When?' asked MacMillan with eagerness.

'Next Saturday. I'm going to need pacemakers.'

'Count me in, Roger!'

'I know it's a lot to ask, Don, but –'

'Listen, mate. *I'm* not likely to be the first man through the barrier, I've accepted that. But it would give me a kick to be in on it as a pacemaker. What's the drill?'

'I'll explain all that when we meet up.'

'Where will the race take place?'

'Motspur Park. We'll drive you down there.'

'Good.'

'Do you think you could be on the corner of Tottenham Court Road and Bray Street at ten o'clock on Saturday morning?'

'I suppose so.'

'A black car will pick you up. Norris McWhirter is taking us.'

MacMillan was puzzled. 'Is this an official meeting?'

'No,' said Bannister. 'It's just a private attempt. I've had trouble with a pulled muscle. We're keeping the attempt quiet in case the muscle doesn't hold out.'

'That's fair enough with me, Roger.'

'So don't breathe a word of this to the press, will you?'

'Of course not.'

'See you on Saturday then, Don. And thanks.'

'Thank *you*.'

He put the receiver down and felt pleased that he had been

asked. While Roger Bannister was by no means a close friend, MacMillan was excited by the idea of being in on the first four-minute mile. It was the kind of experience that might even upstage the Coronation.

Eight boys lined up for the next race and a teacher started them off. They hared around the track at Motspur Park, encouraged by the shrill yells of their schoolfriends. Technique was poor but energy and daredevil abandon were in plentiful supply.

The teacher watched them until they went through the tape at the end of the back straight then he caught sight of the five men who were bearing down on him. They seemed rather irritated. Stopping for a brief discussion, the group then sent one of their number over as a spokesman. The teacher vaguely recognized the strong face beneath the domed bald head but he could not put a name to it.

'Excuse me. We'd like to use this track.'

'Out of the question, I'm afraid,' said the teacher firmly.

'This is rather important.'

'So is our sports. We booked this place two months ago, I don't see why we should move aside just because you chaps want it.'

'There *is* a very special reason.'

'I don't care. These kids have got a right to be on this track and they're staying there.'

Harold Abrahams pointed to the group still standing a little distance away. 'Do you see that young man with the fair hair? That's Roger Bannister.'

'Is it?' The teacher registered immediate interest.

'He wants to make a serious attempt to beat the four-minute mile today so that we can pip the Americans to it. You'd be helping us enormously if we could borrow the track for a short while.'

The teacher could not have been more co-operative. He cleared the children off and sat them down around the track. Instead of simply taking part in the school sports they now had the chance to be present at a historic occasion.

When the athletes had changed they came out on to the track. Roger Bannister was over six foot but he looked short beside the giant figure of Don MacMillan. Chris Brasher, stocky, dark-haired and wearing spectacles, was the shortest of the three.

On the drive down to Motspur Park they had finalized their plan. For the race to be legitimate, all the runners taking part had to finish but there was no limit set on the amount of time that it took them. It was decided, therefore, that Don MacMillan should pace Bannister for the first two and a half laps while Brasher conserved his energy by jogging around a single lap. When MacMillan started to tire, Brasher would still be fresh to take over the pacemaking and pull Bannister along until he was ready to strike for home on his own. After the others had finished, Brasher would then go on to run his own fourth lap alone to comply with the rules.

Chris Brasher, a steeplechaser with the British team in Helsinki, was also an expert mountaineer and had been on the short-list for the Everest expedition. Having missed out on that magnificent triumph, he was grateful for the opportunity to be involved in the conquest of another fearsome peak.

'Good luck!' called Norris McWhirter, holding the stopwatch.

'Let's give the kids something worth watching,' said MacMillan.

'I'm ready,' added Brasher.

Bannister, who liked to feel nervous before a race, was walking around near the starting line. He gave a nod and took his place.

The race went according to plan. MacMillan galloped over the first two and a half laps to be replaced by Brasher, who was so full of running and enthusiasm that he was shouting encouragement to Bannister over his shoulder. When the latter made his move the children cheered wildly. They were completely caught up in the exhilaration of it all.

The first three quarters – run at 59.01, 60.01 and 62.01 – had given Bannister the platform from which to attack and he did so with all the strength and commitment that he could summon. As he lunged past the finishing line with a last effort, he knew that he must be close to four minutes. Exhaustion hit him at once and his sagging frame had to be supported.

'What was it?' he gasped.

'Almost there: 4.02.'

Bannister had given everything but it was not enough. His disappointment was intense but it was cushioned by the knowledge that he had just run the third-best mile in history. Only Gunder Haegg and Arne Andersson had been inside his time and they had now retired.

Roger Bannister was the fastest miler in the world.

That fact, at least, was something to savour.

After long discussion the British Amateur Athletic Board pronounced its verdict. The formality of the language did not weaken its impact.

> The Board wishes it to be known that whilst appreciating the public enthusiasm for record performances, and the natural and commendable desire of athletes to accomplish them, it does not regard individual record attempts as in the best interests of athletics as a whole.

The new record was not ratified because the board felt that the race at Motspur Park was not 'a *bone fide* competition according to the rules'. All that pain and effort had been wasted.

Roger Bannister had to start all over again.

Chapter Thirteen

When John Landy came downstairs in his track suit that evening his father expressed mild surprise.

'You're not going out in this, surely?'

'I have to, Dad.'

'But it's absolutely pouring down, son.'

'Rain never hurt anyone.'

'Can't you miss your training session just for once?'

'I daren't. I must keep myself at peak fitness.'

'But you won't have to race again for months.'

'That doesn't matter,' explained Landy. 'There's still a lot of hard work to do and I'm not going to let the weather stop me doing it.' He recalled something Cerutty had once told him. 'Zatopek trains in the snow when the temperatures are below freezing.'

Gordon Landy ran a hand across his chin and considered for a moment. While he was fiercely proud of his son's athletic triumphs, he did have qualms about the remorseless interval training to which the latter subjected himself on a daily basis. It had become a complete obsession.

'Don't you think you might be overdoing it, John?'

'That's just not possible.'

'Can't you . . . slacken off a little?'

'Dad, I'm on the brink of running the four-minute mile,' argued Landy seriously. 'I'd kick myself if I didn't have a go. You'd like me to be the first to do it, wouldn't you?'

'Nothing would give me greater pleasure, son.'

'Then you must accept that it means rigorous training. These are the maintenance months for me.'

'So it will get *worse* once the season starts?'

'I'll step it up gradually.'

His father sighed. 'Your mother and I are getting worried about you.'

'It's called parenthood.'

'We are, John. I mean, you work all day, study all evening and then go out running in all weathers. It's not much of a life for anyone.'

'I happen to enjoy it, Dad.'

'But you don't have any *fun*. You might just as well be a monk.'

Landy laughed. 'I'd like to meet a monk who can run my times for the mile.' He put a hand on his father's arm. 'It won't go on for ever, Dad. I'll stick it for a couple of years maybe and then, if I haven't made it – wine, women and song all the way.'

'That'll be the day!'

Gordon Landy followed his son to the front door and winced when it was opened to reveal the downpour outside. Rain was slanting down in a torrent and the pavements were awash.

'I bet other athletes don't train in this, John.'

'That's where I have the edge over them,' replied his son. 'Besides, you've got to remember that it's their summer in Europe and America. While I'm paddling about in the rain, people like Roger Bannister and Wes Santee are running on first-rate tracks.'

'Neither of them has cracked four minutes yet, though.'

'Not for want of trying. Bannister's already had a couple of shots at it and Santee won't rest till he's had another attempt.' He shook his head. 'He's the one I fear most. Santee. He's been getting too close to that four-minute mark for comfort.'

'What sort of bloke is he?'

'Off the track, he's very friendly. Bit noisy but then most of the Yanks are like that. No, I got on well with him. I prefer that sort of bloke to some of the English.' He looked out at the rain. 'I must be off, Dad. See you . . .'

'Right.'

'Oh, and you were wrong about me not having any fun.'

He gave a broad grin. 'Winning races is the best fun I know.'

He went out into the night and started to run.

Wes Santee sat disconsolately on a bench in the team changing room at the University of Kansas. Art Dalzell and other athletes were getting into their running gear in preparation for the meeting but Santee was brooding. Bill Easton paced up and down before returning to the attack.

'I explained it all to you the first day we met, Wes.'

'Yeah.'

'You came here as a team man and I took you on as a team man.'

'And I've been a damn good team man, coach. I've anchored the relay team to twenty-seven wins. That's twenty-seven ashtrays as prizes. If they give me any more of those goddam things I'll open a shop and sell them!'

Easton sat beside him. 'Wes, I'm paid to get results for this college. Give me a break, will you?'

'Why don't you give *me* a break?' retorted the other. 'Every time I run a mile the crowd sits there in absolute silence wanting me to do it. And when I fail them, I feel I've let them all down. I feel I've let America down.'

'Yeah. I sympathize, believe me.'

'The way I see it, I'm not even being given a chance.'

'I know, Wes, I know,' agreed the coach. 'You're running too hard, too often, and your competition isn't good enough to push you to the limit.' He shrugged helplessly. 'What am I to do?'

'If you want me to run in the relay,' said the athlete fatalistically, 'I'll run in the relay.'

Easton pondered. 'Listen, if you really want a crack at the mile today, just go out there and do it.'

'I can't let the boys down.' Santee's hesitation vanished in an instant as he hit on a solution. 'I'll run 'em both! Hell, I'm fit enough. Yeah – I'll run 'em both.'

'Wes,' promised the coach, 'as soon as I can, I'll get you across to Europe somehow and you can run the mile and nothing but the mile against the best goddam milers in the world.'

'Wowee!' whooped the other, turning to embrace him warmly. 'Now you're talking, coach!'

Roger Bannister walked along Kings Road between Chris Chataway and Chris Brasher. It was Friday evening and Bannister had finally been inveigled into going along to the Duke of York's Barracks in Chelsea.

A mutual love of athletics had united three disparate personalities. The reticent Bannister was still a medical student at St Mary's Hospital. The ebullient Chataway was now an under-brewer at the Guinness Brewery in Park Royal, West London, and the purposive Brasher, a Geology graduate from Cambridge, worked as a junior executive for an oil company.

Chataway imparted news that had filtered through from America.

'Santee only ran 4.07.'

'Is that all?' asked Brasher with relief.

'The idiot ran a relay an hour before the mile. Slowed him down.'

'Thank goodness,' murmured Bannister.

They turned in through the entrance of the barracks and made for the drill hall. A few other athletes were drifting in and they found almost a hundred or more inside the building. The hall was buzzing with activity of all kinds to give an impression of concerted energy. Bannister looked around with cautious interest.

Because they felt that his vulnerable point was his lack of strength, his friends had persuaded him to come along to a workout. Bannister stood there with mingled curiosity and trepidation until a smiling Franz Stampfl came over to him. Though the two men knew each other well by reputation, they had never been properly introduced. Chataway willingly repaired that situation. Athlete and coach shook hands. Stampfl grinned.

'Welcome to the madhouse.'

'Thanks.'

'Bob a knob.'

'I beg your pardon?'

'Franz means that he charges a shilling a head for a coaching session,' explained Chataway. 'Cheap at twice the price,

Roger. If you slip him a quid, he might help you run a four-minute mile.'

It was a light-hearted remark but it made Bannister look at the Austrian warily. Stampfl became brisk.

'Let's get down to it, shall we?'

Denis Johansson had lost none of his charm and arrogance. Looking relaxed and casually smart, he sat in the lounge of a Melbourne hotel and fielded questions from a handful of journalists. An attractive young Australian girl sat beside him. Jill Webster got in first.

'Mr Johansson, what is your opinion of John Landy?'

'My opinion is that you make too much fuss about him,' he said, reaching for the packet of cigarettes on the table in front of him. 'Ever since I got to Australia, I keep hearing "John Landy this" and "John Landy that" as if he was some kind of god.'

'In athletic terms some people feel that he is.'

'That's only because you've got nobody else down here.' He took out a cigarette and slipped it between his lips while he was still talking. 'With respect to John Landy, I don't think he'd cause more than a tiny ripple in America.'

'What sort of ripple did you cause there?' asked Jill bluntly.

'Oh, I get attention wherever I go,' he replied, lighting his cigarette. 'That's never been a problem.'

'Did you know that Landy has run 4.02 for the mile?'

'Of course I know it. But that was a year ago and he's been marking time ever since.'

'Do you think you'll beat him when you race against him?' said another journalist, through the cloud of cigarette smoke that the Finn was creating. 'How much chance do you give yourself, Mr Johansson?'

'Ask me how much chance I give John Landy because the answer is "No chance". I'll beat him.'

'Then you'll be the first miler to do so for over a year.'

'I didn't come halfway round the world to lose.'

Jill Webster returned to the fray. 'Mr Johansson, your best time, I believe, is around 4.04. John Landy has consistently run below 4.03. How can you possibly win against a man who runs faster?'

'Because I'm tactically superior. It isn't the fastest man who always wins. Look at Wes Santee. To my mind he is the best miler in the world today and makes Landy look like a novice.'

'Can we quote you on that?' asked someone.

'Quote me on anything you like,' offered the Finn amiably. 'To come back to Santee. He was beaten last season by an English runner called Gordon Pirie. I think Pirie ran somewhere around 4.06 to win. Santee was the fastest man in that race and yet he lost.'

'Why was that?'

'Pirie out-thought him.'

'Is that the way you plan to beat Landy?'

'Yes, he's in for a shock. The only reason he's won so many races down here is that he's had nobody good enough to challenge him. That means he's complacent. And he knows next to nothing about the real tactical skill of miling.'

'That's a pretty harsh comment,' said Jill.

'No. It's simply an honest one.'

'Mr Johansson,' began a swarthy journalist with a large moustache, 'you'll be running on grass when you race against Landy at the Sydney Cricket Ground. Does that worry you?'

'Why should it? I'll beat him if we run on grass, cinders, sand, gravel, anything you care to name.' He exhaled more smoke. 'Mind you, this will be the first time I've ever run on a cricket pitch.'

'You don't play cricket in Finland, of course.'

'No, thank you. It would send us all to sleep.'

'Have you ever seen a proper cricket match?'

'Yes. I went down to the Melbourne Cricket Ground a couple of days ago. There were all these men in white just standing around and doing nothing.'

The moustache bristled. 'Cricket happens to be one of Australia's most popular sports, Mr Johansson.'

'You get more action from a game of table tennis.'

'What did you think of the MCG?'

'The what?'

'Melbourne Cricket Ground.'

'Shabby. I couldn't believe it when I was told that you were going to hold the Olympics there. We built a wonderful new stadium in Helsinki for the Games. Can't you do better than a run-down old cricket ground?'

'We happen to be rather fond of the MCG,' warned the moustache. 'And a lot of money is going to be spent on it before the Olympics.'

'So it should be.'

Jill Webster intervened. 'Do you have any more insults for us?'

'It is an opinion, that is all,' he countered. 'We do not begrudge Australia the chance to hold an Olympics. It will do this country a lot of good to have its eyes opened.'

The journalists exchanged a look then scribbled into their pads. Johansson stubbed out his cigarette and immediately took out another one. Fresh smoke billowed.

'You seem to like your cigarettes,' noted the moustache.

'Smoking is a hobby of mine.'

'Doesn't it impair you as an athlete?'

'Listen, sir. My best 1500 metres is only 1.08 outside the world record. Does that sound as if smoking is bad for me?'

'Do you have any other hobbies?' asked Jill.

'Yes, little lady,' he said with a disarming smile. 'I must discuss them over a drink with you one evening.'

'I think we've got all we need,' decided the moustache. 'You've been very frank with us, Mr Johansson.'

'My pleasure. Aren't you going to ask me about the four-minute mile? Every other reporter does.'

'You're on record as saying that Wes Santee will be the first man to beat four minutes. Do you still feel that?'

'Yes. Wes Santee or Denis Johansson.'

'Not John Landy?'

'Impossible.'

'How can you be so certain?'

'Landy has reached his peak and can go no further.'

'What about Roger Bannister?'

'He is not strong enough,' said the Finn airily. 'Bannister is like a lot of English athletes. Their approach is too amateur. They think they can train when they feel like it and then go out and break world records.'

'Gordon Pirie *did* break world records last season,' reminded Jill Webster. 'In the 6 miles and as part of a British

175

team in the 4 by 1500 metres relay. How do you explain that?'

'Pirie is the exception. He's a good, honest, hard-working athlete who lives for his sport. Bannister belongs to the Oxford and Cambridge elite and I do not have a lot of time for them. They are so aloof and superior. They think they are something very special.' He gave a short laugh. 'Helsinki showed them up as floundering losers!'

The journalists stood to go. Jill Webster had a last question. 'Could we have a quote on how you feel to be here?'

Johansson had it ready and waiting. 'I am very happy to be in Australia. It is a paradise. But in every paradise there is a serpent and where I am concerned, that serpent is John Landy.'

They took it down verbatim.

The forthcoming race at the Sydney Cricket Ground was built up into a confrontation between two athletes as if nobody else were taking part. It began to sound more and more like a title fight between two middleweight boxing champions and the grudge element was played up. While Johansson enjoyed sparring in the sports columns, however, Landy could not be coaxed into throwing a single punch. His interview was marked by his composure and honesty.

'Johansson has been saying some very harsh things about you, John. Has it upset you in any way?'

'No.'

'Do you think it was designed to catch you on the raw?'

'Maybe.'

'What answer have you got for Mr Denis Johansson?'

'None. He is entitled to his opinions.'

They were sitting in the comfortable living room of the Landy home in East Malvern. The journalist was a short, stout man with a grizzled appearance that spoke of long years in the stands during countless sporting occasions and long hours in the bar afterwards.

'Johansson thinks that you and Bannister are crumbs,' said the man, trying again to touch on a nerve. 'How would you describe the Finn?'

'He is a very stylish runner.'

'Do you intend to take your revenge on him?'

'I will run my own race. As usual.'

'If we can just look at your training programme, John,' continued the other. 'You did an enormous amount of work in the winter months.'

'Of course. There is a strong correlation between the amount of work done and the speeds recorded in a race. You have to put the miles into your legs.'

'You certainly do that.'

'I find that I have to punish myself to get anywhere.'

'Now, that's always been the basis of Percy Cerutty's philosophy. It has to hurt before it does any good.' He watched Landy carefully during the next question. 'What role has Cerutty played in your running career?'

'He had a significant influence on me at the start,' admitted Landy, concealing his uneasiness behind a smile. 'Percy had a lot of good ideas about running and he also instilled confidence in me.'

'What about all those sessions down at Portsea?'

'I only went there on one occasion for a week.'

'But isn't there a John Landy bunk named after you?'

'I wouldn't know about that.' Cerutty had not missed the opportunity to capitalize on Landy's fame and it embarrassed the athlete. 'Percy and I haven't seen each other for some time.'

'But there's no animosity between you?'

'Of course not. I respect him and what he's done for athletics in this country. He's a pioneer.'

'So if we had more trainers like Percy Cerutty, we'd have more runners like John Landy. Is that what you're saying?'

It was not but Landy nodded. The rift with Cerutty was now a permanent one and he did not like to talk about his relationship with his former coach. Having come to rely on himself so much, he quite naturally wanted to be given credit for his individual dedication. Cerutty had certainly fired him in the early days but Landy now saw, in retrospect, that much of the value he gained from the sessions in the Botanic Gardens derived from the camaraderie of the other athletes. The group dynamic had been a source of help and pleasure.

'You've been reeling off a string of very impressive times

for the mile, John,' resumed the journalist. 'How do you account for that?'

'I set myself a target and I reach it.'

'You haven't yet reached the ultimate target. Four minutes.'

'I'll keep on trying until I do,' he promised.

There was a brief interruption as Mrs Landy came in with a tray. She set the coffee and biscuits down on the table beside the two men, smiled as they both thanked her, then withdrew quietly to the kitchen. The journalist spooned sugar into his cup and stirred.

'I believe that Roger Bannister made some attempts to beat four minutes last season by using pacemakers.'

'That's right.'

'Including our own Don MacMillan during one run.'

'Don's over there at the moment.'

'Wouldn't it have been a bit galling to you if Bannister had actually succeeded in that race?'

'His time wouldn't have been ratified anyway.'

'But if it *had* been, John,' pressed the journalist. 'And if he had finally got inside four minutes. How would you have felt about the fact that an Australian had helped him to do it?'

'I don't suppose I'd have been too thrilled.'

'Have you ever considered using pacemakers?'

'No,' said Landy firmly.

'But there must be athletes here who would run their hearts out to get you past the four-minute mark. Les Perry, Len MacRae and so on. What have you got against the idea?'

'I don't happen to think it's in the spirit of athletics.'

'It's cheating?'

'Put it this way. I might just as well go to a greyhound stadium and chase a hare.' He reached for his coffee. 'When I beat four minutes, it will be in a proper race. I couldn't bear to have the whole thing set up like that.'

'That's very noble of you, John. But is it realistic?'

'We'll have to wait and see.'

The journalist nodded, helped himself to a biscuit and bit into it. He washed down the crumbs with a mouthful of coffee before returning to the subject of the race against Johansson.

'How do you intend to run it, John?'

Landy smiled. 'As fast as I can.'

178

'From the front?'

'Probably.'

'In most of your races the first two laps tend to be the fastest ones. Why is that?'

'I like to get to the halfway mark and feel that I don't have to run any faster,' explained the athlete. 'If you put in fast times early on, you have them in the bag.'

'Could you just talk your way through a race?' asked the other, finishing off his biscuit. 'Lap by lap, I mean.'

'You do the first lap on your nerves. That's why it's the easiest. If you have enough momentum it should carry you through the second lap. The third is the critical one.'

'Why?'

'Because you have to make a relatively greater effort to maintain the same speed,' said Landy. 'You're tired. You have negative feelings. Your legs are starting to go.'

'What about the last lap?'

'That's terrifically hard, of course, but at least you know the end is in sight. That lifts you. Also, if you've run a good time over the first three laps, you get another spur. So you stick in there and try to stave off the fatigue that's eating at you.' He looked over at the journalist. 'It hurts a lot.'

'I'm bloody exhausted just listening to it!'

When the interview was over Landy showed the man politely to the door. The journalist paused on the step and chuckled to himself.

'Strictly off the record, John . . .'

'Yes?'

'Cerutty and the so-called Stotan philosophy,' he said with jocular contempt. 'What did you make of all that baloney?'

'Well,' replied Landy tolerantly, 'nobody believes *every-thing* that Perce says. It's like a walnut. You throw away most of it and eat the good bit.'

'That's it – in a nutshell!'

The man went chuckling all the way back to his car.

Outrage is a good salesman. Because of the derogatory remarks made about Landy by an outspoken Johansson, a potentially large crowd at Sydney Cricket Ground became a huge one as Australians flocked to see the man who had dared to deface one of their national sporting monuments. Support for Landy was buttressed by anger at Johansson. The mile race was seen as a needle contest in which the Australian not only had to win. He had to destroy the bumptious Finn.

Landy himself had no doubts about his ability. He was yards faster than his main rival and he now had the confidence to win a race entirely from the front. His fitness was markedly superior. He had sharpened himself up in a sequence of races while Johansson had flown in from his winter lay-off.

Despite all this Johansson remained cockily optimistic.

'Hello, John . . .'

'Pleased to see you . . .'

They shook hands in the changing room before the race.

'I'm very sorry, John.'

'Why?'

'I said some bad things about you in the press.'

Landy grinned. 'So I noticed.'

'Don't take offence. It's my style. I like to be the villain. All the crowd out there will boo me and that makes me run harder.' He turned on his full charm. 'But don't be fooled. I'm in the race to win today and I will.'

He walked off to get changed and left Landy nonplussed.

The early events in the programme were simply appetizers for the mile. A noisy crowd became clamorous as the athletes came out on to the track and Johansson collected his due of abuse.

'Go back to Finland!'

'Bullshitter!'

'You couldn't win a bloody three-legged race!'

'Murder him, John! Murder the bastard!'

Johansson took it all in his stride and waved nonchalantly to the packed stands. He looked slightly heavier than when he had been in America and did not seem to exude fitness. Landy, by contrast, was lean, tanned and supple.

Rain had left the grass moist and given it a spongy quality. As soon as Landy had run a few yards on the track, he knew that a fast time was unlikely. The wet turf would absorb his spikes and tax his energy.

Landy went back to the starting line and took his place with the other competitors. Johansson had to withstand some hostile muttering in the ranks but it did not disturb his equanimity at all. The gun sent them away and the clamour became even louder.

Three laps later the cheering was still as great but the abuse had died down. Whatever his shortcomings as a diplomat, Johansson had proved that he was a fine athlete by sticking in behind Landy all the way as the latter bounded on. The Finn deserved some respect. Halfway around the last lap he was still in contention and even had the temerity to try to pass the Australian.

Landy responded at once. With an aggression that shaded into brutality he drew on his immense reserve of stamina to kick hard before pulling away decisively. Johansson was broken and the crowd bayed at him. Landy flashed on around the bend with a springing gait and entered the finishing straight with bedlam in his ears.

'Go on, John!'

'Good on you, mate!'

'You've beaten the loudmouth!'

'He's done like a dinner!'

'Faster, faster, faster!'

Landy was no longer running against another athlete. He was racing to beat off the disappointment of his fans. Sydney-siders had come in their thousands to see the young Melbourn-ian and they wanted to see him set a new record. Over the last, agonizing few yards he drove himself unmercifully until the tape gave him release.

Acclamation resounded. Johansson crossed the line to a few jeers but they were drowned out by the applause for John Landy. Press photographers swarmed on to the track to take pictures of the panting victor and humbled loser. The ovation died away so that the announcer could be heard. The time had been 4.05 and there was an audible moan before the cheering resumed.

Crowds at the Olympic Stadium in Melbourne were habitu-ated to seeing what was virtually a solo run by a champion. Sydney Cricket Ground had at least seen a closer and better race.

Johansson took his defeat well, praising Landy to the journalists who surrounded him and making no excuses for his failure. When he had showered and changed he sought out the winner for a quiet word.

'That was a fantastic run, John!'

'Thanks. You gave me a few scares yourself.'

'I take back all I said.'

Landy nodded. 'I appreciate that.'

'But why do they make such a great athlete like you run on such appalling tracks? It would not be allowed in Europe.'

'I know.'

'On a good track, that run of yours today would have produced a new world record,' argued the Finn. 'Perhaps even a four-minute mile.'

'Do you think so?'

'I will prove it, John. When the season is over you are coming to us. I am issuing a formal invitation to you on behalf of the Sports Club of Turku.'

'That's great,' said Landy, flattered.

'Our tracks are first-rate. When you get to Finland you will be able to show that you are the finest miler alive!'

It was a bewitching thought.

Chapter Fourteen

When Britain enjoyed its mildest December for twenty years it knew that it would have to pay for the privilege. The invoice soon came. Within a month intense cold brought sleet, snow, ice, frozen pipes, rising numbers in hospital casualty departments and regular footage on BBC TV News of areas of the country that were suffering the most. It made Lyons' Corner House a very warm place to be.

'Why doesn't Roger ever stay and join us?' asked Stampfl.

'He never has the time,' explained Brasher. 'He always has to dash off straight after the training session.'

'Yes,' added Chataway. 'I'm glad I didn't read Medicine. It seems to be a kind of accelerating treadmill.'

The three of them had come for one of their regular chats in the small upstairs café in the Kings Road. The coffee would not win any awards but it was piping hot and the cakes were a bonus after the rigours of training at the Duke of York's Barracks.

'I still think it is ridiculous,' argued Stampfl.

'That's only because you don't know Roger very well,' said Brasher.

'I know him well enough to realize that he is a very tricky customer. Why must he pretend that he does not need a coach? He knows that he cannot achieve his ambition without professional help.'

'And he's getting it,' reminded Chataway.

'Yes, but indirectly. *I* work out the training schedules and you two pass them on to Roger as if they came from you. It's crazy!'

'No, Franz,' replied Chataway. 'It's very English, that's all.'

'But it would be so much easier and more effective if the four of us could just sit down and work out our plan of campaign.'

'Roger will come round to it,' promised Brasher. 'Just bear with him for a little longer.'

'But everybody *knows* he comes to my coaching scheme at the weekends. If he fails to beat four minutes, *I* will get the blame.' He reached for the last cake. 'And if he succeeds I will probably get no credit at all.'

'You will from us, Franz,' insisted Chataway. 'We'll all be eternally grateful to you.'

'Yes, Chris. *You* may be. But what about officialdom? What about the bigwigs who run athletics in this country in the hopes that they may get a knighthood or something? Will *they* bring themselves to admit that a mere foreigner – an exiled Austrian – can do something that their national coaches cannot do?' He munched the cake ruminatively. 'I have already been in trouble with your officials for daring to coach British athletes. Who *else* can I coach in Britain?'

'I'm afraid that you'll just have to put it down to professional jealousy,' soothed Brasher. 'If you weren't the best in the business, you wouldn't have so many of us after your services.'

'As for Roger,' said Chataway, 'his attitude is slowly changing.'

'Slowly is about it!' complained Stampfl. 'He's been coming to me for months and he still won't acknowledge me as his coach.'

Chataway continued. 'But he realizes now that he was stuck in a rut last season. He lost his sense of direction. Now that the rest of us are involved and it's become a team effort, his enthusiasm has been rejuvenated. He's a much more determined athlete now.'

'And a much stronger one,' observed Brasher. 'Thanks to Franz.'

'Weight-training is valuable for all athletes. He accepts that now.' Stampfl finished his cake off. 'I have two major problems.'

'Yes,' joked Chataway. 'Chris and me.'

'Oh, no. You are just minor problems.'

'Thank you.'

'My first major problem is how to coach someone without letting him see me do it. Second – how do I improve an athlete who is already a basic world-beater? It is easy to take a nobody and improve him a hell of a lot. But a man like Roger Bannister . . .'

'He only needs to be improved by a few seconds,' said Brasher.

'It will still be difficult.' He drained his cup. 'In order to do it, I will have to improve you first.'

'I certainly couldn't run a half-mile in two minutes at the moment,' confessed Brasher. 'I need to work on my basic speed.'

'So will I,' said Chataway.

'You must get him to the bell in three minutes or as near as makes no difference,' emphasized Stampfl. 'Then the rest is up to him.'

'How long have we got?' wondered Chataway.

'That depends on Roger and when he feels ready.'

'The season doesn't start for a few months yet,' commented Brasher. 'That should give us enough time.'

'If you stick to my training schedule and monitor your progress at every stage,' urged the coach. 'And make sure you time *everything*. Down to the last second.'

'I've never trained with a stopwatch in my hand before,' said Chataway, amused at the notion. 'I'll feel like Paavo Nurmi.'

Stampfl smiled. 'If you can only run like him, Chris, then all our worries are over.'

'Unless, of course, Landy gets there first,' Brasher pointed out. 'Their season is not over down under. He still has a few races in which he can do it.'

'No,' said the coach confidently. 'He seems to be stuck around 4.02. He has got close to it time and time again but he has never beaten it. That is his absolute limit on Australian tracks.'

'Who does that leave?' said Chataway. 'Barthel?'

'Lots of European milers will be back in the hunt as soon as spring comes,' remarked Stampfl. 'Then, of course, there is Wes Santee. I believe that he is coming to race in Europe this season in order to find tougher opposition.'

'Santee is good,' conceded Chataway.

'Even though he can't resist telling us about it,' added Brasher.

'Santee is an exceptional athlete,' decided the coach. 'He has everything a miler needs. Speed – strength – stamina – competitive spirit – tactical skill. With a little more experience he could become almost unbeatable.'

'That's nice to know,' said Chataway with light irony.

'It is the reason that Roger must get a move on.' Stampfl looked from one to the other. 'If *he* doesn't break four minutes this season, I have a strong feeling that Wes Santee will.'

Wes Santee relaxed in the college swimming pool by floating on his back on the surface of the water. Other students were cleaving their way up and down and a few were practising their diving from the springboard. Santee found the pool an ideal place in which to unwind after a long session with the weights in the gymnasium.

As he lay there a smile touched his lips. He was reflecting as ever on an athletic ambition that he had nurtured for a long time now. But for certain technical difficulties, he knew exactly how to achieve that ambition and it amused him to go through it all in his mind. His reverie was short-lived.

There was a huge splash right next to him and he was dragged bodily under the water. When he fought his way back to the surface the grinning, wet face of Art Dalzell greeted him.

'You were asleep, Wes!' he accused.

'No, I wasn't. I was thinking.'

'Comes to the same thing!'

Santee lunged playfully at him but Dalzell was too quick. Diving to his right, he swam off down the pool with Santee in pursuit. The friends ended up holding the rail together and laughing.

'Say, you going to grab a few beers tonight, Wes?'

'No.'

'Why not?'

'Because I'm going to see a play.'

'A *what*?'

'A play, Art. You know – drama. On a stage. The guys have got a show opening tonight and I figured I'd go along and check it out.'

'Hey, yeah, it's all coming back now,' said Dalzell, remembering some posters he had seen around the campus. 'The play is by some lousy Russian.'

'Chekhov.'

'That's him. Chekhov. Why do you want to go and watch something written by a stinking Red?'

'He wasn't a Red,' argued Santee. 'And even if he was, you've got to keep an open mind. Hell, I don't know much about drama but I like to try everything that's going on around here.'

'Then how about a couple of beers?'

'After I've seen the play. How's that?'

'Okay.'

'The way I see it, I spend most of my time doing track work or studying. A guy needs to broaden his horizons for when he leaves college.'

'When we leave college, Wes, we got military training to do. And that won't give us any chance to watch plays by Reds!'

'Chekhov *isn't* a Red!'

'Who cares?'

Santee sighed. 'You're right about the draft, though. It sure cuts a hole in your life.' He became rueful. 'I bet some of those European milers don't have to interrupt their season like me to go on a six-week summer camp on the Marine Corps programme.'

'Maybe you won't have to go,' reassured Dalzell. 'Last time you got off because the AAU rang up and said you had to run instead.'

'It's the principle of the thing, Art.'

'They still got the draft in Europe.'

'Yes, but some guys dodge it. Bannister, for instance. He got deferred because he's studying to be a doctor or something. And there's lots of other ways to stay out of uniform so you can concentrate on your event. They get all the luck!'

'What about Landy?'

'What about him?'

'They got an army down in Australia?'

'Sure, they have!' joked Santee. 'Equipped with the latest technology, too. Forty-thousand Aborigines with army-issue boomerangs.'

'Hey, Wes!' called a voice.

'Yeah?'

'Can you spare a minute?'

Bill Easton was on the bank with a worried expression on his face. Santee got out of the pool immediately and went over to him.

'I got it all figured out, coach.'

'What?'

'The four-minute mile.'

'Oh, that . . .'

'Listen, you'll love this.'

'I make no promises,' warned the coach.

'Now – Art Dalzell is my rabbit for the first two quarters, okay? Then I got this fresh half-miler standing by to zip me round the next lap and a half. And away I go to finish somewhere around 3.58. Good?'

'Terrific!' said the other without enthusiasm.

'Except that they don't allow rabbits, I know. If I beat four minutes that way, the AAU would blow their stack.'

'They already have, Wes.'

'What?'

'That's what I came to see you about.'

'The AAU?'

'I've just had them on the line from New York.'

'Why?'

'Did you accept a camera as a prize a couple of months back?'

Santee shrugged. 'Yeah. It was only a small one.'

'You know the rules on this.'

'I got sick of getting ashtrays every time I won, coach. So I said, "Please save up ten of your ashtrays and give me a camera or something instead." What in hell's wrong with that?'

'They'll tell you when they see you.'

'What do you mean?'

'You've got to go to New York. Explain the situation.'

'Why can't I just give them a call and do that?'

'Because they want to see you in person,' said Easton. 'Wes, this is serious. They could get rough.'

'How rough?'

'That depends. All I know is that they've always looked real hard at that word "amateur". Infringe the rules and – boy! – you can be in deep shit.' He shook his head sadly. 'I always remember what they did to poor old Jim Thorpe.'

'Hey, come on!' protested Santee. 'It's not *that* serious. Thorpe took money for playing baseball. All I took was one lousy camera.'

'Jim Thorpe was the finest all-round athlete America has ever seen. Football, baseball, athletics . . . you name it. At the Stockholm Olympics of 1912 he won the pentathlon *and* the decathlon by enormous margins. Then what happens? Because of some half-assed story in a newspaper about Thorpe playing baseball for money one time, they stripped him of his medals and kicked him out altogether.'

'But that was the Olympic Committee not the AAU,' argued Santee.

'Officials are all the same, Wes, believe me,' replied Easton with feeling. 'The thing was that Thorpe didn't *know* he wasn't supposed to take dough for playing baseball. Whereas you *do* know that you're not supposed to accept a camera.'

Santee brooded for a moment. It was, unfortunately, no casual encounter with officialdom but the latest in a long line of hassles with authority. Out of a trivial gift like the camera the AAU could, if it chose, make quite an argument.

'One thing, anyway,' he said. 'At least I got no Olympic medals they can take off me.'

His smile did not have its usual bravura.

Roger Bannister held back his head to gulp in as much air as he could. It was the end of another training session and the exertion had taken its toll. Chris Chataway and Chris Brasher were also trying to get their breath back as they came over to him.

'This is sheer masochism!' complained Chataway. 'Ten

quarters at 62 seconds each with a two-minute break in between.'

'It certainly is nice when you stop,' decided Brasher.

'But we have to start all over again tomorrow,' noted Chataway.

'It's getting easier,' gasped Bannister, still recovering.

'Speak for yourself!' returned Chataway.

'It is, Chris . . . I feel marginally stronger each time.'

'I told you Franz would toughen you up,' said Brasher.

'He has,' admitted the other.

Hands on hips and head still back, Bannister walked around until the pain and the discomfort began to wear off. Regular indoor work with Stampfl had built up his strength and the interval training with his two pacemakers was also starting to pay dividends. In addition, he was still running during the lunch hour at the track near the hospital. Instead of training there alone, however, he now ran with a group of friends who had taken to calling themselves the Paddington Lunchtime Club.

After the setbacks of the previous year, Bannister now felt that he was moving towards his goal in a much more systematic way.

'I have to get changed,' he said.

Chataway smiled. 'We know. You have to rush off as usual.'

'Not today. I thought I'd stay and have a coffee with you.'

'You mean it, old boy?'

'Of course. Lyons' Corner House, isn't it? There are one or two things I'd like to discuss with Franz . . .'

Chataway and Brasher traded a look of minor triumph.

Three middle-aged men sat behind a table in an office in New York and studied the papers in front of them. The next item for consideration was a reported infringement of amateur status involving one Wesley Santee of the University of Kansas. The biggest and oldest of the three men sat between the other two.

'I think we're all agreed on this one, gentlemen.'

'Sure,' said the rotund official to his right.

'Okay. Let's have him in.'

Wes Santee was pacing restlessly up and down the corridor outside. For his interview with the Amateur Athletic Union he was wearing a royal-blue suit, a copper-coloured tie and a pair of flashy cowboy boots. They would certainly see him coming.

The door opened and the bulky official invited him in before resuming his own seat behind the table.

'Take a seat, Mr Santee,' said the chairman.

'Thank you, sir.'

Santee perched on the edge of the chair and appraised the three men in front of him. He was not reassured. They had the stern and unforgiving expressions that he had seen on so many of the faces of officialdom during his athletic career.

'This will not take long, Mr Santee,' explained the chairman.

'Good.'

'Did you accept a camera as a reward for running a race?'

'It was more of a gift than a reward, sir.'

'Did you accept it?'

'Yes.'

'Then you have compromised your amateur status.'

'Hell, gentlemen, are you so out of touch?' challenged Santee. 'There is appearance money being paid all over the country – and I accept one crumby little camera.'

'It was valued at two hundred dollars.'

'I took it instead of ashtrays.'

'Ashtrays are fine. They are only worth twenty dollars.'

'I had one camera instead of twenty ashtrays, that's all.'

'Then it was very irresponsible of you.'

The rotund man took over. 'Amateur athletics is an ideal, Mr Santee. It's an ideal that we happen to believe in and that we are here to uphold. We've devoted our lives to it.'

'I appreciate that, sir . . .' muttered Santee.

'We know all about the abuses that are starting to creep into the sport. And we're determined to stamp them out. We will not have athletes receiving underhand payments.'

'I haven't taken any underhand payments!' protested Santee.

'You accepted a two-hundred dollar camera and broke the rules.'

'Why make such a big deal out of it?' he pleaded.

'Mr Santee,' continued the chairman, 'I'm afraid that we have no alternative but to take firm action on this matter.'

'What do you mean, sir?'

'I mean that you are one of the leading athletes in the United States and we look to you to set a good example. If you are seen to be getting away with an underhand payment –'

'It was just a gift!' argued Santee.

'Let me finish, please,' barked the chairman. 'If you are seen to be getting away with it, others will follow suit. We will not have that in amateur athletics in this country!' He conferred silently with his two colleagues before addressing Santee again. 'The penalty agreed upon is that you're debarred from any international competition for one year.'

Santee was shocked. 'One year!'

'You will not be allowed to run abroad anywhere.'

'You're joking! I'm just about to go over to Europe for a crack at the four-minute mile.'

'I'm sorry, Mr Santee. You will have to make the attempt here.'

'But I can't. The competition isn't strong enough to stretch me.'

'That is not our concern.'

'Of course it's your concern!' urged Santee, on his feet now. 'Jesus, I don't believe this is happening!'

'Calm down, Mr Santee,' advised the chairman.

'How can I be calm when you've just thrown *that* at me? This country is desperate for an American to run the four-minute mile and I can do it if only you give me the chance.'

The chairman was unmoved. 'Some sections of the press might be desperate about the four-minute mile because it is in their interests to play these things up. Personally, I think its significance is overrated. Besides, we cannot change the rules of the AAU simply to further your individual ambitions.'

'It's not just a few sections of the press, sir,' argued Santee. 'When I go out to run a mile there's a silence so profound that I can hear my heart beating. A hundred and fifty million Americans want me to do it, gentlemen, and if you can't sense that, then you're even more out of touch than I thought.'

'I'm sorry, Mr Santee,' said the chairman, quite impassive. 'Our decision is final.'

'You're crucifying me – do you know that!' yelled Santee. 'You're crucifying me and you're crucifying America!'

Everyone who read the sports pages in Australia was well acquainted with Percy Cerutty as a firebrand in the world of athletics. With his flair for publicity and his controversial ideas, he kept himself flitting in and out of the headlines. What most people did not know about him was the generous side to his personality which prompted him to do charity work. During the Christmas holidays he always put on free training sessions at Portsea for the deprived children involved in the Lord Mayor's Camp and he made his facilities available to youngsters at other times as well.

'Catch me if you can!'

'Go on, lads! After him!'

Neil Robbins watched with amusement as Percy Cerutty sprinted off down the beach like a super-charged Pied Piper with a stream of boys in his wake. The trainer loved to involve himself and to give his young charges a day that they would remember. Staying ahead of them all the way, he looped around and came back to the starting point. His own athletes then took over and divided up the boys into small groups so that they could use the equipment at the training camp.

'Some of them nearly caught you up, Perce,' observed Robbins.

'Yes, there's bags of talent there,' agreed Cerutty. 'The tragedy is that it will never be developed. These kids just don't have a chance.'

'I know.'

'The whole structure of athletics is wrong, Neil,' insisted Cerutty, climbing on to a favourite soapbox. 'The vast majority of athletes come out of the public schools and the Old Boys' Clubs. Kids from the poorer state schools don't get a look-in. And what is the AAU doing about it?' He made an obscene gesture. 'What we need is enormous capital expenditure at the grass-roots level. Every school in the country should have a decent running track and a fella like me to make sure the kids use it properly.'

'There *are* no fellas like you, Perce.'

'I know! And that's the trouble with this bloody country.'

A tousle-haired boy came running over with a piece of paper and a pencil. He offered them both to Cerutty.

'Can I have your autograph, please? That man over there says you were a famous marathon runner.'

'I still am, son,' declared Cerutty, obliging with his signature before handing paper and pencil to his companion. 'And this here is Neil Robbins, who'll be representing Australia at the Empire Games in Vancouver.'

'If selected,' added Robbins, appending his signature. 'There you are, son.'

'Thanks,' said the boy, taking back his makeshift autograph book. 'Who else can I get?'

'See that man over there?' asked Cerutty, pointing to another athlete. 'That's Geoff Warren. He'll be at Vancouver as well.'

The boy ran off to get another name for his collection.

'What was I saying, Neil?'

'You were praising the state schools for the way they foster and develop athletic talent,' teased the other.

'If only they would! You've got to catch them young.'

'Otherwise all that potential goes to waste.'

'Give me a promising youngster and I could build him up into a champion,' boasted Cerutty. 'All it takes is time, commitment and patience.'

'Time and commitment, anyway,' replied Robbins. 'Let's be honest, Perce. Patience has not been your greatest virtue.'

Cerutty laughed then gazed around. 'Look at them. These kids are loving it here. There ought to be camps like mine all over Australia. We should take athletics *seriously* for once!'

'It is getting a little better,' noted Robbins. 'John has helped. When you get a guy like him reeling off some of the best times in the world, it gets the sport noticed. He's done athletics a lot of good.'

'Yes,' said Cerutty, his manner changing. 'He's used what I taught him and put it to effect. John Landy is an example of what I mean. Give me the raw material and I can do the rest.'

'It will be great having him with us in Vancouver. Gives a boost to the whole team when they know they've got someone who's a dead cert for a gold medal.'

'He may not be all that much of a dead cert, Neil.'

'Oh, come on! John is the most consistent miler in the world. Nobody can live with that pace. And he'll certainly be the fittest man at the games. Some of his training sessions make Zatopek's look like gentle exercise.'

Cerutty nodded. 'Landy and Zatopek are birds of a feather. Fanatics. Nurmi was the same.'

'All three of them unbeatable in their prime.' Robbins looked over at him. 'Will you be coming to Vancouver, Perce?'

'No, old son. I'm skint.'

'Can't you wangle it somehow?'

'Not this time. If there was any justice I'd be on the trip as the official team coach. As it is, I'll be stuck at home here.'

'I'll write,' promised Robbins. 'Keep you in touch.'

'Thanks.' He shrugged off his sadness. 'Anyway, I'll have plenty to keep me busy. I'll be training tomorrow's champions.' His eye kindled. 'Hey, did I tell you about that new kid I've come across?'

'Which one? You're always scouting around.'

'This one is sixteen and he's run the mile in 4.25.6. With a first lap of 56.8! If he keeps it up next season I'm going to take a really close look at him.'

'What's his name?'

'Herb Elliott.'

They walked across to join the others. The boy who was collecting autographs came back up to them with a look of disappointment. There was one name he wanted above all others.

'Isn't John Landy here?' he asked.

Percy Cerutty for once showed commendable restraint.

'No, son. Not today.'

The four of them gathered once more around a table in Lyons' Corner House to brave the coffee and review their strategy.

A piece of news which had reached them lent an urgency to their discussion.

'If Landy is going to Finland,' said Stampfl, 'he will have excellent running conditions. On those tracks and in that climate, who knows what he might do?'

'We can't let an Aussie get there first,' complained Chataway.

'An American would be bad enough,' added Brasher. 'But if Landy were to beat us to it . . .'

Stampfl laughed. 'Perhaps I should remind you that it was an Australian who helped to found the Amateur Athletic Association here. Bernhard Wise.'

'Yes,' countered Chataway. 'But he was up at Oxford at the time.'

Bannister had been pensive so far. He rubbed his chin and then came to a decision.

'I think we should make the attempt as soon as possible.'

'That means the first race of the season,' noted Brasher.

'Yes, Chris. Oxford versus the AAA.'

Chataway beamed. 'At Iffley Road.'

'You and Roger will get in the AAA team as ex-Oxford men,' said Brasher. 'I'll have to make other arrangements to make sure that I'm in the mile race with you.'

'Good,' said Stampfl. 'Now that we have agreed on a date we can plan everything very carefully around it.'

'We've still got some way to go,' admitted Bannister.

'Yes,' agreed Chataway. 'We still can't run those ten repetition quarters in under 60 seconds.'

'You will if you keep at it,' assured the coach. 'Nothing must be left to chance. Roger must be paced at the correct speed.'

'Of course, we may not get the ideal weather at Iffley Road,' warned Bannister. 'But I feel it would be too risky to delay the attempt any longer.'

'Oxford it must be,' affirmed Chataway.

'It's what I've wanted,' said Bannister.

'And what's the exact date, Roger?'

'Thursday, May 6th.'

'It could become a famous day,' said Stampfl.

'Oh, it will,' decided Chataway with breezy confidence. 'On May 6th 1954 Roger Bannister will become the first man to beat the four-minute mile.' He beamed again. 'Unless I decide to do it myself instead.'

An historic event had been set in motion.

Chapter Fifteen

On the eve of his departure to Finland John Landy sat in the living room at home with his parents. It was a long time before they would see him again and a few anxieties were surfacing at the last moment.

'Where exactly will you be staying, John?' asked his mother.

'They're fixing up the accommodation, Mum,' he explained. 'More to the point, they're paying for the whole trip. I'll be there as a guest of the Finnish Athletic Association.'

'An honoured guest,' corrected his father.

'But what about food and all that?' wondered his mother.

'They have a very healthy diet. We thrived on it when we were in Helsinki. The Finns eat a lot of fish. In fact it's one of the excuses they always give when their athletes don't run so well abroad.'

'Is it?' said Gordon Landy.

'Yes, they claim that once they come off their fish diet they don't run anything like as well.'

His father's eyes twinkled. 'Is that why Johansson got beaten at the Sydney Cricket Ground?'

'We'll soon find out, Dad. I know he's dying to run against me on his home track in Turku. He's convinced he can win.'

'You'll send us a post card as soon as you arrive, won't you?'

'Of course, Mum.'

'It's rather different from the Olympics,' she pointed out. 'You went as part of a team then and you had lots of friends around you. This time you're all on your own.'

'I've got Denis Johansson to look after me,' he reminded

her. 'And the Finns are a very friendly people. I got on like a house on fire with them.' He smiled. 'Most of them had never seen an Australian before. You'd have thought we'd just stepped off the moon.'

They chatted quietly and Landy did his best to still some of his mother's apprehensions while suppressing his own. His natural excitement at the prospect of the visit was tempered by the distant fear that things might not work out altogether as he hoped. He only had the briefest acquaintance with Denis Johansson, after all, and he was not sure how well he would get on with such a flamboyant extrovert over a period of time.

A new worry nudged his mother.

'How will you manage when you don't speak the language?'

'They usually speak English,' he told her. 'The Finns are one of the most educated people in the world. Even the high school kids seem to speak five or six languages. I'll probably be in demand just to give them some practice with their English.'

'That's all right then, John,' she said, reassured. 'Finland does sound like a lovely place. Everything I've read about it says how nice the people are.'

'I admire any country that can stand up to the Russians the way that Finland did,' commented Gordon Landy. 'They had to pay for it, I know, but they showed some guts.'

'They call it *sisu*, Dad.'

'What?'

'*Sisu*. We don't really have an equivalent word in English. It means courage, perseverance, strong will. A sort of readiness to face up to hardship. Well, let's face it. They need it just to survive in that climate. They have to put up with all extremes.'

'What will the weather be like when you arrive?' asked his mother.

'Cold.'

'I hope you've packed plenty of warm things.'

'I have, Mum. Don't worry.'

'This trip of yours has certainly aroused a lot of interest,' observed his father. 'The papers are full of it. They're all saying that you'll make a perfect ambassador.'

'I don't know about that,' denied Landy with a self-effacing grin. 'What really pleased me was all the cards and letters I got to wish me bon voyage.'

'And the phone calls,' reminded his mother. 'Some days, it hasn't stopped ringing.' She turned to her husband and her tone became almost reverential. 'Did John tell you that Marjorie Jackson rang?'

'No.'

'She's married now,' said Landy. 'She's Mrs Nelson. It was lovely to hear from her. She'll be in Sydney when my plane gets there so she's going to come out to the airport to say goodbye.'

'Isn't that kind of her, Gordon?'

'Very kind.'

'That's Marje all over!' Landy glanced at his watch. 'Right. I'm going on up.'

'It's rather early for bed, John,' noted his mother.

'I'm not going to bed, Mum. I'm going up to get changed.'

'You're not training this evening, surely?'

'Try stopping him,' suggested her husband.

'Can't you let yourself off just this once, John?'

'No. I've got a long flight ahead of me, remember. I won't be able to do anything for the next four days so I'd like to get in a session tonight.'

'If you say so, dear . . .'

'My training is the basis of my success, Mum. That's why I have to keep at it. I'm not going to Finland for a holiday, you know. They're expecting me to run in plenty of races.'

'They're expecting a lot more than that, son,' remarked his father. 'And so is the whole of Australia. They're all expecting John Landy to run the first four-minute mile.'

With the merest hint of a sigh, Landy nodded and went out.

It had been a particularly arduous training session at the Duke of York's Barracks and Chris Chataway was bewailing the fact that Lyons' Corner House did not run to anything more restorative than coffee. Bannister had been unable to join them and so it was just the trio who sat around a table. Stampfl was unusually quiet.

'What is it, Franz?'

'Nothing.'

'You're not happy about something. I can tell.'

'It's just a feeling I have,' admitted the coach.

'About what?'

'Our tactics. I wonder if we should change them slightly.'

'How?' said Brasher.

'At the moment, it's like this. You run two laps, Chris takes over the pacemaking for lap three and Roger goes hell for leather over the last quarter.'

'What's wrong with that?' inquired Chataway.

Stampfl turned to Brasher. 'Could you possibly run two and a half laps before you hand over?'

'I'm not sure about that,' confessed Brasher with obvious misgivings. 'That's a tall order, Franz.'

'How far would I have to tow Roger along?' said Chataway.

'Another lap on your own, making a total of three and a half laps before he takes over by himself.'

'I'll be exhausted!' complained Chataway.

'Roger needs all the help that you can give him. He will have a much better chance if he only has to go it alone over the last 220.' He gave the other time to think it over. 'Well?'

Chataway shrugged. 'I can't pretend I like the idea.'

'But you will give it a try?'

'If that's what it needs.'

'Thank you.' The coach looked across at Brasher. 'What are your reservations, my friend?'

'Failure feelings, I suppose. I'm not like Roger and Chris. I have a slight handicap.'

'You can't help having gone to Cambridge,' joked Chataway.

'In view of the fact that Oxford have just won the centenary Boat Race, I wish I hadn't!' Brasher faced Stampfl. 'Roger and Chris are world-class middle-distance runners. I'm just a good steeplechaser.'

'Good enough to get to an Olympics,' reminded his coach. 'Don't underestimate yourself, old boy.'

'My problem is this. I'm not even certain that I can run the first two laps in 1.58 and you're asking me to hang on for another 220 as well. Have I got the basic speed?'

'You will have by then,' promised Stampfl.

'I just feel it may be rather late in the day to make such a radical change in our tactics, Franz.'

'See it as an experiment, Chris. I think it could work.'

'Only if I can hold out that long.'

Stampfl turned large, soulful eyes on him. 'I wouldn't dream of asking you if I wasn't absolutely sure that you could do it. Tell me the truth. When we started, did you really believe that you would be running ten quarters at an average of 60 seconds by now?'

'No, I didn't.'

'There you are, then. We have broken through one barrier. Now we must break through another.' He could see that Brasher was still uncertain. 'As I have told you before, every athlete has an immediate physical potential which determines the limit of his performance. The purpose of training is to increase that immediate potential so that it gradually approaches the *absolute* potential.' He shook his head and smiled. 'You are nowhere near your absolute potential, Chris. What I am asking you is well within your capability.'

'That's very encouraging of you to say so.'

'It happens to be true,' added Chataway. 'Two and a half laps? You could do it standing on your head.'

'Don't let's have another radical change of tactics!' pleaded Brasher with comic fear. He pondered. 'Could I have more time to mull it over, Franz?'

'No,' said the other levelly.

'You want an answer now?'

'I think you can do it, Chris,' said the coach firmly. 'I also believe that it is the right strategy for this race. What do you say?'

'Okay. I'll have a go.'

'Thank you.'

'As long as this is definitely it, Franz,' stipulated Chataway. 'Three and a half laps is my utmost limit.'

Stampfl shook his head. 'No, my friend. It is not. If Roger runs a four-minute mile in Oxford, I'm sure that you will do the same one day.' He chuckled. 'Don't look so glum, the both of you. There are not many more weeks to go. After May 6th it is all over. And nobody will be more relieved than me.'

'Why?' asked Brasher.

'Because of the time it is taking up. I do have other athletes to coach as well, you know.'

'How many of them?' said Chataway.

'Too many.'

'Give us an approximate figure. How many athletes come to your coaching scheme in the course of a normal week?'

'About seven hundred.'

'Seven hundred!' gasped the other. 'All for a bob a knob?'

'Of course.'

'That makes . . .' Brasher did some lightning mental arithmetic and was pleased with the result. 'That makes it your turn to buy the next round of coffees, Franz.'

Stampfl was happy to do so. In altering the tactics for the race he had obeyed his instincts. He now felt confident that those instincts had been right.

There was only time for a brief chat at Sydney Airport but John Landy found it very worthwhile. Marjorie Nelson, as she now was, had been a good and supportive friend to him in Helsinki and he reminded her of it as they sat in a lounge together and tried to ignore the pointing fingers of passers-by.

'You helped me when I was down, Marje. I'll always remember it.'

'I had faith in you, John,' she replied. 'And you've fulfilled it. You went to Finland the first time as a complete unknown but you're going back there as a big star.'

'As a much better runner, anyway.'

'They'll give you a marvellous welcome, I'm sure.' She touched his arm. 'I know you're going to make it over there, John.'

'I don't,' he confessed. 'I'm starting to wonder if *anybody's* ever going to beat four minutes.'

'Of course there is.'

'Maybe there is a barrier there. Haegg's world record is 4.01.4. I keep running around 4.02. Bannister's best is 4.02. So is Santee's. Maybe we've finally hit the brick wall.'

'I know what Percy Cerutty would say to that.'

'Run straight through it.'

'Yes!' She paused to donate a smile to a group of fans who went past waving to her. 'How is Perce?'

'Much the same. I don't really see him these days.'

'What about the others?'

'Oh, he has quite a stable down at Portsea now. According to Les, there's sometimes as many as thirty athletes running up those sandhills.' He gave a reflective smile. 'Last time I saw Perce, he was having a row with an official.'

'That's nothing new.'

'It was at Olympic Park. Neil Robbins was in the race and Perce hopped over the fence to give him some last-minute advice. This big official walks up and tells Perce that he's not allowed to coach on the track. Orders him to get back in the stand.'

'I can imagine what Perce said.'

'I hope so, Marje, because I couldn't repeat that language in public. This official was twice his size but Perce raises a fist at him and says, "I'll punch you on the nose, fella!" ' Landy chuckled. 'I've heard him threaten to do that a dozen times.'

'Have you ever seen him do it?'

'No.'

They shared a laugh then heard the announcement concerning Landy's flight. It was time to go. They stood up and headed towards the departure lounge, collecting even more public attention now.

'How's married life?' he asked.

'Wonderful! You should try it, John.'

'Not a chance!' he exclaimed. 'Running takes up all my time. I won't even be able to think about marriage until after I've retired.'

'When will that be?'

'I don't know. Depends how I get on in Finland. And Vancouver.' A thought struck him. 'Hey, you'll be coming to the Empire Games, won't you, Marje? I hope married life won't get in the way of that.'

'I'll be there,' she vowed. 'I have to be.'

'Why?'

'So that we can win that gold medal in the sprint relay. I still have nightmares about dropping the baton in Helsinki.

It was terrible. I owe it to the other girls to go back and do it properly.'

'And then?'

'That's me finished.'

'For good?'

'The time to quit is when you're at the top so that people remember the good things about you.' She lowered her voice. 'Also, of course, there's the financial side of it.'

'Yes. Athletes don't get a bean.'

'We may win the odd medal or two and travel the world and even end up with a scrapbook of cuttings. But you have to be realistic about it. Stay an athlete in this country and you end up broke.'

'You're not kidding.'

The announcement cajoled him again and he knew that he had to go. He gave his friend a kiss on the cheek and thanked her profusely for finding a moment to send him off. More and more people were watching them now and it made Landy feel very uneasy.

'This is one of the things I'm hoping to escape.'

'What? Fans?'

'Yes. If I walk down a street in Melbourne I get mobbed.'

'You should have been in Lithgow when I got back from Helsinki. The town went completely mad. You'd have thought I was royalty.'

'You are, Marje.' He nodded politely at some well-wishers who went past then leaned in for a last confidence. 'I'm not just going to Finland to run. I want some peace and quiet. In Australia just about everybody has heard of John Landy. Over there hardly a soul will know who I am.'

She laughed.

'What's funny?'

'You'll find out, John.'

The Texas Relays provided a real test for the team from the University of Kansas. As the 4-mile relay approached its climax it was the host quartet who were in the lead by over fifty yards and the result did not seem to be in any doubt. Then Wes Santee was given the baton for the final leg.

'Go get him, Wes!'

'Eat him up, man!'

'He's all yours!'

His team mates urged him on from the infield, sorry that they could not have set up a lead themselves but confident that their star miler would save the day once again. Santee's eyes were fixed on the vest of the tall, stringy Texan up ahead of him and he kept them there all the way. The athlete ahead of him was strong and would not be caught easily so Santee had to whittle away his lead slowly over the first three laps.

At the bell he was only five yards adrift.

'Take him, Wes!'

'Get him on the bend!'

'Come on, Kansas!'

Santee was in control now. He was going to enjoy himself. He ran alongside the Texan and turned to give him a broad grin before pulling away with consummate ease. Yelled home by an enthusiastic college crowd, he pulled out a spectacular finish and crashed through the tape some thirty yards ahead.

'Terrific, Wes!'

'We did it again!'

'You really are something, man!'

'Ain't nobody can whip Kansas!'

His team mates were hugging him and patting him on the back. When they got into trouble in a race they knew they could always rely on their anchor man to get them out of it. Santee went along with the celebrations but his heart was not really in them. Instead of thinking about the relay that they had won he was obsessed with the individual mile race from which he was debarred.

Bill Easton left the timekeeper and came over to Santee.

'How did I do, coach?'

'Unofficially — 4.03 dead.'

'And it's wasted on a lousy relay!'

'We won, Wes. The college won.'

'Sure — and that's nice, coach,' he said angrily. 'But see it from my point of view. I just ran one of the fastest mile times in the world this year and yet I can't get in a proper mile race!'

'Yeah, I know.'

'It's not *right*! There's only a few guys in the States who

206

can run three quarters in three minutes and their coaches are too scared to let them run against me. I finish up racing against punk athletes like that Texan out there. I deserve *better*, coach!'

'That's what I keep telling the AAU.'

'My talent is being strangled to death here!'

'Take it easy, Wes,' advised the coach. 'You got problems and I'm working on them. But it takes time.'

'We don't *have* time.'

'I'll find you the right competition somehow.'

'Can't we raise the dough to invite them here?' pleaded Santee.

'Who?'

'Bannister and Landy. Get them to the States and let me take them on. I don't mean in Kansas. Most of our tracks are like ploughed fields. We'll run on one of those great clay tracks in California.'

'It's a nice idea, Wes,' agreed Easton sympathetically, 'but we just don't have that kind of dough.'

'But it could be a feature race in a big meet. You know – another Mile of the Century. It'd pull a terrific crowd.'

'If it ever happened.'

'They used to fly in athletes to take on Glenn Cunningham. Why can't they do it for me?' He paced up and down for a few seconds then came back at Easton. 'Bannister, Landy and me – we're the three best milers in the world. We've *got* to race each other!'

'Maybe you will, Wes. At the next Olympics.'

'It'll be too late by then. Besides, who's to say one or both of them won't have retired?' His tone became rueful. 'After they've clocked four minutes.'

'You're a victim of the system, I'm afraid.'

'There's just got to be a way to buck it.'

'I been trying for twenty years to find it.'

'You saw me run today. It's *there*. I just need that extra little spur and I'm home and dry. I *feel* it.'

'So do I. You're only strides away.'

'Fix me that race against them.'

'If only I could, Wes.'

'I guarantee one thing,' affirmed Santee. 'Stick me in against

Bannister and Landy and I'd not only win. All *three* of us would beat four minutes!'

He was finding his frustration increasingly hard to bear.

Thirty minutes of interval running had left them drained. After each hard quarter they had trotted back to the start within two minutes and sprinted off again. Because they had put so much effort into it, they were slightly demoralized by the results.

'That last lap was only 61.01,' said Chataway.

'It felt faster,' noted Brasher.

'It was our slowest quarter yet,' complained Bannister.

'We just don't seem to be able to beat 60 seconds for every quarter,' sighed Chataway. 'I don't know why. Everything seems to be going well and then we look at the stopwatch.'

'What shall we do, Roger?' asked Brasher.

Bannister considered. 'Let's have a chat with Franz.'

'But I need a brandy and a good cigar,' insisted Chataway, still blowing hard. 'Not a coffee and a jam tart.'

They went off to get changed.

Seated around a table in Lyons' Corner House, they tried to rationalize their problem. Weeks of unrelenting work had suddenly stopped bringing the slow, steady advances they had achieved before.

'We seem to be marking time, Franz,' said Brasher.

'Maybe we should try going faster over the first 220,' suggested Chataway. 'We can get below the 60 for some quarters but not all ten.'

'What happens when you run alone, Roger?' wondered Stampfl.

'It's the same story. Close, but not quite there.'

'Close is not good enough, my friend.'

'What do you suggest, Franz?' asked Brasher. 'We've only got a few weeks to go now.'

'Do we intensify our training for one last push?' said Chataway.

Bannister had doubts. 'I don't feel that that's the answer, Chris. If we overdo it we could become stale.'

'Right,' agreed Chataway. 'Then we simply try harder next time.'

'No,' said Stampfl. 'Maybe you all need a rest.'

'But that would interrupt our momentum,' observed Brasher.

'A few days' relaxation might freshen you up. Bring you back with a renewed interest. I suggest that you have a break from training.'

'That sounds an attractive idea,' remarked Chataway.

'What do you mean, Franz?' asked Bannister. 'That we just sit at home with our feet up?'

'Oh no. You need to get completely away. A change of scene. Why not take yourselves on a little holiday?'

'We could always go climbing, I suppose,' said Brasher.

'Perfect!' agreed the coach.

'I couldn't take time off,' said Chataway, 'but I'll certainly give myself a well-earned rest.'

'What about you, Roger?' asked Brasher.

'I suppose I could manage it.'

'Have you done much climbing before?' said Stampfl.

'No.'

'It could be just the thing. Fresh air, good exercise, your mind occupied with something else for a change.'

'I promise we won't try anything too difficult,' added Brasher. 'We'll go to Scotland. Glencoe.'

'All right,' agreed Bannister. 'That could be fun.'

'It might just do the trick,' decided Stampfl.

'How big are the mountains up there, Chris?' asked Chataway.

'Small by world standards but they could test us.' He turned to Bannister. 'We'll go up Clachaig Gully and tackle Jericho Wall. It's pretty steep but it's no Everest.'

'That comes on May 6th,' noted Bannister.

They laughed away their doubts and ordered more coffee.

The long flight had left John Landy feeling tired and jaded. Even with stop-overs, the business of travelling over long distances and through different time zones was fatiguing and it made a big difference that he was on his own. As part of the Australian Olympic Team he had not found the journey to Europe half as taxing.

He fastened his safety belt as they came in to land and got

his first glimpse of Turku through the window. Vestigial snow lay about and the sun was glinting on patches of ice. Pine trees stretched out in long carpets. The city itself seemed to be enclosed in water as the River Aura joined the sea to exchange cold greetings.

As soon as he was clear of customs, Landy was pounced upon.

'John! Welcome to Finland!'

'Thanks.'

'Good trip?'

'A bit tiring.'

'You'll be able to sleep it off here.'

Denis Johansson, wrapped in warm clothes, was full of bonhomie as he carried one of Landy's bags and took him towards a small crowd of journalists and well-wishers. A small cheer went up as the two athletes approached and Landy was suitably impressed.

'You must be quite a hero here, Denis.'

'They're cheering for you, my friend.'

'Me?' He was startled.

'Of course. The whole of Turku knows that John Landy is visiting us. These people want to be the first to welcome the great Australian miler. You are famous here.'

Landy was torn between pleasure and discomfort.

Peace and quiet might not be so easy to find after all.

Chapter Sixteen

The Aston Martin was built for speed rather than passenger comfort. As the vehicle powered its way north the athletes took it in turns to crouch down on an inflated Lilo in the luggage space behind the two bucket seats. Chris Brasher had managed to cadge a lift for them from his doctor who happened to be driving to Scotland that day.

'I can't tell you how grateful we are,' said Brasher.

'Glad of the company, old man,' replied the doctor. 'Besides, I'm always willing to help out a medical student.'

'Thanks,' added Bannister from the rear of the car.

'Professional solidarity, Roger. I know what a final year can be like. You're very wise to take a short break like this.'

'I hope so.'

Another fifty miles sped by. An April shower began to sprinkle the windows and the wheels were soon squishing over a wet road surface. Bannister lay huddled in the back and looked forward to the time when he and Brasher could change places again. Apart from the doctor's own luggage, they had crammed climbing gear and haversacks into the limited space. It was not the most dignified way to travel.

'We'll stop for some lunch soon,' decided the driver.

'Good,' said Bannister.

'Give you a chance to stretch your legs.'

'Yes.'

'Nothing worse than for a couple of athletes like you to be cooped up like this,' observed the doctor chirpily. 'I'm surprised you didn't decide to run up to Scotland.'

'How long do you think it will take?' asked Brasher.

'All told? Oh, about ten hours.'

Bannister was alarmed. 'Ten hours!'

'Don't worry, old chap,' assured the doctor. 'We'll make it.'

'Yes, this car has competed at Le Mans,' explained Brasher.

Bannister felt that it had already been going for that length of time. He adjusted his position on the Lilo to redistribute the aches then settled down to wait for lunch.

Bitter cold made it impossible for Landy to run on the track because it was covered in a series of undulating waves of ice. He had to confine himself to light training and took comfort from the fact that warmer weather would be coming in a matter of weeks. Meanwhile he had time to look around Turku at leisure. Denis Johansson proved a lively and well-informed tour guide.

'Turku is Finland's oldest city and it was the capital for a very long time. In 1808 we were "re-united" with the Russian Empire. Soon after that, Helsinki took over as our capital.'

'You've got so many beautiful buildings here.'

'Not as many as we should have, John. There was a terrible fire here early in the last century and almost the whole of Turku was destroyed.' He pointed to some ruined houses further along the street. 'We had a lot of fire damage in the last war, too.'

'It's certainly very different from Melbourne.'

'Much bloody colder, you mean!' said Johansson, laughing.

'Oh, it can get cold down there, believe me. And we always seemed to have that wind blowing in off the Bass Strait. Of course we don't get ice and snow like this . . .'

'It is a big problem for an athlete. In your winter it is still possible to train. Here, there is no chance.'

'I thought that Turku was supposed to have a mild climate?'

'This *is* mild compared to most of the country, John. But I have never been able to use a track here all the year round.'

'Is that why you went to America?'

'Partly.'

'What was the other reason?'

'I like American women.' He flashed a wicked grin. 'More to the point, they seem to like me.'

'What did you choose to study?' asked Landy.

'I started off with Physical Education then changed to Economics. It is very hard work but I will get the hang of it one day.' He turned to his companion. 'And what about you?'

'Agricultural Science.'

'Ah, you must visit some of our farms.'

'I'd like that very much.'

'This is one of the most fertile regions in Scandinavia. There will be plenty for you to see while you're here. You will not have to spend all your time running.'

'Good.'

They walked on into the Luostarinmäki quarter, one of the few areas of the city to survive intact the fire that had devastated the city in the previous century. Landy was fascinated to watch the potters, weavers, wood-carvers, hand-painters and other craftsmen at work in their old houses, continuing family traditions that went back for many hundreds of years. Johansson led his guest on to Samppalinnanmäki Hill, a nearby park in which children were playing.

'It is one of the things I like about your city, John,' opined the Finn. 'All those lovely parks.'

'Yes. Parks and gardens make up about a quarter of Melbourne.'

'That is how it should be. In some American cities they do not seem to know what parks are. You have concrete all around you.'

'Wouldn't suit me.'

'And what about Turku?' asked Johansson as they strolled on. 'Do you think that will suit you?'

'Oh yes. I felt at home as soon as I arrived.'

'I am glad. We want to make your stay a happy one. Except when you get out on the track, that is.' He flashed his smile again. 'I did not only invite you here to break the four-minute mile, John.'

'I know. You reckon you can beat me.'

'You are a faster runner but I have more guile.'

'We'll have to see who comes out on top,' said Landy pleasantly. 'But don't think I was fooled by what happened in Sydney. You weren't really fit in that race. It will be different here.'

'Very different.'

'And I daresay there'll be other athletes dying for the chance to run against me and win.'

'Dozens. You will have plenty of competition, John.'

'That's what I came for, after all.'

'For that – and to enjoy yourself, I hope.'

'Of course.'

'Are you recovered from the flight yet?'

'Yes, I'm fine now.'

'Good. Then tonight you will see something of Finnish culture.'

'Go to the theatre or something, you mean?'

Johansson laughed aloud. 'Not exactly . . .'

Roger Bannister learned that Glencoe was a wild, gloomy valley in Argyllshire on the west coast of Scotland and that it was situated near the head of Loch Leven. The mountains rose steeply on either side to a height of well over 3000 feet. A light drizzle was falling as the athletes went for their first walk but it only seemed to enhance the moody grandeur of their surroundings. Rock faces acquired a moist sheen and, glimpsed through a veil of fine rain, the lazy beauty of the loch was an inspiring sight.

Brasher told the story about the massacre of Glencoe and then the talk, inevitably, turned back to athletics. Bannister was interested in Franz Stampfl.

'Why did you want him to coach you?'

'Because he's the best person for an athlete like me, Roger.'

'He's a fine technician, certainly.'

'Oh, he's much more than that,' said Brasher with enthusiasm. 'He understands what makes an athlete tick. Franz doesn't just get you fit and refine your technique. He coaches you from the inside, so to speak. Reaches down into your soul.'

'That's probably what I have against coaches.'

'They're not all Svengalis, you know.'

'Granted,' said Bannister, 'and I'd be the first to admit how much help Franz has given me. But I could never enjoy that close, long-term relationship with a coach that a lot of athletes seem to need.'

'You're still tainted by the Greek ideal,' teased the other.

'It does have an appeal, I must confess. And I've never found anything to match it. I just think that running is such a marvellous and creative thing. It does so much to bring out an individual's true potential. Or as the Greeks would say, it develops the whole man.'

'The Greeks didn't try to beat four minutes for the mile.'

'There is that . . .'

They went down to the edge of the water and spent a few minutes watching a lone figure rowing slowly across Loch Leven. The man was taking it at his own pace without hurry or urgency. He seemed to have all the time in the world.

'What do you think of Glencoe?' asked Brasher.

'Glorious!'

'Sorry about the rain.'

'You couldn't be expected to lay on fine weather.' He looked around. 'I like it here. It's rugged but it's restful. And it's a vast improvement on the Kings Road.'

'Yes, Roger. No Lyons' Corner House.' Brasher scanned the mountains through his spectacles. 'We'll go climbing tomorrow.'

'Right.'

'Nothing too strenuous.'

'I'm glad to hear it,' said Bannister with relief. 'What made you take up mountaineering in the first place?'

'Lots of reasons.'

'Such as?'

'Excitement. Challenge. The danger element. Also – and this may sound ridiculous – I get a tremendous feeling of liberation when I'm up there, high on a mountain face. It's a new sort of freedom.'

'It doesn't sound ridiculous to me, Chris,' replied Bannister seriously. 'That's very much how I feel about running. I get this extraordinary sense of release somehow. In the mind and the body. It's quite electrifying.' He gave a shrug. 'I suppose I'm a very selfish athlete, really. I run for that personal lift I get, that sense of expansion.'

'All athletes are selfish, Roger,' declared his friend. 'You have to be egocentric to take up an individual sport of any kind.'

'It goes deeper than that with me.'

They turned and made their way along the bank of the loch. After the bustle of London and the discomfort of their car journey north, they were finding the solitude very refreshing.

'Do you still intend to retire this year, Roger?'

'I have to, Chris,' explained Bannister. 'There's no way I can go on running once I qualify. That's why I'm so keen to make another attempt at the four-minute mile. It's my last season.'

'It could be an amazing one for you.'

'It could be,' said the other guardedly.

'The four-minute mile, the Empire Games, the European Championships. You could go out with a bang.'

'I thought that at Helsinki.'

'Something tells me that this could be your year, Roger.'

'Hopefully . . . What about you, Chris?'

'Oh, I think I'll cling in there for a couple more years.'

'Melbourne?'

'I'd love to go to another Olympics. I just didn't feel that I was properly prepared last time.'

'Even if you are, things don't always work out. What struck me most about the 1500-metres final was the crucial part that luck can play. It's unnerving, really.'

'It's also what makes athletics so intriguing to watch.'

'I thought I'd done it all right for Helsinki, Chris. I trained hard, vetted the men I was up against and even went over to Finland well in advance to get some idea of conditions over there. David Dixon, Nick Stacey and I ran all over the place there and had a wonderful time.' He shook his head. 'Then they popped in that semi-final round. I just never got over that stroke of bad luck.'

'We don't have problems like that this time,' assured Brasher.

'That's true.'

'And one thing is certain, Roger.'

'Is it?'

'Whatever happens at Oxford, you're bound to win.'

Bannister smiled. 'I'd be rather surprised if you or Chris did.'

'So would we,' said Brasher.

They strode on as the drizzle began to intensify.

*

The nightclub was a riot of noise and colour as dozens of young men and women threw themselves about to the music of the band. Schnapps and beer were the preferred drinks and nobody was stinting themselves. There was a wildness and exhibitionism to it all that John Landy found irresistible. As he sat at a table nursing his glass, he watched Denis Johansson leaping about with a blonde girl on the dance floor.

The music ended and his host returned to the table.

'Enjoying yourself, John?'

'Very much.'

'A little livelier than Australia?'

'It certainly is.'

'We are descended from the Magyars, you see,' explained Johansson, pausing to down his drink. 'Hot-blooded, volatile people who like to express their high spirits.'

'So I see.'

'Do you go to nightclubs in Melbourne?'

'Not really.'

'Girls?'

'I never have much time.'

'But you do dance?'

'Not like that. You lot really throw yourselves into it.'

'Of course!' shouted Johansson. 'It is the only way!' He flopped down on his chair and poured another drink from the bottle. 'That is why I like Americans. They know how to have fun.'

'So do Australians. We're always kidding around.'

'But not the British.'

'They never seem to let themselves go.'

'The British are too cold-blooded. I do not have a lot of time for them. But I like you, John.' He slapped the other hard between the shoulder-blades. 'I want us to be friends.'

'We are, Denis.'

'You forgive me those things I say in the press?'

'Yes,' Landy told him. 'They're dead and buried.'

'I said far worse things about Santee before I raced him.'

'No wonder he wanted to beat you.'

'But I like you, John,' insisted the Finn, leaning over so that

Landy could smell the drink on his breath. 'Even though I will run your legs off on the track, I like you.'

'Good.'

'I want you to remember your time in Finland.'

'Oh, I will!'

'Whatever you want, just ask.' The band started up again. 'Ah, you can have a dance now.'

'Er, I'll just sit this one out, thanks.'

'That is no good. You must get on the floor.' He beckoned to the blonde with whom he had been dancing earlier and she ran over. 'I have found a partner for you, John.'

'Perhaps she doesn't want to dance with me,' said Landy shyly. The girl spoke to Johansson in Finnish then giggled. 'What did she say?'

'She likes you, too.'

'I see. That's nice.'

'But she won't think very much of Australian men if you don't dance with her.'

'Well,' decided Landy, 'we can't have that.'

He got up, took the girl's hand and led her into the middle of a mass of writhing couples. Carried away by the excitement and the beat of the music, Landy was soon dancing for all he was worth, clearly relishing the change of pace from his austere training routine.

A couple of hours later he and Johansson were walking home together down a road. Johansson, arm around Landy's shoulder to support himself, was in an amiable mood.

'I told you I would show you something of Finnish culture.'

'Now I know what you meant, Denis.'

'Oh, there is something else.' Johansson stopped and turned to the other. 'I have a small confession to make.'

'Keep it till the morning,' suggested Landy. 'I've had far too much to drink to listen to it now.'

'But it's important. The four-minute mile.'

'What about it?'

'I did not bring you here to run the four-minute mile at all.'

'Yeah, I know. You want me to cart you round the track so that *you* can do it. That's your game, mate.'

'How did you guess?'

Landy laughed. 'You're not the most subtle person, Denis. Besides, you're not interested in breaking world records the way that I do. By running into an area of pain and then taking it from there.'

'That is – what's the word? – masochism!'

'Maybe, but it happens to suit John Landy. But not Denis Johansson. You're only happy to attack records if you can thumb a lift on the way.'

'You've found me out!' said Johansson then he guffawed.

They moved on down the road with the Finn leaning more heavily on his prop now. A police car shot across the intersection ahead.

'That's the second one we've seen,' noted Landy.

'Our police are very busy at this time of night.'

'Why?'

'They have to keep the streets clear of drunks. In this country, they take it very seriously. If you are found drunk on the streets, you can go to jail.'

Landy was alarmed. 'Jail? How long for?'

'A couple of years sometimes.'

'Just for having a few beers too many?'

'Some of our young men go too far. They fight, break windows, that sort of thing. So the police round up the drunks every night.'

'We'd better get home quickly,' suggested Landy.

'They won't touch me,' said the Finn confidently. 'I have always been able to hold my drink like a gentleman.'

Landy hurried him along as fast as he could.

It happened so quickly. One second, Chris Brasher was climbing on Jericho Wall in Clachaig Gully and the next, he had slipped and lost his purchase. His fall was broken by a running belay of nylon rope which absorbed the worst of the impact before it snapped. Brasher landed on his feet and rolled over at the bottom of the gully. Anxiety brought Bannister scrambling back down as quickly as he could.

'Are you all right, Chris?'

'I think so,' said the other a little shamefacedly.

'Nothing broken, is there?'

'No. I'll just have a few nasty bruises, that's all.'

'Thank goodness for that! The last thing we need at the moment is a broken bone.'

'Don't worry about me, will you!' protested Brasher. 'Just worry about the bloody race.'

'I didn't mean it that way, Chris,' said Bannister. He thought for a second then grinned. 'Perhaps I did.'

'You'd make me run in crutches, wouldn't you?'

'Let me help you up.'

Bannister took his arm and helped him up from the ground. They were already soaked to the skin from the rain and Brasher was now plastered in mud. He flexed his arms and legs to make sure that there was no serious injury. It was his pride that had been damaged most.

'And I'm supposed to be the expert!' he said.

'It could have happened to anybody, Chris. The rain has made the rocks so slippery.' Brasher laughed. 'What's the joke?'

'Just look at us, Roger!'

'What?'

'We must be crazy. We're tired, drenched, I've just had a fall, we've both got another nightmare journey of ten hours home . . . What a way to prepare for a four-minute mile!'

'I never thought of it like that, Chris. You're right.'

'Come on,' said the other. 'Let's try again . . .'

Franz Stampfl liked to make informal notes about individual training programmes so that he could monitor the progress of his athletes. Though his relationship with Roger Bannister was too ambiguous to be seen as a normal coach/athlete arrangement, he had still jotted down the pertinent details. As he sat in the drill hall one evening, waiting for his athletes to arrive in force, he glanced through his notes and allowed himself a smile of satisfaction.

The brief respite had worked. Within three days of returning from their holiday in Scotland, Bannister and Brasher had run ten repetition quarters in an average time of 58.09. Chris Chataway, too, had benefited from the lay-off and was achieving the desired target.

Since the resumption of training, the severity was reduced. The emphasis was now on giving the athletes speed and freshness, in getting them to learn how to unleash in four minutes the energy stored up over a long period of training. The record here was also encouraging.

Roger Bannister looked good on paper.

April 14	¾ mile solo time trial in 3.02.0.
April 15	880 yards solo time trial in 1.53.0.
April 16/19	Rock-climbing with Brasher in Scotland.
April 22	10 x 440 yards at average of 58.09.
April 24	¾ mile time trial with Chataway in 3.00.0.
April 26	¾ mile in 3.14.0. 8 minutes' rest. ¾ mile in 3.08.6.
April 28	¾ mile solo time trial in 2.59.9.
April 30	880 yards time trial in 1.54.0.
May 1	Easy 4 miles striding.
May 1/6	Rest until day of race.

The sessions with coffee and cake were over. All that Stampfl could do now was to wait for the great day and to pray for fine weather.

It was now in the lap of the gods.

The ice had now melted to reveal a track that felt moist but firm beneath Landy's spikes. His training regime drew gasps of awe from the young Finnish athletes who watched him. While they could stay with him for the first couple of quarters, they could not match his recovery rate between sprints and were soon left panting in his wake. At the end of a session Landy was bombarded with questions in broken English.

'How often you train?'
'Every day.'
'How long you rest in winter?'
'I don't. I keep at it. Maintenance work.'
'You use weights?'
'All the time.'
'How many miles you run a month?'
'About two hundred.'

'Who was last man to beat you in race?'

'I can't remember.'

Landy's natural charm and readiness to answer their inquiries made him very popular among the local athletes. He remembered only too well that it was in this same country that he had been able to approach Zatopek and learn so much from the Czech.

At the end of one session Johansson touched on this point.

'Every athlete models himself on his favourite runner.'

'Up to a point,' conceded Landy.

'Wes Santee followed on from Glenn Cunningham. Over in England, Roger Bannister was influenced by Sydney Wooderson and maybe also by Jack Lovelock. Then there is you.'

'It was Zatopek's *attitude* that I tried to copy,' admitted Landy. 'That ferocious single-mindedness. It impressed me a lot at Helsinki. The other thing I liked was the fact that he had the guts and the strength to win a race from the front.'

'That is a bad habit to pick up from him, John,' warned Johansson.

'Why?'

'Because the positional runner always has the advantage over the front-runner.'

'I don't agree, Denis.'

'It is obvious,' said the Finn. 'When you run a tactical race you can keep an eye on everyone else and choose the right moment to make your break. But when you are out in front you see nobody.'

'You don't need to,' replied Landy.

'But what if someone sneaks up behind you?'

'If you're strong enough and confident enough, that can't happen. Listen, do you remember the 1500-metres final at Helsinki?'

'Of course.'

'Werner Lueg went into that race as world record-holder. I remember saying to Ray Weinberg, a friend of mine, that Lueg ought to run the race from the front in the knowledge that nobody else could touch that time of his. If I'd been him,

222

that's what *I'd* have done. Instead of which, Lueg runs a tactical race and gets beaten into third place by Barthel and McMillen.'

'I still say that front-running is too dangerous.'

'Not if you can live with the danger,' rejoined Landy.

'John, it's so *lonely* out there.'

'That's the attraction.'

Two days later Landy had an opportunity to state his case in public. The first meeting of the season drew a sizeable and very knowledgeable crowd to the stadium in Turku. There were a few international runners in the mile race and although it was only the start of the Finnish season they expected to cause their Australian visitor a few problems. It did not work out quite like that.

Landy exposed their lack of race fitness from the start. Going to the front almost immediately, he let them trail him for two laps before turning on full power. The second half of the race was simply an extended sprint by a supreme athlete at the height of his powers. Connoisseurs of middle-distance running, the Finnish spectators stood to applaud a superb exhibition of miling and Denis Johansson, watching from the infield, was glad that he had not competed. When Landy surged through the tape the nearest man was more than a hundred yards behind.

'That was wonderful!' congratulated Johansson.

'All done from the front,' answered Landy, who did not seem at all taxed by his exertions. 'It may be lonely out there but it's safe.'

His time was 4.05.3. It had been set on an unfamiliar track during his first race for weeks and against opposition that was totally anonymous. When the time was announced the applause increased.

Landy acknowledged it with a grin all over his face. It had been a vital race for him. On a fast track and in calm atmospheric conditions, he had found it all remarkably easy. Without any real effort he had achieved a respectable time. With real competition he knew just how much faster he could go.

The grin remained for a long time. John Landy could see a vision of another mile race on the same track. He was now absolutely certain that he would break through the four-minute barrier at Turku.

And it would happen fairly soon.

Chapter Seventeen

Thursday, 6 May, 1954.

He had another bad night. Restless with anxiety, he awoke more than once to find that he was perspiring freely. Not long after dawn he got up and crossed to the bedroom window to look out. His heart sank. It was a grey, sombre day and the wind was gusting fiercely. In a race, those conditions would rob him of valuable seconds that he simply could not spare. There was no margin for error.

Roger Bannister's immediate reaction was to consider postponing the attempt altogether. It would be difficult enough to penetrate the four-minute barrier in good weather. To try to do it on such a blustery day would turn a calculated risk into a madcap enterprise that was doomed to fail.

He tested his ankle. He had turned it slightly the day before on a polished floor at St Mary's Hospital. It would be ironic if his fitness were impaired by an incident that took place at one of the most famous medical centres in the country. But the ankle seemed fine. No twinges, no discomfort. It was some reassurance.

After breakfast with his parents, he packed his running gear into a bag and went off to the hospital, determined to stick to his normal routine in the hope that it would keep his mind off what lay ahead. To avoid any journalists, Bannister planned to catch a train from Paddington at noon and go up to Oxford early. Rumours about his scheduled attempt had been floating around Fleet Street for days and he had been pestered unmercifully.

Bannister had never enjoyed the happiest of relationships with the press. A private man with a distaste for publicity, he liked to be allowed to get on with his running and not to have it constantly monitored in the headlines. Some British athletes, like Gordon Pirie, courted controversy by making bold predictions about their performances on the track or by offering trenchant criticism of the state of athletics in general. Bannister, by contrast, fought shy of the press conference. He was a Corinthian, a true amateur, a man for whom running was at once a recreation and a preparation for life.

Again, he had never admired Fleet Street's ability to shift between praise and condemnation with no intermediate stops. He was either being hailed as a hero or a villain, the brilliant young miler claiming another record or the misguided athlete who had let his country down at Helsinki.

He had enough to worry about with the weather. He did not want the gale-force wind of the British press blowing in his face as well.

'Roger.'

'Yes?'

'Telephone call for you.'

'Who is it?'

'Someone from the *Express*.'

'Tell them I'm not available.'

'Right.'

Several journalists tried to reach him at the hospital but he kept them at bay. When his morning's work was completed he slipped off to Paddington Station and caught the Oxford train.

'Hello, Roger.'

'Oh. Hello.'

'I thought I would go up early so that I could check the weather conditions. And I want to spend some time with the others.'

Bannister was surprised but not displeased to find Franz Stampfl in the compartment. The Austrian was sitting quietly by a window. On the rack above his head, his duffel coat and flat cap testified to the cold that he was anticipating at Iffley Road. The meeting was not due to commence until 5 p.m. and the mile race, as the ninth event in the programme, was scheduled for an hour later. It was unlikely that it would be any warmer at that time of the evening.

'How do you feel?'

'Fine.'

'Nervous?'

'A bit.'

'Have the press been bothering you?'

'They've tried.'

They made light conversation and then the train started up, puffing its way noisily out of the grimy station and dispersing the pigeons with the venom of its steam. The ugly back gardens of suburban London soon came into view.

Both men felt the uneasiness.

Though Bannister needed advice he did not seem able to ask for it. Years of solo endeavour had reinforced his doctrine of self-reliance and he had never pretended that Stampfl was his coach in the accepted sense. He respected the Austrian enormously and had found his help critical, but he could never bring himself to make that commitment to the idea of being coached that Brasher had made.

Stampfl had his pride. He was not a person to force his opinions on anyone. Much of the assistance he had given to Bannister had been covert and indirect, though no less effective for that. Stampfl was only too willing to offer his counsel but only if it were sought. A highly-strung person like Bannister needed delicate handling so that he did not feel he was being pushed into anything. Stampfl decided to bide his time. If the opportunity arose he knew what he would say.

The train thundered on across some points.

Rain began to fleck the windows. The sky was darker than ever and the wind still blew with unabated ferocity. Bannister looked out through the glass in a mood of dejection.

'It's dreadful out there!'

'This is England.'

'Just look at it!'

'You never know. It may improve.'

'Not according to the forecast.' There was a long pause. 'It's hopeless to expect that I can do it today.'

'Why?' asked Stampfl calmly.

'Because this wind is bound to slow me right down.'

227

'It may take half a second off you per lap but you could still finish in under four minutes.'

'I don't think there's a chance.'

'I do, Roger,' said the other quietly. 'You're capable of running a mile in 3.56. Even allowing for time lost because of the conditions, that will still get you home and dry.'

Bannister sighed. 'I wish I could believe that.'

'Then look at your time trials. Look at your consistency. You're a stronger and faster runner than you were last year, Roger. You must have felt that, surely?'

'Yes, I have.'

'So? Get out there and run. Ignore the conditions.'

'I can't ignore them, Franz. They're a critical factor.'

'Only if you let them be.' Stampfl smiled his encouragement. 'It is all in the mind, my friend. If you have the right mental attitude, you can overcome *any* adversity. Wind, rain, whatever. Believe that you can do it and you will.'

'I'm not so sure,' admitted Bannister.

'Oh, come on now. You're a medical man. I don't need to tell you about the power of the mind, surely?'

'I suppose not,' conceded the other.

'When the body is in pain,' explained Stampfl, 'it reacts against that pain to reduce it. When an athlete hits the threshold of the pain barrier, his natural response is to pull back. But does he? No, something drives him on to withstand that pain and to conquer all his normal instincts. His mind!'

They talked on together as fields and houses and stations raced past the windows. Stampfl's reasoned and persuasive arguments were slowly convincing Bannister. The latter's doubts were not erased but they were at least subdued.

'You simply must take a shot at it, Roger,' urged Stampfl.

'Must I?'

'Postpone it this time and you may never get another chance. You could pull a muscle or go off the boil or find even worse conditions facing you. Also, there is Wes Santee plotting his attack on four minutes over in America. And John Landy doing the same in Finland.'

'I know,' said Bannister ruefully.

'Listen to me,' added the Austrian, leaning forward. 'If you

228

don't do it now, you'll never do it and you'll bitterly regret it for the rest of your life!'

It was the most persuasive argument yet.

The secret was out. Iffley Road Running Ground was invaded by an army of sportswriters and photographers. A BBC film camera was set up in the middle of the track. All pretence that this was another routine clash between the Amateur Athletic Association and Oxford was now abandoned. Wrapped in raincoats, swathed in scarves and huddled under umbrellas, over 1200 spectators were crammed into the tiny stadium to attend upon what they hoped would be a great event. Other items in the programme dwindled into insignificance beside the mile race, which came to seem like the rationale behind the whole meeting.

Bannister's doubts multiplied when he saw it all.

On his arrival at Oxford he had gone to lunch with Charles Wenden, friend, athlete and now Bursar at All Souls' College. Mrs Wenden had prepared a ham salad and stewed prunes for Bannister and he ate the meal gratefully. Unable to relax, he had then sought out Chataway to tell him that they must call off the attempt. Chataway had told him to leave the decision until 5 p.m.

As he looked around now, Bannister made that decision. He could not go through with it. To fail spectacularly in the glare of such publicity would be humiliating. Rain lashed down and the wind whipped on. It would be folly to expect to beat four minutes in such hostile conditions. When he went into the wooden changing rooms to get ready, Bannister felt that there could be only one course of action.

It was off.

'What am I going to say, Franz?'

'Tell him to wait another half-hour.'

'He thinks it's pointless.'

'Tell him to have more faith in himself.'

Chris Brasher had run over to Stampfl to ask his advice. He went back to the changing rooms to have another go at persuading Bannister that a four-minute mile was still viable. Franz Stampfl gave a philosophical smile. He was coaching by remote control yet again.

'He says it's definitely off, Franz.'

'Ask him to hang on just a little longer.'

'It's the wind that's putting him off.'

'Tell him that it won't make all that much difference.'

It was Chris Chataway's turn to run out for fresh advice. The two pacemakers were finding it impossible to convince Bannister to go ahead with the attempt. They were applying to Franz Stampfl for more ammunition to use.

'He just doesn't have enough confidence, Franz.'

'Remind him about all the training you've done.'

'We have but he's still not persuaded.'

'Then tell him what I told him on the train,' urged the coach. 'If he's serious about wanting to run inside four minutes, he simply has to take this chance. He won't get another.'

'Now or never.'

'That's the message, Chris. Now or never!'

But it still did not bring Bannister around.

When he came out with the others at 5.30 p.m. to begin his warm-up he was plagued by the same misgivings. Brasher trotted over to him and put a hand on his shoulder.

'We've got to go for it, Roger.'

'We've *got* to!' reinforced Chataway.

Bannister mouthed a positive 'no' and moved away.

An additional problem intruded. Rain which had eased off since the meeting had begun now returned with a vengeance. There was a heavy shower that scoured the whole stadium and left the athletes looking quite bedraggled. To Bannister it was a final, deciding factor.

While he was agonizing the other events continued. Oxford were struggling against a superior team but Boyd drew cheers from the home crowd by winning a spirited 880-yards race for the university. Immediately before the mile race, Higham gave Oxford more cause to applaud when he recorded a splendid time in the high hurdles to lose by a matter of inches to Hildreth of the AAA.

The storm had now ended. Against a slate-grey sky a beautiful double rainbow arched over the church that stood beyond the ground. And then – suddenly, unaccountably, miraculously – the wind dropped and the flag of St George went limp on its pole.

Brasher and Chataway took fresh heart at once.

'Yes, Roger!'

'We must, we must!'

'Come on!'

'We *have* to!'

Bannister, however, shook his head once more then loped off on his last warm-up run. The pacemakers stood there helplessly. With only a couple of minutes left before the race there was nothing else that they could do. They looked balefully across at Franz Stampfl but it was too late even for his persuasive tongue.

Then Bannister came trotting back to the starting line.

'Yes,' he said.

It was on.

Six names were listed in the programme to run in the mile race: R. G. Bannister, C. J. Chataway, W. T. Hulatt and C. W. Brasher represented the AAA while G. F. Dole and A. D. Gordon wore the university vest.

All the attention, however, was focused on one athlete.

Roger Bannister, a true embodiment of the amateur ideal, an Oxford man who had helped to create the very track on which the race was being run, a tall, thin, elegant miler in the classical tradition.

Tension was so high among the competitors that there was a false start. At the second time of asking, they were away. Chris Brasher took the lead as pre-arranged, with Chataway and Bannister tight in behind him. After five days of rest they were now fresh and able to release the energy that had been built up over so many months of preparation.

The lay-off, however, had another result. It affected Bannister's judgement of pace. Though Brasher was running to schedule, the overwrought Bannister felt that they were going too slow.

'Faster!' he called. 'Faster, Chris!'

The time for the first quarter was 57.04.

Bannister continued to urge his friend on but the pacemaker did not even hear him. He was far too preoccupied with maintaining his rhythm and forward impulsion. They came down the home straight for the second time and Stampfl leaned out from the infield to yell his advice to Bannister.

'Relax! Take it easy!'

The time at the second quarter was 1.58. Bang on target.

As they went into the back straight Brasher knew that his task was done and he waited for Chataway to relieve him. It seemed like an age before the carrot-coloured hair swept past him with Bannister in tow. Demonstrating his characteristic attack once again, Chataway led the way to the starting line once more.

The time at the third quarter was 3 minutes 0.4 seconds.

Bannister was one-tenth of a second behind that time. To break through the four-minute barrier he had to run the last quarter in 59.4. He was running smoothly and the effort was barely perceptible but a question now tormented him. Chataway was slowing. Did Bannister pass him now, on the bend, with 350 yards to go? Or did he wait another 100 yards and overtake in the back straight?

He stuck to plan. Keeping close to his pacemaker as they raced down the back straight with the wind at their back, he chose his moment and then kicked. Like an uncoiled spring he shot forward into the lead and went for home. A concerted roar from the crowd and the other athletes carried him around the bend and into the finishing straight. He was now running on the rim of history.

Head high, fair hair streaming, face tight, chest thrust forward, long arms pumping hard, Bannister surged on majestically. His slashing stride was taking him where no human being had ever been before and his ambition to do one thing in life supremely well was now on the verge of fulfilment.

There was no pain. Just a strange unity between body and mind that drew him forward down the long avenue to the tape. One final thrust, one final stab at the impossible, one final act of madness.

And he was there.

Exhaustion ambushed him at once. While Bannister collapsed into the arms of his friend, the Rev. Nicholas Stacey, the whole stadium acclaimed what had been a run of epic proportions by a British miler. He had forced himself to breaking point and now had to be supported as he gulped and sagged and suffered the tortures that had stayed their hand during the race itself. It was minutes before he could muster up enough breath for one hoarse question.

'Did I do it?'

'I think so,' said Stampfl.

But the official confirmation still did not come.

Arms around the shoulders of two friends, Bannister now had to endure the additional agony of waiting to hear if his headlong run into physical oblivion had been worth it. When the loudspeaker eventually crackled, a silence descended on the crowd.

Norris McWhirter, who was on duty as the results announcer, only increased the suspense. In a calm, flat, unemotional voice he read out the result that had brought them all to Oxford that day.

'Ladies and gentlemen, here is the result of event number nine, the one mile. First, number forty-one, R. G. Bannister, of the Amateur Athletic Association and formerly of Exeter and Merton Colleges, with a time which is a new meeting and track record and which, subject to ratification, will be a new English native, British national, British all-comers, European, British Empire and world record. That time is THREE . . .'

Exultation drowned out the rest of the announcement. Bannister hugged his two pacemakers then waved to the crowd. Friends, journalists and photographers swarmed around him. Franz Stampfl looked on and smiled.

The mythical barrier of four minutes had at last been breached.

Roger Bannister's time had been 3.59.4.

He had done it.

Initial celebrations took place at Vincent's, the club frequented largely by Oxford's sportsmen which takes its name from the printer's shop below its premises. When Bannister had been first elected to the club he had been almost too shy to visit it. Three years later he had become President of Vincent's and realized what an enjoyable and valued institution it was. Now he entered it in triumph.

'Well done, Roger!'

'What will you have?'

'Break out the champagne!'

'Fantastic achievement!'

'Out of this world!'

Bannister's first need was to replace some of the salt that he had lost during the race and so he drank a saline solution out of a wine glass. Chataway and Brasher toasted him but Bannister insisted on paying tribute to them first. Without their pacemaking and their readiness to make the attempt in such unfavourable conditions, he knew that he would never have made it.

Journalists continued to surround him for interviews and quotes but the most persistent voice came from a BBC sports reporter.

'We've got a car waiting outside, Roger,' he said. 'We'll drive you straight to London in time to get you on *Sportsview*. All you have to do is to sit in front of the cameras and say a few words. Nothing else to it.'

'I don't know,' replied Bannister shyly.

'Go on, Roger,' urged Chataway. 'Speak to the nation first and then we'll hit the town.'

'Yes, don't be a spoilsport,' added Brasher.

'But it's not *that* extraordinary,' argued Bannister. 'Someone was bound to do it sooner or later.'

'Yes, but you're the one who happens to have done it,' the BBC man pointed out. 'Please say you'll come.'

Chataway laughed. 'He's the world's most reluctant hero.'

'No, I'm not, Chris.'

'You're famous now, Roger, and you're stuck with it.'

'And don't give us all that stuff about it being nothing special,' warned Brasher with a broad grin. 'If it wasn't so important to you, why have you spent over seven years of your life trying to do it?'

Chataway slapped his back. 'Get down to London and do your duty ... Oh, and don't forget to mention that I came second!'

Everybody in the room was encouraging him to go and he finally gave in. He finished his drink and turned to the BBC man.

'All right, I'll go and play the hero. But this is the first and the last time.'

'Don't you believe it!' said Brasher.

'Off we go, Roger,' added Chataway. 'I'll be driving right on your tail. You're the pacemaker this time.'

'Okay. Cheerio, everybody . . .'

The entire room shouted its farewell to Bannister.

Minutes later he was being driven at speed along the A 40 in a blue sports car. Leading the cavalcade of vehicles that followed was an old pre-war Austin with Chris Chataway at the driving wheel.

He removed his cigar to beam at the world in general.

'We did it!' he yelled then beeped the horn in triumph.

The Oxford Union filled up that evening for another debate. Before it could begin, however, a young man rose to make a suggestion.

'I move that the House adjourns for three minutes, fifty-nine and four tenths seconds . . .'

The laughter went on for almost that long.

Ralph Bannister and his wife sat in front of their television and watched the familiar credit sequence of *Sportsview*. After a last-minute decision to see the race in Oxford they had come back home to Harrow to see his interview. Strident theme music played and a stopwatch appeared with its second-hand circling rapidly. Superimposed on the face of the watch was a rapid montage of sporting action. As the sequence ended the smiling, moustached face of Peter Dimmock told the viewers that the programme had exclusive film of the first-ever sub-four-minute mile.

The Bannisters watched with pride and fascination as the film was shown. Their son's face then came up on the screen. He was sitting in a corner of the studio with an interviewer and had clearly enjoyed the recording of his historic run at Iffley Road.

'Congratulations, Roger,' said the interviewer.

'Thank you.'

'The whole world will be celebrating your achievement but there will, of course, be especial delight here in Britain.'

'I'm glad about that.'

'Tell us about the race.'

'The main problem was the weather. We were worried about the very strong winds which might slow us down so much that we would not be able to run it under four minutes.' He smiled at the camera. 'I particularly wanted someone from this country to do it . . .'

'And you did, son,' said Ralph Bannister.

Later that night, having shaken off the pursuing newshounds, Bannister, Chataway and Brasher slipped into the Royal Court Theatre in Sloane Square. Unrecognized by theatre patrons who were flooding out, they went upstairs to Clement Freud's club for a very special dinner together. Chataway and Brasher were accompanied by their girlfriends and an attractive, fair-haired young woman in an off-the-shoulder green gown soon arrived to sit beside Bannister. Seated in a dark corner, they enjoyed the meal and savoured their success.

It was an appropriate venue. Just down the road, but now closed for the night, was Lyons' Corner House. This was an occasion that merited rather more than coffee and cakes.

They ate and drank and danced until the club finally shut down then went off to Chataway's car. It had not been designed to accommodate six laughing adults but they squeezed in somehow.

'Where now?' asked Brasher.

'Home?' suggested Bannister.

'The night is young yet!' announced Chataway. 'Come on, we'll see if we can find another place. I think I know one . . .'

The car drove off and meandered through the streets until it eventually finished up in Piccadilly Circus. Chataway pulled up and lowered his window to beckon a policeman over.

'Lost your way, sir?'

'Yes, constable. Isn't there a club around here that's still open at this time of night? It's called the –'

'I know what it's called, sir,' interrupted the policeman with a frown. 'You gentlemen are no gentlemen if you take these ladies to *that* club.'

The remark caused a lot of hilarity inside the car. Bending

236

over to peer in at the passengers, the policeman reached up to his top pocket to take out his notebook and pencil. They fell silent as they feared that they might be booked. But a smile softened the constable's face.

'Perhaps I can have your autographs, gentlemen?'

Chapter Eighteen

To a man with such a keen interest in the natural world as John Landy had, Finland was an inexhaustible source of wonder. After visiting endless low, forested hills and ridges, he saw something of the bare-topped fells further north. Much of the landscape was raw and untamed with an occasional town or village thrown in as an afterthought. He was impressed with the high quality of the farming and found as much time as he could to discuss agricultural problems with the Finnish farming community. In addition to a holiday and a chance to run on first-rate tracks, he was improving his knowledge in his chosen field.

Most of all, perhaps, he had come to love the lakes.

'I didn't believe you when you told me there were sixty thousand of them in Finland,' he admitted.

'At least that number, John.'

'That must mean you're more water than land.'

'In some parts of the country that is absolutely true.'

'It's marvellous!' decided Landy. 'You can have your own private lake up here and nobody would ever bother you.'

They were sitting in a skiff on the placid waters of a lake to the north of Turku. Denis Johansson was pulling on the oars and taking them along at a leisurely pace towards the far shore. After spending so many wild nights at bars in Johansson's company, Landy was glad of a more muted expedition.

'Does it worry you that much, John?'

'What?'

'The news.'

'Oh that . . . No, not really. Good luck to the bloke, I say!'

'Yes,' agreed Johansson. 'I am not a big fan of Roger Bannister but I take my hat off to him. You have got to admire an athlete who can run a mile that fast.' He smiled ruefully. 'I only wish he had waited until I had beaten four minutes first.'

'That was my feeling as well!' added Landy with a laugh. 'The funny thing is that it doesn't hurt as much as I thought it would. I mean, I'm still disappointed that it wasn't me – I wouldn't be human if I wasn't. But I've sort of coped with the idea quite easily.'

'Why is that?'

'Because I'm having such a bloody great time here, mate!'

'Good.'

'It's true, Denis. If I'd been stuck at home in Melbourne with no chance of a race for months, I'd have been pole-axed by the news. But not here somehow. It doesn't seem as massively important to me as it did back home.'

'I'm glad Finland has done something for you, John.'

'There is another way of looking at it, though.'

'Is there?'

'Yes,' explained Landy. 'If I hadn't come to Turku, then Bannister mightn't have been pushed into having another go at four minutes. I bet he was dead scared that I might beat him to it.' He laughed again. 'He's proved one thing, anyway. It is possible. And now that Bannister has opened the door the rest of us can charge through it.'

'I want to be first in the queue,' confessed Johansson. He rested on his oars and grimaced slightly. 'If only it hadn't been a British athlete!'

'Why do you say that?'

'Because they will have to crow about it, John.'

'Wouldn't you?'

'Of course. I'd tell everyone how wonderful I was!'

'But you do that anyway,' joked Landy.

'It's different with the British,' continued Johansson. 'They have this lordly attitude. As if they were somehow better than the rest of us. And they will rub our faces in this four-minute mile.'

'The Poms might but Bannister himself won't. Too shy.'

'How well do you know him, John?'

'Oh, not very well at all. Met him briefly in England when we first arrived. Some track in Paddington, I think.'

'What about Helsinki?'

'Hardly spoke to the fella there even though we ran in the same heat of the 1500. No, he kept himself to himself there. I did spend a bit of time with Chataway, though.'

'Oh?'

'Yes,' recalled Landy. 'I broke this 2-mile record in England and Chataway couldn't really believe it. Came and chatted to me about it. Pleasant bloke.' He chuckled. 'Though he obviously thought I was just another colonial upstart.'

'They are such a strange people, the British,' said Johansson. 'This terrible class thing. You just don't get it in America. Nor in your country, really. But over there!'

'I know. I wonder if it's that damn class system that's made poor old Bannister like he is.'

'What do you mean?'

'Well, you get your upper-class fellas. Your blokes like Lord Burghley and that who are born to it. Chataway has a touch of it as well. You know, this sort of relaxed, English public school charm.'

'Except that it's not very charming.'

'Then you get your ordinary guys. Bill Nankeville, say. Jim Peters.'

'Or Gordon Pirie.'

'Yes. Pirie's an even better example. Doesn't give a stuff. Just goes ahead and does his own thing.'

'A bit like you Australians!'

'Maybe,' conceded Landy. 'Anyway, you've got your blokes in the middle like Bannister. They come from good backgrounds but not all that swish so they've had to work to make it. Those people are always sort of brittle and defensive.' He hunched his shoulders. 'Ah well, that's only my theory. Bannister's a likeable person when he's had a few beers. Good, honest bloke.'

'If only he hadn't run that bloody four-minute mile!' complained the Finn, lifting his oars again. 'I wanted it for *me*!'

'It's not the end of it, Denis.'

'What?'

'We've still got a challenge left. *I* have, anyway.'

'Challenge?'

'Yes,' affirmed Landy. 'I can't beat Bannister to four minutes now. But I'll do my damnedest to take that world record off him.'

Johansson laughed his agreement and rowed them to the shore.

Wes Santee lounged on a chair in the sun and concentrated on his paperback novel. He did not see Bill Easton come up to him and did not even look up when the coach sat down beside him.

'It must be one hell of a good book, Wes.'

'What?' He glanced up. 'Oh, sorry.'

'What are you reading?'

Santee handed the paperback over. 'Norman Mailer. *The Naked and the Dead.* I finally caught up with it.'

'What's it like?'

'Terrific! That guy's got a real way with words.'

'I don't read many war stories.'

'This one's great,' said Santee. 'Though it sure puts you off the idea of joining the military. They go through hell.'

'Can't be any worse than being on the college relay team.' He handed the book back. 'You sent that cable yet?'

'Yeah. Right away.'

'Good.'

'Bannister deserves it. I'm as mad as hell at him for doing it first but you got to hand it to the guy.'

'Sure.'

'That time is still not as low as it can be run but it was a great performance. Even if he did use rabbits.'

'They were clever this time,' noted Easton. 'It was a *bona fide* race so they stayed within the rules. Just.' He gave Santee a playful punch. 'Anyway, don't let it get you down. The cards were always stacked against you.'

'I know,' accepted Santee resignedly. 'It was a shock at first but it's wearing off. I just sure would love to run against that guy some time! Especially now.'

'We got other targets, Wes.'

'Yeah – more relays.'

'A few, maybe. But I want us to spend more time on the 1500.'

'Suits me, coach.'

'You'll be running in Compton in a few weeks. One of those fast Californian tracks you always do well on.'

'That race has got my name on it, coach.'

'I think you can manage more than a win, Wes.'

'You want me to throw in a national record as well?' asked Santee with an obliging grin. 'Why not?'

'You'll be up against some good athletes at Compton,' said the coach. 'They could give you something to fight against.'

'I sure need it.'

'Then use it to your advantage, Wes. You've been waiting for the big time long enough. It's time to go out there and grab yourself a piece of the action.'

'What are you saying, coach?'

'You lost your chance to beat four minutes. Bannister got there first and you've got to respect the guy for that.' He looked hard into Santee's eyes. 'Let's make him respect *you* now, Wes. When you get out on that track, don't just settle for a national record.'

'All the way?' He was excited by the idea.

Easton nodded. 'I think you can do it.'

'Well, I'll give it my best shot, anyway! We got to work on this, coach. We got to work on it like I never worked before!'

Norman Mailer had been cast aside for the rest of the day.

Franz Stampfl flicked through the press coverage of the mile race at Iffley Road. With the impetus of a long-jumper, Roger Bannister had leapt from the sports pages to land right in the middle of the front pages. Every newspaper featured the story as a British triumph and all of them spent more time describing the actual race than looking at the intensive preparation that went into it. As an Austrian he found some of the jingoistic attitudes rather offensive but he had learned to get along with such things in his adopted country. What he still found difficult to accept, however, was what he saw as the national inability to give credit where it was due.

The names of Christopher Brasher and Christopher Chataway appeared with justifiable frequency but there was no mention of the months spent at the Duke of York's Barracks or of the critical decisions taken around a table in a Lyons' café.

Stampfl looked again at a front page which typified press reaction. Bannister had eclipsed everything. Beside the running of a sub-four-minute mile, even peace overtures from Molotov, tantrums from Aneurin Bevan and the imprisonment in Buenos Aires of a British journalist were minor events. The triumph was something to shout about.

AT LAST – THE 4-MINUTE MILE
Bannister Does It
English Victory Beats World

The dream of world athletes was achieved yesterday by an Englishman – 25-year-old Roger Bannister, who became the first man on earth to run a mile in under four minutes.

His feat at Oxford last evening – against a 20-mile-an-hour cross-wind – was equal in dramatic achievement to the crashing of the sound barrier.

YES, I MIGHT DO EVEN BETTER
by Roger Bannister

I have never felt so good in all my life and I am so glad it took an Englishman to do this thing before America's Wes Santee and the other chaps got down to it.

Three photographs adorned the front page. The main one, hanging beneath the banner headline like a Union Jack, showed Bannister at the instant when he broke the tape, head back, mouth open, fatigue imminent. A smaller photograph showed his limp body being held by friends and surrounded by anxious faces.

But it was the third photograph that interested Franz Stampfl. A still exhausted Bannister was being supported by two figures. To his left was a big, hefty man in raincoat, trilby and spectacles; to his right was a concerned individual in duffel coat and check cap.

The caption was the interesting thing.

Bannister, eyes closed, has a support escort. He was the last to
know he had made sports history.

In the duffel coat, Bannister's adviser, Franz Stampfl. On the
right, George Truelove, A A A team manager.

'Adviser!' murmured Stampfl with wry amusement. 'Well,
that's something, I suppose . . .'

The camp at Portsea was a scene of peak activity as athletes did
out-of-season training in preparation for the Empire Games.
Presiding over it all with his usual air of manic commitment,
Percy Cerutty drove his men on to realize their full potential.
Publicity was an important factor and he made sure that he
got plenty of it.

'How often do they run up that big sandhill?'

'Every day.'

'Someone told me that you only use that when press photographers come down here.'

'Then that someone is a bloody liar!'

Jill Webster had paid a visit to Portsea to study Cerutty's
training methods at first hand. She found him as prickly as
ever.

'What's your view about the four-minute mile?'

'I'm still waiting for someone to do it properly.'

'Don't you recognize Bannister's achievement?'

'I recognize that he ran four quarters with the help of
pacemakers. That was no proper race!' He snorted with
contempt. 'The last two runners didn't even bother to finish.'

'Only because the track was invaded by the crowd.'

'I still say it was illegal!'

'But the record has been ratified, Mr Cerutty.'

'Yes!' shouted the other. 'And that's the difference between
Britain and us. Do you know, I watched a shot putter break
an Australian national record last January only to have it
disallowed by the zombies who run athletics in this damn
country. And *why*?'

'Because they said the throwing circle wasn't perfectly
round.'

'Exactly. In Britain that record would've stood and the fella
would've been a hero. Down here they go out of their way to

make him feel like a cheat.' He waved an angry arm. 'The attitude in Australia is so damn *negative*!'

They were on the beach. Although a persistent wind was blowing in their faces it was still warm enough for a stroll. In the distance a group of athletes could be seen on their morning run to the rock pool at Sorrento further up the coast. Out in the bay several yachts were skimming over the water.

Jill Webster continued. 'Officialdom here has come in for a fair bit of criticism lately.'

'And so it should!'

'What was your view of this Shirley Strickland business?'

'Disgraceful!'

'You think she should be in the team for the Empire Games?'

'Of course. Strickland is the best hurdler in the world. You don't win an Olympic gold medal unless you've got one hell of a good motor under your bonnet.'

'You haven't always been the most enthusiastic supporter of women's athletics,' noted Jill.

'I believe that running is primarily a case of man against man in a basic physical contest.' His index finger did some pointing exercises. 'But that doesn't mean I don't sympathize with Strickland. The way they've treated her is bloody disgusting.'

And he proceeded to tell her why. In full Technicolor.

Shirley Strickland's illustrious career had hit a road block. After taking time off the previous year to give birth to her son, she resumed training and, well before the deadline for entries, she was twice able to manage the hurdles qualifying time for Vancouver.

Troubled by influenza at the Australian Championships in February, she did not run in the 100 metres and was unplaced in the hurdles following a break which the starter failed to notice. Shirley Strickland remained on the blocks and waited for a recall gun that was never fired.

Since she had failed to get a place in either event she had been omitted from the Empire Games team. Officials added insult to injury by telling her that she had not been selected because she had not made the qualifying time. Yet she had done so twice in December. When it was revealed that one of the hurdlers chosen instead of her had not, in fact, run the stipulated qualifying time, press controversy raged for a long while.

'And you know *why* Strickland stood down from the 100 metres at the championships, don't you?' demanded Cerutty. 'Because the Western Australia officials told her to save her strength so they could be sure of a hurdles win.' Both his arms went into the waving routine. 'They forgot to tell the girl that the first four place-getters in the 100 got automatic selection to Vancouver!'

'She's entitled to feel bitter about it,' agreed Jill.

'Bitter! If it was me I'd be suing those bloody officials.'

'Why do you think the Australian Women's Amateur Athletics Union turned down her application to compete in the games at her own expense as an independent?'

'Because they didn't want Strickland around to remind them of the complete mess of it they've made! They didn't want her to show them up by winning a gold medal!' Fury made him strut around in a circle. 'Can you believe it? They would prefer to *lose* than take Strickland with them! How mad can you get?'

'There is another side to it,' returned Jill.

'Is there?' he challenged.

'Strickland is thirty next year. A lot of people think that she might be over the hill.'

'Over the hill!' Cerutty became apoplectic. 'I'm getting on for sixty and I'm not over the bloody hill yet. Strickland will be at her peak for years yet!' He remembered someone else. 'Look at that Fanny Blankers-Koen in the London Olympics. Four gold medals and she was thirty years old and pregnant at the time!'

Jill gave him a few moments to calm down and then they continued their stroll. Though some of her colleagues dismissed Cerutty as a crank, she always enjoyed the cut and thrust of their discussions and she knew that nobody in athletics could provide her with such a fund of pungent quotes.

'What sort of chance do you give our team in Vancouver?'

'Not a very big one. Once again we'll be doing it on the cheap so that will mean they won't have a proper coach.'

'Do you see any definite gold medals among the men?'

Cerutty shrugged. 'Gosper in the 440, maybe. Achurch in the javelin. And Lean could do well in the 440 hurdles.'

'What about Landy?'

'Well, he'll be up against Bannister.'

'Isn't Landy a better competitor?'

'He's a fitter one, I know that. Something I taught him.'

'What advice would you give to him for that race?'

'Oh, he'll run it his way no matter what I say,' retorted Cerutty with irritation. 'Why do people only ever think about Landy? Don MacMillan is going to be in that race in Vancouver as well. I think he could very easily be the dark horse.'

'Do you think Landy will have been upset by the fact that the four-minute mile has been broken by somebody else?'

'Well, he won't be jumping for joy, I know that! Bannister's time will have shaken them all up. Landy, Santee, Barthel, the whole lot. They'll all want to come straight back and take Bannister's world record off him.'

'And will they succeed?'

'Santee might.'

'Not Landy?'

'He's a great runner but I don't think he's got enough killer instinct. I can't see him doing it somehow.'

'But he's running on good Finnish tracks now. And he'll have tough competition from Denis Johansson.'

'Johansson!' Cerutty sneered. 'That bloke could win a gold medal in the Scandinavian Bullshit Championships.' He put an arm around her shoulders. 'Let me tell you something, Jill. If there's one sort of fella I can't stand, it's the kind that shoots his mouth off to the press all the time!'

Jill Webster was proud of her self-restraint.

The conditions were perfect. Fine weather, fast track, testing opposition, large crowd. Wes Santee felt good as he began his warm-up. At the end of his first run he was joined by another competitor in the 1500 metres. The athlete, a wiry negro in a blue vest, was an old acquaintance and track rival. They slapped their right hands together in a greeting.

'Welcome to Compton, man!'

'Thanks.'

247

'I figure it's my turn to beat you today, Wes.'

'No way!'

'Hey, man. What do you think about this Bannister guy? That sure must have been some run over in England. I always thought Wes Santee was going to get there first, though.'

'So did I!' replied the Kansan ruefully. 'But Bannister had something I never did have.'

'Luck?'

'Help.'

'Yeah, those two rabbits.'

'Without them he'd never have done it.' Santee's tone was edged with bitterness. 'Where would I find two Americans who'd do that for *me*? Nobody helps anybody in this goddam country. It's dog eat dog and patriotism can go to hell!'

By the time that he lined up with the others, aggression was surging inside him. He felt strong, positive, sharpened for combat. The gun sent them away and he was into his stride at once, finding himself a comfortable berth near the front of the pack.

The pace was hot. At the end of the first quarter Santee permitted himself a smile. He was going well. Energy was coursing through him. Confidence was high. His will to win was like a flame-thrower inside his head. He was in a real race.

Santee knew he would run faster than ever before.

John Landy came into the changing room with his ovation still ringing in his ears. Before a packed audience at the Turku stadium he had won yet another mile race from the front in emphatic style. Not even Denis Johansson had been able to stay with him over the final lap. It was a fine victory in an excellent time but it had somehow left him very dissatisfied. As he sat on a bench to brood on it all, Johansson joined him. The Finn read his thoughts.

'You are disappointed, John.'

'Only 4.02.8. I've been quicker than that in Melbourne.'

'It is still a good time when you have nobody to push you,' said Johansson. 'I did my best but I am still not as fit as I should be.'

'Try laying off the beer and cigarettes,' joked Landy.

'But they keep me alive, my friend!'

The athletes stripped off and went into the showers with the others. As Landy let the hot water cascade all over him, he felt at once revived and saddened. He was having a wonderful time in Finland and had made many friends but he was still nowhere near achieving the aims that had brought him there in the first place.

'It is a pity we have no snow,' said Johansson.

'Why?'

'After a hot shower like this we could run outside and roll over in it. Very invigorating!'

'I'm sure,' replied Landy. 'I bet that crowd out there would enjoy watching us!'

They laughed, switched off their respective showers and came out to their towels. The Finn could see that his companion's disappointment was still lingering.

'Tonight we will go to a nightclub!'

'I need to get to bed earlier, Denis,' decided Landy. 'It may be these late nights that are slowing me down.'

'But 4.02.8 is hardly slow!'

'It is by my standards. I came to Turku in the hope of running a four-minute mile before Bannister or Santee. And what happens?' He pursed his lips and shook his head. 'Bannister beats me to it and now Santee has just broken the world record for the 1500 over in California.' He turned to the Finn. 'They've *done* something, Denis. I haven't.'

'You've seen much more of our country,' reminded the other.

'Oh yes, and that bit has been fantastic. I love it here. I really believe that I could come and live here.'

'Then why don't you?' invited Johansson. 'You've settled in so well here, John. You're one of us now.'

'My own country still has first claim on me.' A sigh escaped his lips. 'In more ways than one, I'm afraid.'

'What do you mean?'

'Australia is looking to me for something very special, Denis. They want a world-champion miler. I'm expected to deliver the goods.'

'And you will!' encouraged the Finn.

'Not if it goes on like this.'

'All you need is someone to make you run faster.' He walked around naked for a few moments as he considered. Snapping his fingers, he came back to Landy. 'Do what Bannister did!'

'I could never use pacemakers,' insisted Landy.

'You won't have to, John. He used Chataway and you could do the same. Except that in this case, Chataway would be trying to win.' He laughed to himself. 'Do you see? He is a brilliant runner and will give you a close race. I think that Chris Chataway is our man.'

A slow smile spread across Landy's features.

'I think you may be right.'

Chapter Nineteen

Fame intruded more deeply into his life than he had either anticipated or wanted. As well as making him a prime media target, his celebrated run at Iffley Road stadium had turned Roger Bannister into something akin to a national institution. The problem was that the British public expected to be admitted free of charge.

It was difficult for him to walk down a street in London without being recognized and approached, and he had lost count of the number of times he was asked to give impromptu autographs. The pressures of his fame were becoming annoyances. When he could not avoid a public situation, therefore, he learned to minimize the dangers by taking a few precautionary measures.

For an evening meal with Chris Chataway he chose a very quiet restaurant and sat in a corner with his back to the room. Subdued lighting was an extra defence against well-intentioned but tiresome fans. Bannister glanced through the menu as he waited.

'Roger . . .'

'Hello, Chris!'

'Sorry I'm a bit late. Got held up.'

'That's all right. I haven't been here long.'

'Well?' asked Chataway, sitting opposite him. 'How were the exams?'

'Not too bad at all, thanks.'

'Have you passed?'

'The results won't be out for a while, Chris.'

'But you feel cautiously optimistic?' He chuckled as Bannister nodded. 'Good! That calls for a drink.'

He summoned the waiter and they ordered drinks. The man scuttled away through bead curtains at the rear of the restaurant. Chataway turned back to his friend.

'I don't know how you managed it, Roger.'

'What?'

'Studying for your final exams with all that publicity going on. It must have been sheer hell.'

'It was problematical,' agreed Bannister. 'I just had to keep my head down. These exams were pretty vital. I didn't want six years' work to go down the drain.'

'When can we start calling you "doctor"?'

'Not yet.'

They chatted until the drinks arrived then Bannister guided the conversation around to another topic. There was the faintest hint of irritation in his voice.

'I hear you're going across to Finland.'

'Ah, yes. They invited me over.' He sipped his drink. 'I was going to give you a buzz and tell you about it.'

'Will you be running against Landy?'

'That's the general idea.'

'*His* idea, I suppose?'

'No, it was Denis Johansson who set the whole thing up. Turku. They've got quite a flourishing athletics club there.'

Bannister looked into his glass. 'You'll probably push Landy to a very fast time. That's what he's after.'

'Then he's in for a surprise, Roger. I'm going there to run a very fast time myself and not to do Mr Landy any favours.' He produced his familiar, warm grin. 'You said yourself I'd be the next man to beat four minutes. This is my chance.' Bannister remained silent. 'I can see that you don't agree.'

'It's certainly possible, Chris.'

'But you think it's unlikely. Well, stop looking so betrayed,' urged Chataway, shaking the other's arm. 'This is not a conspiracy against *you*. If Landy or anyone else wants a race I'm not going to turn my back on a challenge.'

'It's not in your nature,' said Bannister with a smile.

'My pacemaking days are over, believe me. I was happy to play second fiddle to you at Iffley Road – so was Chris – but we're athletes in our own right with our own careers to consider.'

'I accept that.'

'You have your targets for this season and I have mine.'

'Gold in the 3 miles at Vancouver?'

'That's only for starters, Roger. I want a world record all to myself. Then, of course, we've got the European Championships in Berne. I'll be after my revenge in the 5000.'

'Zatopek?'

'I was too raw and eager at Helsinki. I've learned a lot in the last two years, though, and I'm sure I can turn the tables on him.'

'What about this Vladimir Kuts? The Russians are saying that *he's* the next Zatopek.'

'Never believe Russian propaganda,' suggested Chataway before draining his glass. 'Anyway, I'm ready to take Kuts on or anyone else. Which is why I can't pass up the opportunity of running in Finland.'

'Landy won't be easy to beat,' warned Bannister.

'I wonder. He's been stuck around 4.02 for so long now that he can't get off it. I'm not afraid of him, don't worry. If anybody's going to take your record off you in Turku, it'll be me!'

They laughed then reached for the menu to make decisions.

Franz Stampfl was attending to his own fitness with a series of sit-ups when Harold Abrahams strolled into the drill hall at the Duke of York's Barracks. Abrahams, wearing the dark suit he favoured for his court appearances, put down his briefcase and watched. Stampfl completed his allotted number of sit-ups and paused to regain his breath.

'It's a question I often asked myself, Franz.'

'What is?'

'*Quis custodiet ipsos custodes.*'

'I don't speak Welsh.'

'It's Latin.'

'I know,' said Stampfl, getting up. 'I was joking.'

' "Who will guard the guards themselves?" Or – in your case – who will coach the coaches?'

'You've got your answer now. We coach ourselves.'

A few athletes had arrived to begin their gym work but the session had not really got under way. Abrahams had called in for a chat with Stampfl before the latter was too involved with his duties.

'It still gives one a glow, Franz, doesn't it?'

'Fifty sit-ups?'

'No. Roger Bannister. The four-minute mile.'

'That was last month, Harold. Athletics moves on.'

'It was such a splendid achievement and it gives me such endless pleasure to recall that it was done by an Englishman.'

'Who was helped by an Austrian and paced by someone who was born in Guyana.' Stampfl smiled at Abrahams' surprise. 'Brasher was born in Georgetown. But don't look so alarmed. He's British and not South American.'

'It was so vital that an Englishman got there first.'

'Only to other Englishmen.'

'We could not have chosen a more suitable athlete than Bannister.'

'Oh, I don't know,' said Stampfl. 'Chataway is capable of beating four minutes and Pirie will do it as well one day.'

'That's not what I meant, Franz,' explained the other. 'Roger Bannister epitomizes the amateur ideal. He believes that when sport of any kind is played by selfless amateurs like himself it's a positive force for good in the world. You once called him a romantic and you were right. It's what gives this feat its special lustre.'

Stampfl chuckled. 'You English will hold on to this ridiculous idea of playing the game for the game's own sake! I can see the appeal. You want to make Bannister into an idol. A person who runs the four-minute mile and then casually goes back to his medical lectures.'

'It's the quintessence of the sport, Franz.'

'No, Harold. It *used* to be. Times have changed.'

'Not all that much. We still hang on to certain principles in this country. And they inform our approach to athletics.'

'I know,' agreed Stampfl. 'It's the reason why you got no gold medals in the last Olympics. America and Russia wiped the floor with your so-called "principles". They play the game to *win*.'

'Yes,' rejoined Abrahams forcefully. 'But look how they do

it. Athletics in America is an arm of business and athletics in Russia is an arm of politics. Take your pick – they're both repulsive.'

'You may enjoy the luxury of being high-minded about it, Harold, but changes will have to come here. British athletics is desperately in need of money.'

'You don't need to tell me that,' murmured the other.

'So where does the finance come from: private sponsorship or government? The American way or the Russian way?'

'Neither as long as I have anything to do with it. We don't have to be commercialized or politicized.' About to speak, Stampfl checked himself. Abrahams urged him on. 'Say it, Franz. Go on.'

'As soon as you charge people to watch athletics, you have commercialized it,' argued Stampfl. 'As soon as you have international meetings like an Olympic Games, then politics comes into it.'

'I don't agree.'

'Each country pits itself against the others.'

'Yes, but in the true spirit of the Olympic ideal.'

'I'm sorry but I think that attitude is a little naive today.'

'Not as long as we can produce athletes like Roger Bannister.'

'Now wait a moment, Harold. I don't want to tarnish his image as a model amateur but he did accept advice from a professional coach and he did use two pacemakers in that race.'

'I can see we'll have to agree to differ here.'

'It won't be for the first time.'

Several more athletes had come into the hall and Stampfl broke off to call out instructions to them. Recognizing Abrahams, the athletes got stuck into their respective training routines with real vigour. Stampfl was amused by the sight.

'You must come more often. They all want to impress you.'

'Why not? That's part of the fun of athletics.' He paused to watch a short, stubby young man working out with a pair of dumb-bells. 'What did you think of our Mr Santee?'

'Very impressive. That world record for the 1500 has stood since Haegg set it in 1944. Strand equalled it, so did Lueg, but Santee's the first to crack it.'

'He made so many bold claims in the papers, before failing, that I was beginning to wonder if he'd ever really come good.' Abrahams smiled. 'He's been able to justify his brashness for once.'

'Santee will also beat four minutes one day soon.'

'That only leaves John Landy, then. Bannister and Santee have set their world records. What can Australia do?'

'It really depends on Chataway.'

'Do you think he can win in Turku?'

'On his day he can beat anybody.'

'But the mile is not his best distance,' said Abrahams. 'Over 5000 metres, I'd take him to beat Landy hollow but not over a mile.'

'Chataway is one of the most competitive athletes in this country,' replied Stampfl. 'He's got bags of talent and – what's more important – lots of guts. When he's in the right mood Chataway is a handful over *any* distance.'

'Are you saying that he's going to win?'

Stampfl grinned. 'I'm saying that it'll be an interesting race.'

When Chris Chataway arrived at Turku Airport he found John Landy and Denis Johansson there to greet him. They were soon heading towards the city, which was some thirteen kilometres away.

'It's marvellous that you could come!' remarked Landy.

'I was glad to be asked,' said Chataway. 'How long have you been here, John?'

'Ages. I'm really acclimatized.'

'We have made him an honorary Finn,' observed Johansson. 'He has got used to our ways here and gone along with them.'

'When in Finland do as the Finns do, eh?' noted Chataway.

'They're terrific hosts, Chris,' said Landy. 'As they were in Helsinki. Only even more so when you live amongst them.'

'I'm looking forward to a spot of sightseeing.'

'We'll take you around,' volunteered Landy. 'There's a few days before the race and we can't spend all the time training.'

'Training?' asked Chataway. 'What's that?'

When they had reached the town and shown the Englishman his accommodation, they gave him some time to settle in. That evening found all three of them in a pleasantly noisy bar. Cigar in mouth and brandy on the table in front of him, Chataway relaxed happily in the convivial atmosphere. He nodded towards the other side of the room.

'Who's that ravishing young creature with Denis?'

'I don't know,' said Landy. 'He has so many girlfriends.'

'Bit of a ladykiller, is he?'

'He's a wild bugger, Chris!'

'Nobody could say the same about you,' added Chataway with a grin. 'I'm having a real problem with you.'

'Why?'

'Because I'm finding it very difficult to dislike you.'

'I thought I'd disarm you by asking you out for a few drinks,' explained Landy light-heartedly. 'Show you what a nice guy I am.'

'But you *are* nice – that's the trouble. All that rubbish we've been fed about John Landy being modest and unassuming and gentlemanly turns out to be disgustingly true!'

'No, it's not,' teased the other. 'It's an act.'

'Really?'

'Underneath it all, I'm a killer. I smile when I pass my rivals in a race just to make them feel worse.'

'That's sadism.'

'No, it's the competitive instinct. I've got it just like any other athlete. Most of the time I manage to disguise it.'

'Well in that case,' promised Chataway benignly, 'I'll have no compunction at all about wiping you out.'

They were at ease in each other's company. Music started up and a few couples began to dance. Landy bought another round of drinks then brought them back to the table. Chataway eyed him shrewdly.

'Do you actually like running?'

'Of course. Don't you?'

'I find it rather boring,' confided Chataway. 'Sometimes I think it's a very stupid and pointless thing to do.'

'Then why do it?'

'Because I like beating other runners. It gives me a weird sense of power. I put in all those hours of blood, sweat and grind so that I can go out there and beat some other poor devils.' He rested his cigar in the ashtray while he enjoyed his drink. 'I'm not one of your cold-blooded athletes. I run on emotion. I like to *hate* the other competitors before a race. That way I get more of a kick out of beating them.' He grinned. 'Basically, I'm not a very nice person out on the track.'

'Who is?' asked Landy. 'We're all out there to destroy the other blokes. It's part of the attraction.'

'I want to beat you, Landy,' warned Chataway. 'So let me hate you. Stop being so damned sociable.' He picked up his cigar again and inhaled the smoke. 'Is that why you do it?'

'What?'

'Because of the kick you get from winning?'

'It's one of the reasons.'

'What are the others?'

'Well, it gives me a chance to fulfil myself. Achieve certain ambitions. It gives me tremendous confidence. And then, of course, there's the fun side of it.'

'Fun?'

'In Australia, anyway – and here in Finland. There's this wonderful camaraderie. You're part of a special little group.' He pondered. 'But I suppose the main reason I run is because of the exhilaration I get. When you're going fast and smooth and everything seems to be meshing perfectly, you feel this sort of . . .'

'Aesthetic pleasure?' suggested Chataway.

'Yes. Aesthetic pleasure. You feel that everything's co-ordinating and your body is working as it's meant to work. I think I get as much pleasure out of running like that and improving my times as I do out of winning.'

Chataway laughed. 'You *are* nice, Landy. You've just damned yourself out of your own mouth.'

'Have I?'

'You obviously don't enjoy beating people as much as I do.'

'Maybe not,' agreed Landy with a smirk. 'But I'll thoroughly enjoy beating you, Chris.'

The regime at Portsea Training Camp was exhausting. When Neil Robbins and Les Perry came into the cabin from a session with the weights they were glad to flop down and reach for a bottle of milk. They were spending another weekend with the maker of champions.

'Do you feel conditioned, Les?' asked Robbins.

'Yes, mate. Conditioned to drop.'

'You know Perce's philosophy. We have to push ourselves beyond what we think our capabilities are.'

'I've certainly done that.'

'Me, too.' He drank some milk. 'If only we didn't have to listen to all that stuff about Plato and Wordsworth into the bargain.'

'Ah well, that's Perce, isn't it? Always hunting around in books to pick up a little piece here and a little piece there. I don't believe half of what he says, Neil.' He considered. 'Three-quarters.'

'I'm not sure that *he* does!' They laughed. 'Whenever I have a weekend down here, though, I go back feeling better for it. When the pain wears off, that is.'

'It never does wear off with me.'

They finished their milk and dropped the bottles back into the crate. Robbins looked down at it and became reflective.

'How good do you think he really is, Les?'

'Who?'

'Perce. As a coach.'

'Best in Australia!' affirmed Perry loyally.

'I know but that's not saying much. Top coaches are pretty thin on the ground down here.' There was a pause. 'They say this Arthur Lydiard is damn good, though.'

'He's just another version of Percy Cerutty.'

'Short, mad and bursting with energy.'

'A bit like me,' noted Perry with a grin.

'Lydiard certainly gets results in New Zealand, though. He's brought Murray Halberg right on. What was his time for the mile?'

'Around 4.04. Eight seconds below his best time.'

'And Halberg is still only a kid. Apparently he sometimes helps Lydiard on his milk round in Auckland. It was in this interview he gave. Everybody thinks of Lydiard as this dynamic guy who's always in a hurry. But Halberg said how the guy used to put the bottles back in the crate very gently and drive as quietly as he could so that he wouldn't disturb people who were still asleep. That's a different side to Lydiard altogether.' He chuckled. 'Can you imagine Perce being so considerate on a milk round?'

'He'd bang the bloody bottles together to wake *everybody* up!'

'Yes! And beep the horn!' They got up and went outside again. 'Murray Halberg will be running in Vancouver. We'll be able to see if he's all he's cracked up to be.'

'He won't bother John in the mile,' decided Perry.

'Bannister might, though.'

'Oh, I don't know. When he's in the right mood John Landy will beat anybody.'

'Even the world record-holder?'

'Anybody, Neil. I think that this is the year that John will really come into his own.'

'I hope so,' said Robbins. 'But he seems to be taking his time about it. He needs to get a move on.'

It was a beautiful evening. Warm, crisp and clear in the Scandinavian twilight. Six thousand spectators were jammed into the little stadium in Turku. Expectation was high. The main event was at hand.

The six competitors were doing their warm-up.

'Perfect weather for it,' observed Landy.

'I promised you the best of everything,' replied Johansson.

Landy indicated Chataway. 'Who's that bloke with the short legs?'

'Don't let him hear you say that!'

'Why not? He likes to feel hostile to his rivals. Wasn't he one of Bannister's rabbits?'

'That's right, John.'

'We've got millions of rabbits in Australia. They're a pest.'

Landy went for a final sprint and then came over to the starting line. Johansson was exuding his usual pre-race confidence. Chataway had the quiet concentration of a man who was there with only one aim. Three other Finns were also competing.

The people of Turku had come to know and admire Landy very well, and he did not want to let them down. At the same time he was cautious and not prepared to run his usual gruelling race from the front. He respected Chataway too much to take any risks.

They crouched, tensed, waited. They were off.

Kallio, one of the Finns, raced into an immediate lead and set a testing pace. Landy rode in behind him. Though uneasy that he was led at someone else's speed, he did find that the strain had been taken off him slightly. After two swift laps behind the Finn he looked for his moment to ease into the lead.

When he finally did so, Landy took Chataway with him. The English athlete was running with that cavalier determination that had become his hallmark and he would not be easy to dislodge. At the bell, however, Landy was given just the stimulus he needed. When the time was announced over the loudspeaker he realized that he was within striking distance of a world record.

'My God!' he thought. 'Is that fair dinkum?'

But Chataway was still sticking to him like a limpet.

Landy produced his spurt on the first bend and pulled away from the red-headed Englishman. It was the first time since Helsinki that Landy had ever really been challenged in a mile race and he now responded to that challenge with graceful urgency.

His moment had finally come. He took it like a champion.

Lengthening his stride, he drew further ahead as he coasted down the back straight and around the bend. The sight of the tape, the cheers of the crowd and his own inner promptings lent him extra incentive and he stretched himself even more.

But there was another spur that goaded him on. Fear.

Fear of defeat. Fear of humiliation. Fear of running below his best. Fear of betraying his talents. Fear of letting others down. Fear that he would never crash through the four-minute barrier. Fear that he might never get such a chance again.

As he tore through the tape, he had conquered his fear.

'Landy! Landy! Landy! Landy!'

The chanting of the crowd was a salute to a champion.

Chris Chataway, in second place, was almost fifty yards behind. Olavi Vuorisalo was third while a puffing Denis Johansson led in the two backmarkers. But the spectators did not notice the others.

'Landy! Landy! Landy! Landy!'

Officials were crowding excitedly around the timekeeper. Landy, feeling no real distress after his run, was walking up and down the track, receiving the congratulations of the other athletes as they came past the line. Silence for the announcement, which was in Finnish.

The crowd went berserk.

'Did I beat four minutes?' asked Landy, bemused.

'You did better than that, John,' said Johansson, clapping him on the back. 'You broke the world record.'

His time had been 3.57.9. Delirium ensued.

Chataway came racing over from the timekeeper. 'Jesus! You've broken the 1500 record as well!'

Landy was seized by the others and hurled in the air with joy. Everyone was trying to get at him to congratulate him and touch him. The press fought to get close. The spectators demanded a lap of honour.

'Come with me, Chris,' urged Landy.

'No, old chap. This is your day.'

'But you pushed me to that time.'

'You were the one who ran it, though.'

'Come on.'

'No,' said Chataway. 'If I'd won I'd do a lap of honour on my own. Go and take your plaudits. You've earned them.'

A small band struck up as Landy was about to start.

'What on earth is that, Denis?' he asked.

'That's the Finnish National Anthem,' said the other. 'They don't know the Australian one. You're a Finn now, John.'

Landy grinned and went on his lap of honour. Tumultuous applause followed him all the way round. Because split seconds were not officially recognized his time would be rounded up to 3.58.0. It was still a world record. Faster than Bannister. Faster than Santee. Faster than anybody had ever run a mile. As Landy enjoyed his ovation, he was glowing with happiness and sense of achievement.

This was why he did it.

Gordon Landy and his wife were having breakfast when the telephone rang. She hurried over to answer it.

'Hello? . . . Yes, speaking . . . he's done *what*?' Excitement made her voice querulous. 'Oh, that's wonderful! . . . Thank you. Thank you so much for letting us know.' She put the receiver down and turned back to her husband. 'John's broken the world record in Turku. He's just run 3.58.0.'

'Thank God for that!' said Gordon Landy, getting up to hug her in his delight. 'It's all been worth it! This will make those lousy reporters change their tune!'

The party was held on an island but Landy had no idea where it was or how they had got there. All he knew was that he was sitting in a room with a crowd of rowdy Finns and drinking a lethal combination of aquavit and schnapps. Chataway was there too, and Johansson was conducting the proceedings at what was essentially an all-male celebration. Landy was the acknowledged guest of honour.

'Give us a song, John!'
'Waltzing Matilda!'
'Sung in Finnish!'
'In under four minutes!'
'Stand on the table!'
'Get up there and sing!'

Landy waved them away. He had neither the strength nor the inclination to clamber up on to the table. After so much to drink, he was beginning to wonder if he would ever be able to rise from his seat. As the Finns continued to exhort him to sing, he raised his glass.

'To Christopher Chataway!'
'Chataway!' came the concerted shout.
'I'll drink to that!' added the Englishman himself.

'Only two four-minute miles have ever been run,' continued Landy, 'and this great athlete was involved in both of them!'

'Hurrah!'

'Unfortunately I didn't win either of the races,' complained Chataway. 'Always the bridesmaid, never the bride.'

'Have some more, John,' encouraged Johansson, topping up his glass yet again. 'We haven't started yet.'

'But I couldn't touch another drop, Denis.'

'Of course you could. We'll dry you out in a moment.'

'You'll what?'

Ten minutes later he got his answer. As most of the Finns

got close to the paralytic stage, Johansson called out in his own language and they all struggled up to undress. Landy was helped to his feet and made to strip as well. The whole party then plunged into the sauna and collapsed on the pine benches in a mood of communal abandon.

Landy found the heat overpowering at first but he learned to adjust to it. Perspiration soon streamed down his body and his throat became parched. Impossibly, he now wanted another drink. They withstood the cleansing power of the sauna as long as they could then tumbled out and fell upon the aquavit and schnapps with renewed vigour. Hardier souls repeated the process a few times, drinking to the edge of collapse, lumbering into the sauna, laughing hysterically all the time. One man evolved his own technique.

He took a bottle into the sauna with him.

Landy would never know how he got back home after the party. All that he could remember was that it was well after dawn. Johansson woke him by shaking his shoulder.

'We have to go out, John!'

'Now? I want to sleep for a week.'

'Later. This is important.'

'Why?'

'Our friends are in trouble. The police.'

Mention of the police brought Landy fully awake and he struggled out of his bed. When he had washed and dressed he went with Johansson to the central police station. It had a solid, unwelcoming air to it.

'What happened to them, Denis?'

'They fell by the wayside.'

'Arrested?'

'We must get them out.'

Landy followed him into the police station and did his best to look poised and sober while his friend argued in Finnish with the desk sergeant. Eventually the man nodded and took some keys from under the counter. He led them both down to the cells.

'He's not locking *us* up as well, is he?' said Landy in alarm.

'He wouldn't dare to touch you, John. You're a star.'

Landy had further proof of the fact almost immediately. They went down a corridor and paused outside a large holding cell that looked like nothing so much as a cage in a zoo. A mass of bodies lay on the floor and there was a general stink of alcohol. Johansson spotted the three friends who had gone astray. When he called to them they surfaced long enough from their stupor to wave back.

The policeman unlocked the door and opened it. He turned to Landy and gave him a reverential smile.

'You are the great John Landy?'

'Yes.'

'Choose any three you like,' invited the man. 'They're all yours!'

Breaking a world record had its advantages.

Chapter Twenty

As soon as the news hit England the telephone started to ring at a certain house in Harrow. Roger Bannister found himself repeatedly asked for his comments. He dealt with all the calls in his usual polite and gracious way.

'What was your immediate reaction, Roger?' said yet another voice.

'It was a most wonderful achievement and I sent John my heartiest congratulations.'

'Did you expect your world record to be broken?'

'It was inevitable. Times can always be broken.'

'Are you looking forward to racing against Landy?'

'Very much,' replied Bannister. 'I look forward to running in Vancouver but I don't expect that the time will be broken there.'

'Why not?'

'Twelve men will be in the race and the prime consideration will be winning and not setting a world record.'

'Are you disappointed by what happened in Turku?'

Bannister paused briefly. 'It would have been nice to hang on to my record a little longer,' he admitted, 'but one has to acknowledge a superb athlete. When I beat four minutes at Oxford, John Landy sent me a cable saying, "This is great, great, great. I think the brilliant achievement will be bettered." He went out and bettered it.'

'Have you any comment to make about Chris Chataway's role in the race?' probed the voice.

'Chris ran well but it was not his day. He was up against a superhuman performance. I am sure that he found the race a memorable experience.' Bannister was getting tired of saying the same things. 'Look, is that all? I'm in rather a hurry, I'm afraid.'

'Thank you for your time, Roger,' said the voice.

'My pleasure. Goodbye.'

He replaced the receiver and heaved a sigh. Ralph Bannister had overheard his son and was immediately sympathetic.

'I'll answer it next time, Roger, and say you're not at home.'

'That's all right, Dad.'

'Why don't you point out to them that your time is probably the faster one, all things considered?'

'I'm not sure that it is.'

'But you ran under four minutes in atrocious conditions. Landy had a much better track and perfect weather.'

'That doesn't matter,' returned Bannister. 'He did it.'

'Ah, well. You'll get your revenge at Vancouver.'

'I hope so, Dad. And I hope that Chris will be able to help me.'

'Because he's just run against Landy?'

'Yes. He'll know exactly how good the man is and what sort of tactics he uses. When I ran against Landy in Helsinki I hardly noticed him. He's improved out of all recognition since then.'

'So have you, Roger.'

'Yes,' said Bannister in slight surprise. 'So have I.'

The telephone rang again and he braced himself.

Australia rejoiced when it heard of the triumph achieved in Finland. John Landy had made the difficult journey from hero to legend and his name was on everyone's lips. Portsea Training Camp was agog at the news though it threw Percy Cerutty into a state of ambivalence.

'It's bloody marvellous!' argued Les Perry in delight.

'You can bet your boots he won't acknowledge *my* help,' said the other in hurt tones. 'If it wasn't for me he'd be nowhere.'

'Aw, come on, Perce!'

'Landy walked out on me.'

'This is no time to bear grudges. Enjoy it.'

'I would if they'd give me some credit for it.'

'Look, it's the best thing that's happened to Australian sport for ages. Given the whole damn country a lift.'

'I know,' agreed Cerutty, 'and I've sent him a cable to add my congratulations.' He smirked wickedly. 'I hope it makes him feel guilty.'

'Let's face it, Perce. You and John were never going to be a permanent team. Be realistic.'

'Are you saying I wasn't *good* enough to coach him?' demanded the other, bristling at once. 'That your opinion, Les Perry?'

'Of course not. It's just that you and John were such different types. He's much . . . quieter than you.'

'I can be quiet when I want to!' yelled Cerutty.

They were standing outside the athletes' cabin. The sky was cloudy and the first hint of rain was carried in the wind. Waves rolled more purposefully out in the bay. It was not the ideal time of year for training but that did not deter Cerutty. He kept his men at it in all weathers.

'This could do us a lot of good, Les.'

'What?'

'Landy's world record,' said the coach. 'How many people realize that he started with me?' He waved an arm around. 'That he came down here to Portsea. How many know?'

'Just about every man, woman, child and kangaroo in the whole bloody country, I should say,' mocked Les. 'You've certainly told them enough times.'

'Here, yes. But what about abroad? Landy's international now.'

'Somebody ought to tell them about you, Perce,' said Perry.

'Don't snigger at me!' ordered Cerutty, adopting a threatening posture. 'Or I'll punch you on the nose!'

Perry guffawed. 'Coach Batters Defenceless Athlete. It would make a good story.'

'I've got an even better one. Landy Owes It All to Cerutty. Someone *should* tell the world's press and someone bloody well will!'

He strutted off towards the house to do his duty.

Percy Cerutty was not only ready to blow his own trumpet. He was prepared to become an entire brass section.

*

Bill Easton strolled across the campus and tried to offer sympathy and encouragement to his companion. Wes Santee was in a resigned mood.

'It was just bad luck, Wes.'

'Yeah!'

'That's the way it goes sometimes.'

'Haegg's record stood for eight years,' reminded the athlete. 'Mine didn't even stand for eight days.'

'Seventeen, to be exact,' corrected Easton. 'You snatch a world record in Compton then, less than three weeks later, Landy snatches it off you. There's no justice.'

'There will be,' decided Santee. 'When I snatch it back.'

'That's the attitude!'

'And I can't bad-mouth Landy. He's a great runner. Any guy who collects two world records in one race has got to be up there with the immortals. You know?'

'I go along with that. Landy got inside four minutes during a proper race. No rabbits and no set-up. You got to admire him for that.' They went around the angle of a building and headed for the college track. 'Big question is – who's going to win in Vancouver?'

'Bannister or Landy?'

'Landy or Bannister? Should be a great race.'

'I'd give *anything* to be in it!' affirmed Santee.

'You left it about a hundred and seventy years too late.'

'Why?'

'We're not in the British Empire any more.'

'Maybe I can still get up to Vancouver in August,' said the athlete, his enthusiasm rolling. 'Bannister, Landy, me – hell, we're the three best milers in the world. Ever, probably. We ought to get together somehow. I feel I *know* those guys. The three of us have been chasing the same times and the same records for so long, it's like we're brothers or something!' His eagerness firmed up into a resolve. 'I *will* get up to Vancouver somehow!'

'That could be difficult, Wes,' warned Easton. 'You won't be wearing a track suit in August: you'll be in uniform.'

'They *got* to release me for this!'

'Don't count on it.'

They had reached the track now and paused at the side of

269

it. Bill Easton gazed nostalgically at a spot further down the straight.

'Remember the first time we ever met?' he asked.

'Sure thing. I was so scared of you, coach.'

'It was just over there,' said Easton, pointing to the track. 'I was trying to put some numskull straight about his training schedule and you stroll up.' He looked Santee up and down. 'Who'd have thought then that a future world record-holder was coming to the college?'

'A *former* world record-holder,' amended Santee.

'It was future then and it's future now.' He looked up at the athlete. 'You're the guy who'll outlast them, Wes. Bannister finishes this season and you got a couple of years in hand over Landy. They may have it now but – take it from me – you'll have it soon. *All* of it!'

Santee brightened at the prospect. 'Yeah! All of it!'

'See you, Wes . . .'

'Thanks!'

As Bill Easton set off towards his office Santee threw down his bag and sat on the ground beside it. He took out the latest issue of a sports magazine. It had only arrived that morning and it was already out of date. He found the relevant page.

WORLD RECORDS – 1500 metres
(1500 metres is just under 120 yards short of a mile)

TIME	RECORD-HOLDER	DATE	VENUE
3.55.8	Abel Kiviat USA	8.6.12	Cambridge, Mass.
3.54.7	John Zander Sweden	5.8.17	Stockholm
3.52.6	Paavo Nurmi Finland	19.6.24	Helsinki
3.51.0	Otto Peltzer Germany	11.9.26	Berlin
3.49.1	Jules Ladoumegue Fr.	5.10.30	Paris
3.49.1	Luigi Beccali Italy	9.9.33	Turin
3.49.0	Luigi Beccali Italy	17.9.33	Milan
3.48.8	Bill Bonthron USA	30.6.34	Milwaukee
3.47.8	Jack Lovelock NZ	6.8.36	Berlin
3.47.6	Gunder Haegg Sweden	10.8.41	Stockholm
3.45.8	Gunder Haegg Sweden	17.7.42	Stockholm

3.45.0	Arne Andersson Sweden	17.8.43	Gothenburg
3.43.0	Gunder Haegg Sweden	7.7.44	Gothenburg
3.43.0	Lennart Strand Sweden	15.7.47	Malmo
3.43.0	Werner Lueg Germany	29.6.52	Berlin
3.42.8	Wes Santee USA	4.6.54	Compton, USA

The record had first been set in America, wandered off around Europe and then been repatriated by Bill Bonthron, one of a clutch of great milers in the United States in the 1930s. Scandinavia had then kept its hand on the record for a long time before Santee had prised it clear. It was now back in Scandinavia. At Turku.

Soon it would be exported to Australia along with the world mile record. Wes Santee vowed that he would one day bring them both back home where they belonged.

If American officialdom would let him.

He put the magazine away in his bag.

John Landy was paying a valedictory visit to the lakes north of Turku. As he gazed across the shimmering expanse of water that was fringed with forests of dark pine, he knew that he was going to miss Finland. Living there had been a profoundly happy experience in every way and he was sorry that he was now about to leave.

'Come back again some day,' suggested Johansson.

'I will, Denis. It's a home from home.'

'You are very welcome, my friend. After your performance at Turku Stadium my whole country is at your feet.'

'I've loved it here.'

'Shall I make a confession?' said Johansson with a sheepish grin.

'What?'

'When I first came to Australia I did not like you.'

Landy laughed. 'You made that pretty clear.'

'It was because of your reputation, I think. The way Australians went on about this magnificent sportsman who was so honest and straightforward and modest. I did not believe it.'

'No, you thought I was a naive hick or something.'

'I was mistaken,' admitted Johansson. 'You're everything they said you were. And now you are also the greatest miler in the world.'

'Only because you invited me here,' reminded Landy with gratitude. 'Back in Australia I'd just have been pounding around Central Park.'

'We were honoured to have you, John. You mixed in so well here and you even learned something of our language and customs. We all appreciated that.'

'Good.'

'I hope you did not feel too cut off.'

'But I did,' said Landy, 'and that was the beauty of it. I'm looking forward to running in the Empire Games but I don't relish the prospect of all that publicity. There were no pressures here, Denis. In Vancouver there'll be nothing but pressure.'

'I still think you will win the mile.'

'So do I,' agreed Landy with a quiet smile. 'I have to.'

Percy Cerutty sat at the table and read through the article once more. Several copies of it were scattered about in front of him.

FOOTBALL HIS 'FIRST LOVE'

John Landy would rather be playing football than running around an athletics track.

People who saw John play as centre half-back and centre half-forward with the Dookie College team say he would have become a star League footballer.

Landy, a noted high mark, won a best and fairest award while playing with Dookie in 1950.

It took high-pressure talking by two Victorian athletes – Gordon Hall and Percy Cerutty – to swing Landy from football to athletics.

Late in 1950, Hall, who was then captain of Geelong Guild Harriers, pressed Landy to train seriously for the mile, and induced him to be coached by Percy Cerutty, who had improved Hall from a running nonentity to star ranking.

Under Cerutty's guidance Landy improved his mile time by 17 sec. within a few months to clock 4.14.6.

Landy has now become not only the world's fastest miler, but the most consistently brilliant middle-distance runner the world has ever seen.

. . . His breaking of the four-minute mile probably is a greater triumph of character than of physical ability.

Surely no other athlete has sacrificed more and stuck to his objective with such unflagging purpose.

Using a pen to underline the three mentions of his name on each copy of the article, Cerutty then reached for some envelopes and began to address them.

The AAA Championships that year were again used as a shop window for a major international event. With the Empire Games only three weeks away, British athletes were able to give a full White City a foretaste of what was to come in Vancouver. Since the four home countries would be competing separately in Canada, the focus of interest was very much on the English contingent. They did their best to oblige.

'Well done, Roger!'

'I wish the crowd thought the same!'

'But you won the race easily.'

'Yes, in 4.07.6. They all expected a four-minute mile.'

'Now that's sheer greed,' remarked Chataway. 'You can't be expected to serve up a four-minute mile every time. Besides which, you were husbanding your resources for Vancouver.'

'Tell that to them, Chris,' suggested Bannister, a little upset by the muted reception he got for his stylish win in the mile. 'I've never run a last lap as fast as that: 53.8. And still they're not satisfied.'

'Don't worry,' said Chataway. 'The British public is very fickle towards its heroes. Ignore them.' He heard the announcement of his own event. 'I'll get out there and see if *I* can't cheer them up a bit.'

The event of the championships was without question the 3 miles. It was enlivened by the audacious and uninhibited running of a Kenyan, Nyandika Maiyoro, who set such a fiery pace that he made possible a new world record. As the race neared its dramatic climax Chris Chataway, eager to regain the title he had won in 1952, was battling it out with the moustached and dark-vested Freddie Green.

At the bell Green appeared to give in because he waved his rival past. The bobbing red head moved into the lead and the crowd began to cheer home one of their favourite athletes. But the early pace had had its effect on Chataway and he began to fade slightly. Sensing that he could catch him up, Green rallied and put in a spirited burst for the line. A camera had to separate them and, though Chataway was given second place, he shared the world record for the event.

With the help of Freddie Green, Chataway had more than cheered the crowd up. Disappointment over the mile time was forgotten.

There was a lone win for Ireland in the high jump and quadruple success for Hungary in the hammer, discus, pole vault and long jump. But it was the English athletes who dominated and delighted on the track. Setting a seal on the whole meeting was the signal victory of the indefatigable Jim Peters who set yet another world's best performance in the marathon.

English hopes for the Empire Games were justifiably high.

'We could have a clean sweep on the track, Franz.'

'Don't get carried away, Harold,' warned the other.

Abrahams chuckled. 'I know you're remembering what happened in 1952 but this is different. An Empire Games is a severe challenge but it doesn't compare with an Olympics.' He looked happily around the stadium. 'No, I am very confident.'

'I think you have cause to be,' admitted Stampfl.

'Have you been drinking or something?' teased the other.

'Why must you always misunderstand me?' protested the other. 'I have a lot of admiration for British athletes.'

'Only if you coach them.'

They were standing on the edge of the track as the stadium was slowly emptying. The championships had left Abrahams in buoyant mood but Stampfl, as usual, was more sceptical.

'What did you think of Jim Peters? Sterling performance!'

'I agree.'

'That's one gold medal we must be assured of, Franz.'

'I don't agree.'

'Peters is unbeatable over that distance.'

'Your journalists thought the same in 1952.'

'He's even stronger and faster now,' argued Abrahams. 'And he can draw on a wealth of experience. Did you know that he made his first appearance at these championships way back in 1946 when he won the 6 miles? Astonishing how he's kept going.'

'Even so, there is never a certainty in a marathon.'

'I'd still put my shirt on him.'

Stampfl grinned. 'Make sure you take a spare one to Vancouver.'

They began to stroll along the track itself and it revived memories for Abrahams of his own days as a competitor. He found it difficult to be on any track without regretting the accident that had shortened his career and moved him sideways into the rewarding, but far less exciting, world of athletics administration.

'Give me athletes who want to run!' he announced.

'I prefer those who want to win.'

'It's the enthusiasm for the sport that's important, Franz. Look at that Kenyan in the 3 miles. It was inspiring to see the chap take off like that. Marvellous advertisement for athletics!'

'I think we'll see a lot more African runners in the future,' predicted Stampfl. 'They'll inject excitement.'

'We weren't short of excitement today. It's always the same,' confessed Abrahams. 'Whenever I come to a meeting like this, I find myself wishing that I could still compete. Do you feel that urge?'

'I still do compete.'

'Do you?'

'Through my athletes.'

Abrahams nodded. 'Fair comment. You must have been disappointed for Chris Chataway. Beaten by inches.'

'Oh, he will be back,' assured Stampfl. 'Chataway is a great fighter. He lost in Turku and he lost again today. That won't please him. He'll want to make up for it in Vancouver and he'll do it.'

'Freddie Green will be against him,' reminded Abrahams.

'That is one of the reasons I am sure he will win. Revenge is the best coach in the business.'

'And what about Bannister? Rather a low-key performance.'

'The crowd expected too much of the poor man. He was here to win a race and not to run himself into the ground just to satisfy them. Besides, if they knew anything about miling, they would have been pleased with what he achieved today.'

'Pleased?' questioned Abrahams. 'It was a let-down, Franz.'

'Not from where I was sitting. His last lap was under 54.0 and that is bad news for John Landy. Vancouver will be a slow track. In a slow-run race where it all depends on the last lap, Bannister has demonstrated that he has the advantage.'

'I have every faith in his winning at Vancouver,' asserted Abrahams patriotically. 'Landy is good but Bannister can beat him.'

'I know that he can. He has a secret weapon.'

'What's that?'

'Me,' said Stampfl. 'I will tell Bannister how he can win.'

Abrahams chuckled but he felt quietly reassured.

The Marine Base at Quantico, Virginia kept its commanding officer busy and he did not have much time to deal with minor problems. He was a big, heavy man with iron-grey hair and the kind of peremptory voice that sounded as if it was reining in a deep anger. When a young man entered his office, stood to attention and saluted, the CO was anxious to get the interview over as soon as possible. His voice barked.

'At ease.'

'Thank you, sir.'

'You have a request, Lieutenant?'

'Yes, sir.'

'Make it snappy.'

'Permission to go to Vancouver, please, sir.'

'Vancouver?'

'It's in Canada, sir.'

'I know my geography, Lieutenant,' retorted the CO.

'Of course, sir. I wish to visit the Empire Games, sir.'

'The what?'

'It's a big athletics meet, sir. Like the Olympic Games. Only this one is only for the countries in the British Empire.'

'So?'

'I wish to attend, sir. To see some friends.'

'Permission refused.'

'But this is important, sir.'

'You're in the Marines now, Lieutenant. Nothing is more important than that.'

'It would only be for a couple of days, sir.'

'Why not take a week?' offered the CO with thick sarcasm. 'Maybe you'd like us to fly you up there and handle all your expenses for you?'

'I'm just requesting furlough, sir.'

'Request turned down.'

'But I'm an athlete myself, sir,' persisted the other. 'I need to meet some guys who'll be coming to Vancouver next week. They're the two best milers in the world.'

'Get their autographs another time.'

'You don't understand, sir.'

'That will be all, Lieutenant.'

'Just let me explain, sir.'

'You heard me,' growled the older man.

'But I've been running against those two for the last couple of years. I hit a world record out in California. We got this *bond*, sir. It's vital that the three of us meet. Sort of symbolic.'

The commanding officer bit back his irritation and gave himself time to appraise the tall, uniformed figure in front of him. He decided to mix authority with tolerance.

'I *know* you're a great athlete, Lieutenant,' he said pleasantly, 'and we're glad to have you at the base. But you're not the only star we got. There's guys here from every sport – track, baseball, football, boxing, ice hockey, basketball. If I start letting them sneak off to meet up with their pals for a couple of beers I'm not going to have a single Marine left at this Base.' He stood up to reinforce his announcement. 'Permission refused.'

'Yes, sir. Thank you, sir.'

'Goodbye, Lieutenant.'

The officer came to attention and saluted. Then he left.

Wes Santee stood in the corridor outside and tried to contain his disappointment. It was frustrating. John Landy was already in Canada and Roger Bannister would be arriving there within a matter of days. For the first time since they had achieved world renown, the three of them were on the same continent. They had to meet.

A similar chance might never come again.

Outfitting sessions were always lively events. As the members of the Australian Empire Games team met for the final fitting of their uniforms there was the usual horseplay and hilarity. Short men tried on huge blazers and big men got laughs with tiny hats. The female athletes joined in the fun, trying on anything and everything that they could lay their hands on. It put them all in a cheerful mood.

'I bet other countries don't have this kind of fun,' observed Neil Robbins. 'It's great for team spirit.'

'I can't imagine the English team letting itself go like us,' said Marjorie Nelson. 'But the New Zealand boys do. We had some good times with them at the last Empire Games.'

'Yes, Marje, you picked up three gold medals in Auckland. And I daresay you'll be taking home another three from Vancouver.'

'As long as we don't drop the baton in the relay.'

'You won't,' Robbins assured her. 'How do you feel?'

'I'm in good shape.'

'That's bad news for the other sprinters.'

'What about you?'

'Oh, I've been training hard,' he explained, 'and I feel fine in myself but I keep getting these twinges in my tendon.'

'How serious is it?'

'Well, it won't stop me running or anything like that.'

'Good.'

'But it's one of those niggling little worries at the back of your mind. I dropped a line to Perce. He always gives good advice.'

'If I can help, just let me know.'

'Thanks, Marje.'

'We'll train together, if you like,' she suggested. 'Then I could keep an eye on that tendon for you.'

Neil Robbins was grateful to her. Marjorie Nelson would almost certainly be the outstanding female athlete in the track events and she would be feted by the world's press but she could still find time to offer moral support to a team mate in trouble.

'How is Perce these days?' she asked.

'Lunatic as ever.'

'Pity he's not coming. He'd liven up Vancouver.'

'They'd have the Mounties out after him within five minutes!' He considered. 'Anyway, perhaps it's just as well. I wouldn't want there to be any tension between him and John.'

'I can't imagine John being tense with anyone,' she commented. 'He's the nicest bloke in the world.'

'Even the nicest bloke in the world can get a bit hot under the collar with Perce yelling at him. I do sometimes. Besides, John's going to be under enough pressure as it is. Ever since that amazing run in Turku the spotlight has been turned on him.'

'Quite rightly, too.'

'Roger Bannister against John Landy. The only two men ever to beat four minutes. It's going to be the race of the games, Marje.'

'I know. You can't help feeling a little sorry for Bannister, though. To come all that way in order to be beaten.'

'Yes,' agreed Robbins confidently. 'We've got a certain gold medal in the mile. And nobody deserves it more than John. He's a super bloke and a super athlete.'

'I've seen those training schedules of his. Frightening.'

'He's a running machine, Marje. And he's unstoppable. Bannister and the others are going to find that out in Vancouver. When that gun goes they won't see John Landy for dust!'

It was a foregone conclusion.

Chapter Twenty-One

The coffee at Lyons' Corner House had not improved. Franz Stampfl opted for a cup of tea instead and took it across to the table to join the others. Chris Chataway was relaxing with a cigarette and Roger Bannister was nibbling at a cake. It was time to plan the ascent of another peak.

'You have to admire the Finns,' said Chataway. 'They certainly take their athletics seriously. How many other countries would give you such a detailed time breakdown of a race?'

'Not this one, for a start,' remarked Stampfl.

'I expected lap times in Turku,' continued Chataway, 'but they split the whole distance up in 100-yard segments and timed each one. That's why I brought the information about Landy back. I thought you'd be interested to see his splits.'

'It was very thoughtful of you, Chris,' thanked Bannister.

'But it only confirms what we already know,' added Stampfl. 'Landy is a very fast athlete.'

'He's also a superbly fit one,' recalled Chataway. 'I was wheezing like a grampus at the end of that race, but he was hardly troubled at all. He must have iron bellows instead of lungs.'

'Landy has immense stamina,' conceded Stampfl, 'but he has not yet learned to push himself to the absolute limit. Roger has, and that is why he will win.'

'It will depend very much on his tactics,' said Bannister.

'What are the possibilities?' replied the Austrian. 'He can stay in the pack and risk everything on out-sprinting you over the last quarter. Or he can go to the front at the start.'

'Landy won't hang back,' insisted Chataway. 'Not his style.'

'In that case, we should have the race in the bag.'

Bannister smiled. 'Nobody could accuse you of defeatism, Franz.'

'You must go out on to that track knowing that you can do it, Roger. Not hoping that you might. But knowing in your heart. It's all a question of strategy. Look at the four-minute mile.'

'That was different,' argued Bannister. 'I was only up against the clock there. This time there'll be other athletes trying to get to that tape first. There are so many imponderables.'

'I don't think so,' said the Austrian with measured calm. 'Let us be realistic here. Nobody else in that field is in the same class as you and Landy. Murray Halberg may have run 4.04.4 but he is only twenty and totally inexperienced at this level of competition. No, you can rest assured that it will be a two-horse race.'

'England versus Australia,' said Chataway.

'And we can also rest assured that Landy will run it from the front. He is not going to change his tactics for such a vital race as this. He will play hare to your hound, Roger.'

'That will make for a very tense situation.'

'Of course. But there is always more tension for the hare. He's out there in front and he starts asking questions – "Am I going fast enough? Should I be increasing the pace? Are they still there?" The hound only has to ask himself one question – "Can I hang on?" If he does – he wins.'

'You make it sound easy.'

'And it's not, Franz,' intervened Chataway. 'I was the hound in Turku and I didn't get a sniff of that damn hare in the last lap.'

Stampfl leaned forward. 'There is a crucial distance. In this case, I think it is about twelve yards. You must never let Landy get further ahead of you than that.'

'Twelve yards?'

'I can't be precise but you'll know what it is when you're out there. It's like an elastic rope. It can stretch but once it breaks he's cracked you and you'll never catch him.'

'That's an encouraging thought,' murmured Bannister.

'The most dangerous lap for you is the third one, Roger.'

Chataway nodded in agreement. 'He ran an incredibly fast third lap in Finland.'

'Yes,' said Bannister, '58.2. If he sets that kind of pace in Vancouver I doubt if I'm going to have the reserves to kick from 300 yards out.'

'Save it until later,' urged Stampfl. 'Go round the final bend and *then* produce a burst of speed. To go past a runner at that stage of a race is like a knockout punch in a boxing ring.'

Bannister accepted the soundness of the advice but he still had his doubts. Sensing this, Chataway gave him a warm grin and patted him on the shoulder.

'You'll do it, Roger,' he said reassuringly. 'After all, you're the man who broke four minutes.'

'So did Landy.'

'Yes, but you got there before him and that should give you a psychological advantage.' His grin broadened. 'You're the star. Who ever remembers the *second* man to climb up Everest?'

It had been a long but enjoyable flight for the New Zealand team and they arrived at Vancouver airport in high spirits. Murray Halberg, a thin, pale young man with a left arm that had been paralysed by a rugby accident, moved down the aisle with his close friend, the likeable and ebullient Bill Baillie. Both were coached by Arthur Lydiard and both were hoping to be in the final of the mile.

Baillie winced as a strange wailing noise hit his ears.

'What the hell's that, Murray?'

'I don't know. They've shut the engines off now.'

'It sounds as if they're strangling a cat out there.'

They emerged from the plane to learn the explanation. At the foot of the gangway was a kilted figure with a set of bagpipes, blowing for all he was worth to give them a rousing welcome to Canada. When Baillie got level with him, he glared at the man.

'Drop dead!' he yelled.

'You're wasting your time,' shouted Halberg. 'He can't hear.'

The bagpipes continued to drown out any other sound.

When the athletes had gone through customs they were besieged by a group of journalists. One of them got in the way of the two friends and thrust a question at them.

'Who are you?'

Bill Baillie grinned. '*I'm* the man who wants to murder that bloody piper back there and *this*,' he added, 'is the man who's going to show Landy and Bannister how to run a mile. Meet Murray Halberg.'

The journalist was startled. '*You* are Murray Halberg?'

'Feel free to use any insults you like,' said Halberg amiably. 'When I was in America earlier this year I was described as "that wizened, triangular-faced guy" and a man who looked "more like a refugee from a prisoner-of-war camp than an athlete". Any other offers?'

The journalist rose to a feeble smile and backed away.

Though he would not be in Vancouver in body, Percy Cerutty made sure that he would be there in spirit. Invited to take part in a radio discussion of Australia's chances in the Empire Games, he was quick to promote himself and his ideas. Opposite him in the studio – in every sense – was a corpulent representative of the Amateur Athletic Union. The interviewer was a glib young man with a ready smile.

'Could you enlarge on that, Mr Cerutty?' he invited.

'Yes!' replied the coach. 'What's the point of sending a bunch of good athletes to a foreign country without a proper coach?'

'We feel that the team manager and masseur can handle any problems that might arise,' said the official with reflex pomposity.

'What do they know about athletics?' demanded Cerutty.

'Jim Eve is vastly experienced.'

'Balderdash! He knows nothing about coaching. About helping an athlete through a difficult time. Look at John Landy. That boy has got to be made to feel like a winner. Have you any idea what it's like to have a whole nation's hopes on your shoulders? There's terrific pressure on the poor young coot.' Cerutty thumped the table and the stand microphone vibrated. 'He needs me.'

'Percy,' reminded the official, 'you haven't coached Landy for two years now.'

'That's a complete lie! I write to the boy every week!'

'But does he ever write back?'

'Listen to me, you great –'

'Gentlemen, gentlemen,' interrupted the young man, 'let's keep this discussion on a friendly level.'

'How can I be friendly when he's trying to belittle my efforts?' yelled the coach. 'John was one of my boys at the start and he's one of my boys now. He's got the Cerutty hallmark – he's a champion!'

The official laughed. 'I'm not trying to belittle you, Percy. Everyone knows you've made a valuable contribution to athletics in this country. But they can survive in Vancouver without you.'

'That's a matter of opinion!'

'You know ours.'

'Every athlete needs a father figure!'

'They've *got* a father figure,' insisted the official. 'He's the team manager. I think you ought to be trying to back an Australian team for a change, Percy, instead of doing your best to sabotage it.'

'I just want to make it better!'

'Well, listeners,' said the interviewer, jumping in smartly as he felt things were getting out of hand. 'As you can hear, that old fighter Percy Cerutty has lost none of his fire.'

'Don't you patronize me, young fella!' snarled the coach.

'Mr Cerutty –'

'I'm putting over a serious point here. Self-seeking officials are ruining athletics in this country and the public ought to be made aware of it!'

'Cries in the wilderness!' observed the official.

'One final comment from both of you, please,' asked the interviewer. 'Mr Cerutty? Will you go first?'

'We've sent a fine team to Vancouver but we've put chains on their hands and feet!'

The official disagreed. 'We've sent a fine team and it will prove itself in the face of ill-informed comment.'

'I'm the most well-informed coach in Australia!' argued

Cerutty. 'I will not have you saying rubbish like that about me over the air!'

But it was not over the air. A worried producer had faded the programme out. Soft music was playing to soothe the listeners' ears.

The English team arrived at Vancouver airport and had to run a press gauntlet. Roger Bannister was a prime target and he kept on the move as they hit him with questions.

'How do you feel about being here, Roger?'

'Have you ever run in Canada before?'

'Any special training for the games?'

'Do you mind that Landy is the clear favourite?'

'What will your tactics be?'

'Are you worried?'

'Please,' said Bannister with polite firmness. 'We've had a long flight and we're tired. If you don't mind . . .'

'At least say you're glad to be here,' asked one man.

'I'm delighted to be in Vancouver. I hope this sunshine lasts.'

'Let me put this to you . . .'

Chataway came to the rescue. 'Roger is here to do his best. *I* am here to do my best. Is there anything else I can tell you? We had muffins for breakfast and three cups of tea on the flight over. Roger has a mole in the middle of his back and he's having a passionate affair with Lana Turner.'

'Where did he meet her?' asked one credulous journalist.

'The fool believes me!' hissed Chataway.

Another journalist butted in. 'Everyone is calling this the Mile of the Century. Do you think the world record will be broken?'

'Yes,' said Bannister tolerantly. 'It will be broken but not by me and not at Vancouver.'

'Why not?'

'Competitive races are different to record-breaking attempts. Tactical manoeuvring usually slows the times down.'

'Doesn't anyone want to ask *me* a question?' said Chataway.

'Who do you think is going to win?'

'*I* am going to win, my friend.'

'But you're not in the mile.'

'No,' agreed Chataway. 'I'm in the 3 miles and I'm going to win the 3 miles. Roger's race is not the only one in the games.'

'But who do you think will win it?' persisted a voice.

'I think that Landy will lead for the first three laps then Bannister will make his move. I'm absolutely certain that one of them will win.' He beamed at the press. 'With the 3 miles, however, there is no question. *I* will win.'

The two athletes swept away and made good their escape.

John Landy was delighted to see Marjorie Nelson again. They met at the Games Village which was based around the campus of the University of British Columbia. There was an involuntary hug.

'Marje! Great to see you!'

'Congratulations, John!'

'I was beginning to think I'd never do it,' he admitted.

'I said that you'd run through that brick wall, didn't I?' she stood back to look at him properly. 'You seem to be in good shape. How long have you been in Vancouver?'

'About three weeks. Getting acclimatized.'

'I'm surprised they've given you a moment to yourself.'

'The press have been a nuisance,' he said. 'But I have a foolproof technique.'

'What is it?'

'I outrun them.'

'Just as well you weren't back in Australia when the news broke about your two world records!' she told him.

'Why?'

'Because you'd never have outrun the press there. They'd have organized a full-scale manhunt for you!' She squeezed his hand. 'Have you any idea how big a splash you made down there?'

'My parents said there was a lot of coverage.'

'You were on the front page of *everything*, John,' she said. 'It was the *Sun News-Pictorial* that really went overboard, though. Front page, sports page, centre spread. They even had a photograph of you chasing butterflies.'

'Thank goodness I wasn't there at the time!'

'And they had this picture to show just what a mile looked like. There was a line traced along Elizabeth Street in Melbourne. It went from Flinders Street Station almost as far as Victoria Street. Honestly, it seemed like an enormous distance.'

'That's only because you're a sprinter.'

'But one of the biggest tributes they paid you was to fly the flag over Melbourne Town Hall. It was the same flag we had at the Australian camp in Helsinki.'

He gave a shrug. 'I think I'd have been a bit embarrassed if I'd been there, Marje. It's just not me somehow.'

'Because they don't have all that much to celebrate back home, they make the most of it when a rare chance comes along.' She smiled happily. 'I found that out. They cheered me for weeks after the Olympics.'

'They'll be doing the same after this games, Marje.'

'No,' she insisted. 'The mile is the major event here. You're the one who'll be going home to the crowds, John.'

'We'll see.'

'How was Finland?'

'Magical. I could have stayed for ever. They were so incredibly kind to me. Every one of them.'

'Even that Denis Johansson?'

'Denis, most of all.'

'But he said some lousy things about you in the papers.'

'We got past all that and became friends,' explained Landy. 'He's really in my corner now. Sent me a cable to tell me how I can beat Bannister.'

'How?'

'Denis thinks I should sit on him for most of the race and then thrash him over the last 300 yards. That's not John Landy tactics. I'm not like Denis, all cunning and artful. I prefer to attack from the front and burn the rest of them off.'

'And that's what you'll do,' she confirmed.

'I know, Marje. I want that gold medal more than *anything*.'

Police outriders escorted the English team to the Games Village. The athletes found the accommodation comfortable and clean, and they were pleased by the proximity of the training track. There was another element that appealed to

Roger Bannister. As he was starting to unpack, Chataway called him over to the window. Down below them, a member of the Canadian Royal Mounted Police was on duty.

'That should keep the press away, Roger!'

It was a comforting sight.

The New Zealand team loved everything about Vancouver except the twilight. It seemed to stretch on for ever and made sleep difficult. They managed some sightseeing before the Games officially opened and they discovered that Vancouver was a large, beautiful, well-planned city with ample parks and endless scenic attractions. They saw the totem poles in Stanley Park, marvelled at the civic buildings, shredded their nerves by crossing the Capilano rope-and-wire bridge and experienced the delight of a chairlift up Grouse Mountain. When one of the athletes, Lawrie King, sat in his chair and sang Maori serenades in his fine voice, the sound was almost overpowering in the eerie stillness of the warm night air. It was a memorable moment.

Socially, the New Zealanders were enjoying themselves.

'Did he tell you the one about the Mother Superior?'

'Yes, Bill. And the one about Father O'Farrell.'

'I've never met a guy who knew so many jokes.'

Their neighbours in Acacia camp were the Northern Ireland team and an immediate bond was formed. Bill Baillie and Murray Halberg became very fond of the Irish miler, Vic Milligan, whose sense of humour was a constant source of pleasure.

'I hope he doesn't start telling jokes during the race,' said Baillie. 'I'll fall about laughing.'

'He's just like I always imagined a Northern Irishman to be,' reflected Halberg. 'In fact most of the teams are like that. More or less as I expected. The Canadians are warm and friendly. The West Indians are terrific entertainers once they get going. The Africans are so open.'

'And the English just don't want to know,' added Baillie.

'Most of them don't, anyway. I haven't seen Bannister since he arrived. He hasn't been anywhere near the track.'

'He trains over on the golf course so that the press can't pester him so much.' Baillie was not an Anglophile. 'Why doesn't the English team mix in more? That's the whole bloody point of coming!'

Halberg nodded. 'The bloke who's impressed me is Landy.'

'Yes. I've seen those amazing training runs of his.'

'I didn't mean that, Bill,' explained the other. 'What I was impressed with was the guy himself. So friendly. When I told him who I was, he shook my hand like I was some long-lost mate of his. Yes, and he'll give you any amount of free advice on the training track.'

'That's more than Bannister would ever do!'

The two athletes were sitting over the remains of their lunch in the dining hall at the Games Village. Halberg ran a finger around the rim of his glass as he pondered. An idea was forming.

'Bill.'

'Yes?'

'Can we get into the final of the mile?'

'Of course!'

'Can we win it?'

'Of course!'

'Against two four-minute milers?'

Baillie considered. 'There's still a bronze medal.'

'I'm thinking about the gold,' said Halberg. 'If *I* can't win it – and I've got to be realistic – I'd much prefer that Landy did.'

'So do I, mate!'

'In fact, I'd do my level best to help him beat Bannister.'

'I think I would as well . . .'

Roger Bannister maintained his sprint for another 100 yards over the crisp turf and then he slowed down. Chris Chataway crossed over to him and showed him the reading on the stopwatch. Both were satisfied with their training session on the golf course. When Bannister had recovered his breath he went back to his track suit and found a handkerchief. He blew his nose hard and Chataway registered mild alarm.

'Have you got a cold, Roger?'

'It's only a sniff.'

'That's all you need at a time like this!'

'It's no problem.'

'You should see a doctor.'

'I do,' said Bannister with a smirk. 'Every morning, when I shave in the mirror.'

Chataway laughed but his concern was not allayed.

The opening ceremony of the fifth British Empire and Commonwealth Games was conducted with all due pomp and circumstance in Vancouver stadium. Flags were paraded, national teams marched past, stirring speeches were made and the darker aspects of imperialism were buried beneath the drama, colour, excitement and overwhelming sense of fellowship that prevailed. In size and scope it could not match an Olympics, but the athletes were energized by the whole occasion and they would be trying just as hard to win. At Helsinki the thrill had come simply from taking part. Here it arose from belonging to the empire.

Canadian organization was excellent. A capacity crowd watched the events with keen interest and everything flowed smoothly. The gold medals began to fall one by one.

Agostini won the 100 yards for Trinidad and Jowett stole the 220 yards for an ecstatic New Zealand contingent. Kevin Gosper, friend of Landy, coasted to victory in the 440 yards.

Marjorie Nelson showed her usual devastating pace to win both of the women's sprints and began to keep herself in trim for the relay later in the games. The 80-metres hurdles, won by Shirley Strickland four years earlier, went to Northern Rhodesia in the absence of the defending champion.

Gold for Gosper and double gold for Nelson put Australia into an early lead. England replied with a triple success in the 880 yards where a stylish run by Derek Johnson brought him ahead of his two team mates. In the field events, too, English athletes started to show their mettle. Ken Wilmshurst took gold in the long jump while Geoff Elliott in the pole vault, and John Savidge in the shot, were impressive winners. Competition intensified.

It was the mile which commanded major respect and attention.

'How do you feel, Roger?'

'Fine.'

'You don't sound it. What have you taken for that cold?'

'I'll be all right, Chris.'

Bannister had declared himself fit for the race and hoped that he would not have to push himself too hard in his heat but the pace was faster than he had anticipated. Geoff Warren, from the Cerutty stable, took them around the first half-mile at a punishing speed and then he dropped out. It was Murray Halberg who was ahead at the tape with Ferguson, the Canadian, at his heels. Bannister eased off over the last few yards, having qualified in third place and his colleague, David Law, reserved himself a place in the final by finishing fourth.

Halberg set a new games record of 4.07.4. Bannister, though forced to rouse himself, nevertheless gave promise that he had much in reserve for Saturday's final.

'Good luck, John!'

'Thanks, Marje.'

'You don't need to win. It's the first four.'

'Leave it to me.'

The second heat was a much slower affair and Landy did not have to produce anything like his top form. He crossed the line alongside Bill Baillie and Vic Milligan in a shared time of 4.11.4. Landy, too, had signalled that he was holding plenty back for Saturday.

The final now took on even more lustre and resonance.

Distance was no object to a man of Percy Cerutty's iron determination. He continued to coach. In response to Neil Robbins' request for advice about his tendon, Cerutty sent a long and detailed letter that told him exactly how to bind and treat it. The missive had the coach's authentic voice.

Listen, old son, things aren't bad. Everyone has setbacks. What *is* wrong is sending a bunch of well-trained fellows away, spending so much money and no coach to act as guide, comforter, backstop and friend and remedier of all the aches and pains. If you really want to let off steam, have a crack at the management both of the team and at home here.

. . . I've turned another corner myself. I am planning to lift Australian times up to new levels. I expect to have thirty at Portsea for Christmas and am laying out the dough to make it a real training camp. I am no longer waiting for the A A A's. After all, the rewards will be mine and my athletes'. Portsea will become world-famous and will attract athletes from overseas within three years.

... Boy, this old athletics world is going to hear a lot more about Cerutty and his world-beaters than it has heard about Landy. After all, he is only the Big Star. Les and others were the pathfinders ...

Regards, Perce

P.S. Regards to Geoff and Johnnie Vernon. Tell Don Mac it is important to keep handy in the mile final, he can easily with his strength beat a fading Bannister who will be nearly dead through trying to keep up with Landy. But I am afraid he will give it away before he starts. Show him this privately. It could be, and should be, Australia 1 and 2. And if Landy *did* weaken, Don can still fill the breach but he must keep up. I can run a 440 as fast as some of his firsts. I've 63s in training and 53s in a race.

P.P.S. To serve our purposes Steve could make the story: Urgent Advice From Coach Too Late. Is it wise to take these risks . . .?

Neil Robbins folded the letter and put it back in its envelope. The advice about the treatment of his injury had been just what he needed and he felt restored after hearing from Cerutty again. The man was so much more than a coach. When he was not around at a major international meeting like the Empire Games, there was a dimension missing.

Wes Santee was on the parade ground learning drill when the sergeant approached. He was taken off to see the commanding officer and spent the journey to the latter's office puzzling over what it could mean.

He marched in, stood to attention and saluted. The CO was studying some papers in front of him. His face was impassive when he looked up and his manner was as stern as ever.

'Wesley Santee?'

'Yes, sir.'

'You came in to see me once before.'

'Yes, sir.'

'Some cockamamie story about going to Vancouver to see two friends. Permission refused.'

'Yes sir.'

'They tell me you're a good runner, Santee.'

'I like to think so, sir.'

'You ran the mile?'

'Everything from 220 metres to 5 miles, sir.'

'Seems there's a big mile race up in Vancouver between an Englishman and an Australian. Are those the two guys who beat four minutes?'

'Yes sir. I missed it by six tenths of a second myself.'

'That's tough.'

'I'll make it one day soon, sir.'

The CO appraised him. 'That's a pretty shabby uniform.'

'It's the one I was issued with, sir.'

'We're going to have to get you cleaned up, Lieutenant. I'm not having you letting the Marines down.'

Santee was bewildered. 'Sir?'

'Your request is being granted,' said the CO with a half-smile. 'You'll see that mile race after all.'

'I'm going to Vancouver, sir?' asked a delighted Santee.

'Not exactly,' explained the other. 'You're going to New York to take part in the *Dave Garroway Show* on TV. They want you to commentate on this famous race.' The half-smile matured into a grin. 'Looks like you drew the easy job. *They* do the running – you do the talking!'

Chapter Twenty-Two

Dazzling success attended the English team at the Empire Games. They achieved regular wins both inside the stadium and in some of the other sports as well. Sixteen gold medals helped to take them to the top of the scoreboard. Australia, with fifteen golds, were over a hundred points behind in second place. Canada, South Africa and New Zealand followed in that order. Northern Ireland, Scotland and Trinidad had so far managed two golds apiece while Jamaica, Nigeria, Southern Rhodesia and Northern Rhodesia had each secured one.

Roger Bannister was very conscious of the fact that he was a member of a team. His visit to the London Olympics in 1948 had taught him the importance of national – as well as individual – aspiration and he was as anxious as anyone to make his contribution to the team's overall success. A win in the mile would not only add another gold medal to the tally. It would be an enormous psychological blow to the Australian team who were starting to take Landy's victory for granted.

Hampered by his cold and by lack of sleep, Bannister nevertheless felt confident. His reluctance to train in public was seen by many as proof of his unease about his form but this was not the case at all. Stampfl had helped him to plan the final with meticulous care and he had also instilled the need for more competitiveness and aggression.

Fitness. Strategy. A positive mental attitude.

Roger Bannister's preparations had been thorough.

'You're the underdog, Roger,' observed Chataway. 'That

can only work to your advantage. The pressure is all on Landy.'

'I intend to keep it there.'

'How's that cold?'

'I'll live.'

'It's rotten luck!'

'I only have to put up with it for four minutes.' He gave a wistful smile. 'Perhaps even less.'

'You don't expect a doctor to catch a cold,' chided his friend humorously. 'It's rather like a brewer going teetotal.'

'I don't see you doing that somehow, Chris.'

They were enjoying a quiet walk together around the campus. A hot day had shaded into a warm evening and it was very pleasant to stroll beneath an avenue of trees. Bannister was meditative.

'I suppose I should be grateful to Landy in one way.'

'Well, *I* wouldn't be grateful to him if he took a world record off me,' admitted Chataway with typical candour.

'It woke me up, Chris,' said Bannister. 'After the race at Iffley Road I felt the most extraordinary sense of freedom. As if a huge weight had just been lifted off me. I'd beaten four minutes at last. It was all over. I just can't describe the happiness and the sense of release.'

'Then a reaction set in.'

'It was inevitable. I relaxed, concentrated on my exams and my running got neglected. Looking back now, I can see that I was in the doldrums as an athlete. And then you went to Turku.'

'The decisive factor yet again!' said Chataway.

'The shock made me sit up,' confessed Bannister. 'I honestly hadn't expected Landy to run that fast that soon. It was a remarkable performance and I sent him a cable to congratulate him, but I got some benefit out of it. It gave me that short, sharp jab I needed.'

'As Landy will find out in the final.'

'I hope so.' He turned to his friend. 'You must be bored to death with all this ballyhoo about the race.'

'Press hysteria is always annoying,' said Chataway. 'They make it sound as if the whole Games is built around one track event. It's rather dispiriting for the rest of us.'

'I'm sorry.'

'It's not your fault, Roger. You loathe publicity.'

'It's so distorting.'

'Not to worry,' added his friend, brightening. 'I'll make them sit up and take notice. When they've seen the Mile of the Century, I'll give them something even better.'

'What's that?'

'The 3 Miles of the Millennium!'

John Landy was also very much aware of the fact that he carried national responsibilities into the final. It was not just a personal issue that was at stake. An Australian triumph in the mile would be a telling thrust against a country with whom they would always have a special rivalry. Wearing his nation's vest meant an enormous amount to Landy and it was his dearest wish to take it first through the tape.

While Bannister had confined himself to training runs, Landy had continued with his taxing programme of interval running. Consistently high times had lulled every observer into making him a clear favourite for the final but Landy did not allow himself to get carried away by all the talk. Privately, he gave himself an even chance of winning.

Or of losing.

'There must be a hell of a lot of money changing hands back home, John,' commented Neil Robbins. 'Nobody loves a bet as much as us and they'll certainly be betting on this one.'

'I hope they don't overrate my chances.'

'That would be almost impossible to do.'

'No, it wouldn't, Neil. I'm only human.'

'Not according to those training times,' said Robbins. 'Ten quarters at 58 seconds each with only a minute and a half in between them! That's super-human, John.' He gave a laugh. 'And you ran barefoot most of the time.'

'I prefer it.'

'Bannister can never live with a pace like that.'

'Running from the front is bloody hard work,' reminded Landy. 'It takes it out of you over four laps. I think it's going to be a tough race, Neil.'

'Tough for Bannister and the others, anyway.' Robbins put

a hand on his shoulder. 'As I see it, John, there's only one thing that can stop you winning.'

'What's that?'

'Yourself.'

'How do you mean?'

'Don't be too much of a gentleman out there,' advised the other. 'Like Perce always says, work up some hatred, some aggression. Want to win and want to show the rest of them no quarter.'

'Don't worry,' promised Landy with sudden resolve. 'I just love the idea of getting out there and thumping the bastards!'

They had just left the stadium on their way back to the Games Village. Someone ran to catch them both up. It was Marjorie Nelson.

'Wait for me!'

'Hello, Marje,' said Robbins. 'Just telling John what a certainty he is for the mile race.'

'He would be if the press would only let him alone.' She turned to Landy. 'Are they still hounding you?'

'Worse than ever. We had one of them in the bedroom last night.'

'Of all the nerve!'

'Yes!' recalled Landy, torn between annoyance and amusement. 'This bloke named Dwain Richards comes and sits right on the end of my bed. Says that his editor sent him to do "a day in the life of John Landy" from sunrise to sunset!'

'I hope you kicked him straight out,' she said.

'John Vernon did it for me, Marje. That reporter took one look at John towering over him and he was out of the door like a shot.'

'Thank goodness for that!'

'John's taken a real battering,' agreed Robbins. 'Because old Bannister does his training in secret, they all descend on John. It's not fair. They seem to think he's public property.'

'Well, I'm keeping clear of them tonight,' vowed Landy. 'I've got the most important race of my life tomorrow and that means early to bed. The press can stay right away!'

'Yes,' agreed Marjorie Nelson. 'You need your sleep, John. This time tomorrow you'll be polishing your gold medal.'

*

Though the English team had been slightly aloof, some of its individual members had been fairly gregarious. Murray Halberg and Bill Baillie had struck up an acquaintance with Jim Peters, the veteran marathon runner. They were always pleased to chat with him over a meal. Peters was a slight, spare man with a gaunt face and a top-knot of brown hair. He was one of the oldest athletes at the Games but he had somehow retained his youthful enthusiasm for his event.

'How many marathons have you run, Jim?' asked Halberg.

'Not enough.'

'What was it like having Zatopek up against you in Helsinki?'

'Murder. He was in a league of his own, that man.'

Baillie grinned. 'They say that Jim Peters will be in a league of his own tomorrow. I know that *I* wouldn't care to take on the world record-holder over 26 miles.'

'Don't forget the 385 yards,' reminded Peters.

'I could just about manage that bit,' said Baillie.

'What made you take up the marathon, Jim?' wondered Halberg.

'Finest race of them all, Murray. The real test. If you want to find out all about yourself, try a marathon. Nothing like it.'

'You don't get enough credit for it,' decided Baillie. 'We'll have a full stadium here for our race and all we're running is four laps of the track. Whereas you lot keep it up for two and a half bloody hours!'

'My record is 2.17.40, Bill,' said Peters with a smile.

'That's fantastic,' added Halberg. 'I agree with Bill. The marathon should get more recognition. Be more of a feature event.'

Peters was realistic. 'We can't compete with this so-called Mile of the Century. That's the big one. I only hope the crowd have still got breath to cheer when I come into the stadium not long after the mile is over.'

'*We'll* have breath to cheer, anyway, mate,' volunteered Baillie.

'Thanks.'

'What do the English boys feel about the mile, Jim?'

'Oh, well. Bannister is the golden boy. Four-minute mile and all that. They think he'll win.'

'Landy will slaughter him,' Baillie forecasted.

'Don't underestimate Bannister,' warned Peters. 'He's good.'

'What sort of a bloke is he?'

'Oh, he's all right, I suppose. Pleasant enough. But he's like the rest of that lot, really.'

'That lot?' said Halberg.

'The Achilles Club. Oxford and Cambridge blokes.'

'You seem to have quite a few of those buggers in your team,' observed Baillie. 'They're the ones who keep their distance.'

'Not only from you, Bill,' replied Peters sadly. 'There's the ordinary club runners like me and Gordon Pirie and so on. We never really mix with the Achilles mob. Always been the same. I remember Bill Nankeville going on about it years ago. Why can't we be more like you and the Aussies? You all muck in as a proper *team*.'

'Of course,' said Halberg. 'We all root for each other.'

'Must be nice.'

'It is, Jim. Keeps you going through the bad times.'

Peters gave a wan smile. 'I've had a few of those.'

'But you've come good at just the right time, mate,' noted Baillie. 'Everybody believes you'll end up on that rostrum.'

'Jack Holden won it for us in Auckland. I've got to do the same here.' Peters let out a sigh. 'I certainly won't get another go at an Empire Games gold. This is it.'

He stood up and took his leave of the others, planning an early night against the ordeal that awaited next day. Peters was about to move off when Halberg found a last question.

'When you run all that way, Jim . . .'

'Yes?'

'What the hell do you think about all the time?'

Peters smirked. 'Winning.'

Peter Wilson, the doyen of British sportswriters, sat in his hotel room and plucked at his moustache as he sought for words to describe the situation. Having peered through the ropes at many title fights, covered Wimbledon on several occasions and seen countless dramas in other individual sports, he had learned to relish a contest between apparent equals. The confrontation between Bannister and Landy seemed to him to have all the indications of a titanic struggle. He began to write.

As I write this, it is 2 o'clock on Friday morning at Vancouver – Mile-of-the-Century Eve.

Two in the morning is a lonely, doleful time to be working – you should be in bed or out celebrating with old friends. And then you think that there are two fellows very much lonelier than you are . . . for now the pressure is on. Tomorrow each one of them will run the race of his life against the only other man to run a mile in under four minutes since the first cave man decided he couldn't give weight away to a sabre-toothed tiger . . .

His words were curiously prophetic.

Roger Bannister coughed himself awake and sat up in bed to blow his nose in a handkerchief. He noticed that he was slightly fevered as he had been on the eve of other big races. Reaching for the glass of water on the bedside table, he used it to swallow a few aspirins and then snuggled down once more. It was some time before he could sleep.

In the Australian camp, another athlete was having a bad night. John Landy twisted and turned in the bed in an effort to find the position in which he could sleep but it was all to no avail. Tense and preoccupied he eventually got out from under the sheets and slipped on his track suit in the dark. He padded quietly out of the room in bare feet.

When he came out into the night air he began to jog along the road in the hope that the exercise would relieve his tension and enable him to get some rest. Prone to sleepwalking, Landy had become notorious among his friends for his nocturnal wanderings but this was a journey of a different order. Anxiety was keeping him awake and he was trying to dispel it in the best way that he knew.

A car approached with its headlights blazing and Landy quickly hopped off the road and out of the glare behind a bush. As his foot made contact with something sharp and fragile, pain stabbed him. Blood flowed immediately. He had trodden on a photographer's discarded flashbulb and he was in trouble.

When he got back to his room he dabbed at the wound with a handkerchief. John Vernon, the lanky high-jumper, heard the noises in the bathroom and went to investigate.

'Christ! What have you done to yourself, John?'

'Oh, I stepped on something out there.'

'Give me a look.'

'Oh, it's nothing much,' insisted Landy, not wanting his friend to see. 'Just a scratch, really.'

'Come on,' insisted Vernon and knelt down to look. He whistled to himself. 'That's a bad one, mate. We've got to get you to a doctor.'

'I'll be okay,' argued Landy. 'I'll just put a plaster on.'

'It's too big for that. What the hell did you step on?'

'Glass of some sort. My own stupid fault for running barefoot in the dark.'

'I'll get dressed,' decided the other, going out.

'There's no need . . .'

But Vernon knew that there was. He reported to one of the Mounties on patrol outside and cadged them both a lift to the nearest hospital. Dr Hiddlestone, an amiable young Canadian medic, was on duty in the Casualty Department and he cleaned the wound carefully.

'That's nasty,' he diagnosed. 'What did you step on?'

'I don't know.'

'Glass,' announced the doctor, extracting a fragment with his tweezers. 'You've stepped on some sort of bulb.'

'Probably a photographer's flashbulb,' decided Vernon with disgust. 'They're always throwing them away in the bushes.'

'It'll need stitches,' said Hiddlestone.

'I can't have stitches,' protested Landy. 'I have to race.'

'Not with a wound like that.'

'I've *got* to,' stressed the athlete. 'Just put some sticking plaster on and bind it up.'

'You can't run with a wound like that, young man.'

Vernon interceded. 'Doctor, this is John Landy. He simply has to run, believe me.'

'It's not underneath my foot,' said Landy. 'Put some sticking plaster on and bind it up. I'll see how it feels.' He stilled the doctor's protest with a raised palm. 'Please. Just try it this way first.'

'Very well, Mr Landy.'

Hiddlestone took some plaster from a cabinet and started to stick a piece on the patient's instep. Landy winced slightly but tried to hide the discomfort from the others.

'Could I ask you to keep this quiet, Doctor?' Landy pressed. 'If I can't run, I'll drop out. But if I can run, I don't want any excuses made. Okay?'

Hiddlestone nodded in agreement and so did Vernon.

Roger Bannister received attention from the team doctor who used a stethoscope to listen to his chest. The athlete gave a pale smile.

'It feels much better. It really does.'

'You're not looking any better, Roger,' remarked Chataway.

'There's still some congestion,' said the doctor, standing back.

'That won't hurt me,' argued Bannister.

'It won't help you either.'

'Well, I'm going to run. No question of that.'

'You're a doctor yourself, Roger,' reminded the man. 'What would you advise a patient who came to you in a condition like this?'

Bannister brightened. 'If England and Australia were neck and neck in the medal count, I'd order him to get out there and run.'

'Are they neck and neck?'

'The Aussies are right behind us,' said Chataway.

'Right,' consented the doctor. 'Then I suppose you'd better get out there and run.'

'I will. Nothing on earth would have stopped me.' Bannister stood up. 'This is the most important race of my life. I must win.'

Andy O'Brien was a shrewd, experienced Canadian reporter who had been granted a brief interview with John Landy that morning. He found the athlete in his room, sitting on the bed with a blanket over his legs.

'John Landy?'

'Yes.'

'Andy O'Brien. *Montreal Star*.'

Handshake and civilities were exchanged and the questions came. Landy involuntarily swung his legs off the bed to the floor. O'Brien's eyes bulged as he saw blood seeping from beneath the plaster.

'A slight cut, that's all,' said Landy.

'Looks bad.'

'I don't want this to come out,' emphasized the athlete. 'Okay? It's not as bad as it looks. I don't want the sympathy vote out there.'

'Looks pretty serious to me.'

Landy ripped off the plaster and used cotton wool to stem the flow of blood. He glanced up at his visitor and spoke firmly.

'It's not on the heel and it's not going to affect me.'

'If you say so.'

'I want your word of honour that you won't tell a soul about this. Right?'

'Sure,' replied O'Brien. 'Sure.'

But the temptation was going to be hard to resist.

Wearing a smartly cut uniform that made him an even more striking figure, Wes Santee arrived at NBC Studios in New York. Dave Garroway, the veteran commentator, gave him a warm welcome and used his relaxed professionalism to put Santee at his ease.

'Thanks for coming, Wes. I appreciate it.'

'Great to be here.'

'I'd sure love to see you in that race with them.'

'So would I, Dave,' agreed Santee. 'But since I can't get to Vancouver I guess that this is the next best thing.'

Dr Hiddleston put in the last of the four stitches as he talked.

'When's the race?'

'Not till this afternoon.'

'I should have done this when you first came.' He finished

the stitching and stood up. 'You're going to need pain-killers, John.'

'We're not allowed to take drugs.'

'Pain-killers are allowed. I'm sure.'

'I'll be fine.'

'But you won't be able to run properly like that.'

'I'll have to, Doctor.'

'You're a brave man,' admired the other. 'And a foolish one.'

'No,' replied Landy. 'I'm an athlete.'

Heat and humidity greeted the eager spectators who swarmed into the Vancouver stadium on that Saturday, 7 August 1954. Though there were many intriguing contests to watch on track and field, it was the prospect of the Mile of the Century which magnetized the attention. Everything was ready.

The Duke of Edinburgh sat in the royal box with dignitaries from many lands. The flags of the competing nations hung from their poles. Speculation and debate kept the stands buzzing and even the officials seemed to be caught up in the electric atmosphere of a very special day in the history of athletics.

Media coverage was enormous. Television and radio would carry the race to an international audience. Journalists and photographers would give it worldwide currency. Unforgettable memories would be forged. Myths would be created.

Alarmed by the temperature and the threats it contained, the runners in the marathon set off with caution and took to the streets of Vancouver. For the next couple of hours and more, theirs would be an offstage drama.

When the competitors for the mile finally appeared on the track they were given a resounding cheer. Spectators who had been in suspense for months now released their emotions freely and jubilantly. A great race was at hand and they wanted to discharge their part in it.

While announcements and introductions were made, the athletes limbered up and tried to ease some of their nervous strain and to banish some of their last-minute doubts. Two men monopolized the interest. The other competitors earned no more than a cursory glance. What the crowd had come to see – and what the sporting world was waiting to hear about – was a clash between two sublime athletes who had each broken through what had seemed an impenetrable barrier into the realm of legend.

This was no ordinary race. It would answer the most important question in athletics. It would decide supremacy. It would be charged with tension, touched with magic and lit with high endeavour.

It would be a duel to the death.

As the pictures on the screen were sent all over America, Dave Garroway kept up a smooth commentary and invited comments from his studio guest.

'They look fit and eager to me, Wes.'

'Yes, they're both great guys.'

'How do you read this one?'

'Well, I tend to favour Landy. His training times have been sensational and he's on top of the heap at the moment.'

'What about Bannister's famous finishing burst?'

'I think that John Landy will try and draw the sting out of that burst by setting a fast pace. You can't find that kick when you're exhausted, Dave.'

'I guess you'd like to be in there with them, Wes.'

'This has got to be the finest mile race most of us will ever see. It will be a privilege to watch it. But – my God – it would have been an even greater privilege to be in it. Those guys would push me, Dave. In all my career, I was never really pushed hard enough.'

Track suits came off. Final preparations. Advice from coaches, friends and well-wishers. Officials clustering. Expectation building. Pressure mounting inexorably. Hearts pounding. Minds racing. Nerves dancing.

Contrast was immediate.

The tall, fair-haired, pale-skinned Bannister looked almost sickly beside the tanned, upright, curly-headed Landy. English elegance versus Australian power. Strategy against speed. The amateur ideal taking on a running machine. Hound chasing hare.

Roger Bannister had brought himself to a peak in athletics

and found that he needed an inspirational coach to take him all the way. Launched by an inspirational coach, John Landy saw that he had to free himself in order to soar alone. They were moving in opposite directions.

Yet there were similarities.

Shy, thoughtful introverts from middle-class backgrounds, they had both sought in athletics a focus and a means of expression. Both had come to epitomize the sporting aspirations of their respective countries. Both of them had suffered a setback at an Olympic Games and wiped out its memory with bright achievement. Each found running an act of self-discovery.

As they were called to the line, both were hoping that they would not be troubled by a physical hazard. Bannister had been assuring his team mates that he was completely fit and Landy had stamped his foot in front of inquisitive journalists to prove that it was not injured. Each strove to subdue discomfort.

'Take your marks . . . set . . .'

The wheels of history were rolling again.

'Go on, Roger!'

'Come on, John!'

The stands were polarized in an instant.

Hoping to assist Landy by taking on some of the pace-making, Bill Baillie spurted away in the black vest of New Zealand. Landy did not want relief. Attack was his normal mode. He seized the initiative and usurped the lead with Bannister trailing him closely. The pattern of the race was set. Front runner trying to burn off tactician.

'Keep it up, John!'

'Hang in there, Roger!'

On a slow track and in baking heat, Landy's cracking pace took him around the first quarter in 58.02 seconds. Bannister was still behind him but a gap had opened. Punishing himself with brutal unconcern, Landy steadily inched away to lead by some twelve yards at the half-mile. A time of 1.58.3. Competitors further back had already lost hope.

'You've cracked him, John!'

'Close the gap, Roger!'

'He's fading!'

'You're catching him up!'

Contradictory claims amid a roar of sheer passion.

Landy's confidence was high now as he pummelled his way around one more gruelling circuit. Bannister, having feared that he was too far adrift, now began to haul himself slowly in on the invisible rope. Twelve yards became ten. By the end of the back straight it was down to six. In the finishing straight it became four.

When the bell was rung at the astonishing time of 2.58.4 there was joy and pandemonium in the stadium. All expectations had been surpassed. Incredibly, the race was transcending itself.

'Now, John! Go for it now!'

'You're there, Roger! Almost there!'

'Landy! Landy! Landy! Landy!'

'Bannister! Bannister! Bannister! Bannister!'

The stark contrast in their physiques and running styles was accentuated more than ever now. Landy increased the pressure with shuffling, urgent steps while Bannister responded with his long, loping stride. Only a yard of space separated them as they went into the final bend. Both men had given everything unstintingly. They were running on courage through a fog of pain with a tumult in their ears.

Landy felt that he had done enough. Unaware of how close his rival was and certain that he had broken the Englishman's challenge, he permitted himself a look over his left shoulder. It was a look of hope. He expected to see his pursuer twenty yards behind. But he did not.

At the very moment that Landy looked round to the left, Bannister surged past him on the right. That split second encapsulated the whole race. It dealt a hammer blow to the Australian.

When his head swung round to the front again he saw the back of Bannister's vest as it accelerated away down the home straight. By the time that he had recovered enough to mount a response, it was far too late. Running through a chasm of noise and exultation, Roger Bannister scythed his way through the tape five yards ahead and fell with utter exhaustion into the arms of the English team manager.

He had delved even deeper into himself than during the

epic run at Iffley Road and the resulting torment was pro-
portionately greater. He was helpless for minutes while officials thronged around him and Landy and impeded the other
competitors.

Rich Ferguson of Canada was a surprise bronze medallist.
Vic Milligan came next and Murray Halberg, struggling to
hold off David Law of England, practically had to fight his
way through a seething mass of officialdom to reach the line.

The Mile of the Century was exactly that.

The winning time was 3.58.8 and Landy beat four minutes
as well. With that remarkable sportsmanship that had illu-
mined his whole career, the Australian shook Bannister's hand
and praised him openly. He had no excuses. On the day, he
had been beaten by the better man.

When Bannister had regained his strength and composure
he linked arms with Landy and they waved to the crowd
together. With the sustained magnificence of their contest
they had raised the whole Empire Games to a new level of
excellence.

Unhappily, it did not remain there for long.

Within twenty minutes of their stirring encounter, tragedy
stole upon the scene. Blinded by the heat and racked by
exhaustion, Jim Peters staggered drunkenly into the stadium
at the head of the marathon to complete the last 385 yards
of the race.

It took him eleven minutes to cover half that distance.

He fell on the track six times, fought to get up, then lurched
on crazily into nowhere. A horrified silence had fallen on the
stadium as another face of the sport was revealed. The mile
had enhanced the reputations of its competitors: the marathon
– run in murderous conditions – had destroyed with a vengeance.

Driven on by a hopeless desire to win, Peters stumbled and
groped and zigzagged his way around the track. When he
fell yet again, a voice in the stand implored someone to help
him but he was not finished yet. Crawling on like a maimed
animal, he somehow got up again to lunge the last few yards
to what he believed was the finishing line.

He collapsed in a faint and the English trainer dived to his
aid. When they dared to move him, he was rushed off to

hospital. It had been a sickening spectacle and it was compounded by the announcement that he had been disqualified for not reaching the finishing line. A stadium which had echoed to cheers for the mile now vented its spleen on an officialdom which had forced the marathon runners to compete in such a cauldron.

The gruesome performance overshadowed the mile for a while but its quality could not be denied for long. Its drama and significance were thrown into sharp relief by the grotesque charade that followed it. Within the space of half an hour the beauty and the beastliness of athletics were demonstrated with vivid effect.

Sympathy for Jim Peters was universal and deeply-felt.

But there were cheers in every heart for Bannister and Landy.

Their Mile of the Century would never be matched.

Epilogue

Chris Chataway took possession of his gold medal in the 3 miles with a brilliant run that secured him an Empire Games record into the bargain. Marjorie Nelson helped the Australian women's sprint relay team to a fine victory. Canada won its only gold medal in the stadium during the men's sprint relay. And the powerful, versatile Yvette Williams of New Zealand emerged as the outstanding performer of the games with a hat-trick of gold medals in the long jump, shot and discus.

Behind these triumphs lay many personal disasters. As the few packed their medals, the many stuffed setback and disappointment into their suitcases but there were gifts to take back as well. There was goodwill and trust and international friendship. By measuring themselves against others, everyone had learned and grown.

Notwithstanding individual regrets, therefore, the British Empire and Commonwealth Games broke up in a spirit of happiness and optimism. Its closing act of celebration was a superb banquet at a leading hotel.

'Order, please! Can I have your attention for a second, please!'

The secretary of the British Amateur Athletics Association was a man who could make himself heard. Supplemented by the banging of his spoon on the table, his voice gained a respectful silence among the assembled athletes and officials.

'These games have been a landmark in athletics history,' he continued. 'There have been many brilliant and fine performances and I, and all my team, feel privileged to have taken part. While it is invidious to pick out any one event or performance, I think that none of you will begrudge my making special mention of the two remarkable athletes sitting here in front of me.' He introduced them with a wave of his hand. 'Dr Roger Bannister of England and Mr John Landy of Australia.'

The applause was thunderous. He had to wait a full minute.

The secretary continued. 'We were promised a Mile of the Century. We got more than that. We got a Miracle Mile. Other runners will undoubtedly run the mile faster in years to come because athletics is always on the move and always improving.' He gazed down at the two heroes. 'But I don't think we are ever likely to witness a finer display of athletics and sportsmanship than we saw when these two gentlemen met on the track. One had a heavy cold, the other a cut foot. Yet both of them gave us the first mile in history in which two men have gone under four minutes.'

Applause again prevented him from speaking for a while.

'To the winner, Dr Roger Bannister, the plaudits have gone and they have been justly deserved but we at the British Amateur Athletics Association felt the games would be incomplete unless we paid some lasting tribute to the sportsmanship of the other gentleman sitting here – Australia's Mr John Landy.'

A shorter, intense round of applause interrupted him.

'The British team have therefore prepared a specially engraved plaque which they hope he will accept to remind him in a small but tangible manner of the extremely high esteem and regard in which he's held by all of us.' He looked slowly around the room. 'With professionalism becoming rampant and with the situation looming where athletes will not appear – let alone run – without substantial financial reward, we should perhaps remember at this point when men and women would still compete to the utmost of their capacity – not for glory, not for gold – but for the sheer joy of doing something as well or better than it has ever been done before.'

Tumultuous applause greeted these sentiments and it focused on the two men who most seemed to embody the secretary's words. Overcome with emotion but trying not to show it, John Landy stood up and shook the hand of a smiling Roger Bannister.

Fierce rivals were signalling their friendship. United by the true spirit of amateur endeavour, they were rising above national differences. Having fought to the death out on the track, they had created a mutual bond for life.

In that symbolic handshake, Franz Stampfl met Percy Cerutty.

Everyone in the room rose to acclaim the two milers. As they stood side by side and waved their acknowledgement, their proximity reminded many of the moment that would make their race part of legend.

John Landy looking over his shoulder one way as Roger Bannister swept past him on the other. A breath-taking sequence that would be replayed endlessly in the minds of all who cherished athletics.

Truly, Roger Bannister and John Landy had given themselves with total commitment to the sport they both loved.

Not for glory, not for gold . . .